Cultural Dilemmas of Progressive Politics

Styles of Engagement among Grassroots Activists

Stephen Hart

THE UNIVERSITY OF CHICAGO PRESS
CHICAGO AND LONDON

STEPHEN HART works in medical research at Frontier Science and Technology Research Foundation and teaches sociology at State University of New York, Buffalo. In the past he has worked as a peace organizer in the religious community and as director of survey research for the Lutheran Church in America. He is author of *What Does the Lord Require? How American Christians Think about Economic Justice* (1992; expanded ed. 1996).

The University of Chicago Press, Chicago 60637
The University of Chicago Press, Ltd., London

Printed in the United States of America
10 09 08 07 06 05 04 03 02 01 1 2 3 4 5

ISBN: 0-226-31817-6 (cloth)
ISBN: 0-226-31818-4 (paper)

Library of Congress Cataloging-in-Publication Data

Hart, Stephen, 1946–
Cultural dilemmas of progressive politics : styles of engagement among grassroots activists / Stephen Hart.
p. cm.—(Morality and society)
Includes bibliographical references and index.
ISBN 0-226-31817-6 (cloth : alk. paper)—ISBN 0-226-31818-4 (pbk. : alk. paper)
1. Political participation—United States. 2. Social movements—United States. 3. Religion and politics—United States. I. Title II. Series.

JK1764.H39 2001
323'.042'0973—dc21

00-009876

⊗ The paper used in this publication meets the minimum requirements of the American National Standard for Information Sciences—Permanence of Paper for Printed Library Materials, ANSI Z39.48-1992.

Cultural Dilemmas of Progressive Politics

MORALITY AND SOCIETY SERIES

Edited by Alan Wolfe

THE NECESSITY OF POLITICS: RECLAIMING AMERICAN PUBLIC LIFE
Christopher Beem, with a foreword by Jean Bethke Elshtain

CHILDERLEY: NATURE AND MORALITY IN A COUNTRY VILLAGE
Michael Mayerfeld Bell

BEYOND CARING: HOSPITALS, NURSES, AND THE SOCIAL ORGANIZATION OF ETHICS
Daniel F. Chambliss

HEALING POWERS: ALTERNATIVE MEDICINE, SPIRITUAL COMMUNITIES, AND THE STATE
Fred M. Frohock

MORE THAN VICTIMS: BATTERED WOMEN, THE SYNDROME SOCIETY, AND THE LAW
Donald Alexander Downs

THE END OF THE LINE: LOST JOBS, NEW LIVES IN POSTINDUSTRIAL AMERICA
Kathryn Marie Dudley

RATIONALITY AND POWER: DEMOCRACY IN PRACTICE
Bent Flyvbjerg (translated by Steven Sampson)

FOR THE SAKE OF THE CHILDREN: THE SOCIAL ORGANIZATION OF RESPONSIBILITY IN THE HOSPITAL AND THE HOME
Carol A. Heimer and Lisa R. Staffen

MONEY, MORALS, AND MANNERS: THE CULTURE OF THE FRENCH AND THE AMERICAN UPPER-MIDDLE CLASS
Michèle Lamont

SPEAKING OF ABORTION: TELEVISION AND AUTHORITY IN THE LIVES OF WOMEN
Andrea L. Press and Elizabeth R. Cole

PUBLIC AND PRIVATE IN THOUGHT AND PRACTICE: PERSPECTIVES ON A GRAND DICHOTOMY
Edited by Jeff Weintraub and Krishan Kumar

For Ann Webster Hart and Albert Gailord Hart

Contents

Preface

Since the 1970s American national politics have moved decisively to the right. Yet polls indicate that there has been no corresponding shift in the values of most Americans. What explains this disparity? In this book I argue that part of the problem is that people working for social justice have largely—but unnecessarily—ceded the moral high ground to the right. Too often progressive activists present their proposals in a cool and technical tone, avoid articulating broad social visions, and fail to make links between politics and the cultural traditions to which Americans are attached. In short, the compassionate and even egalitarian values found at the grass roots, and the public-spirited energy seen every day in local communities around the country, have not been adequately connected to our national political debates. To address these failings, we need to pay greater attention to the cultural dimension of political activity and to "styles" of political discourse.

While the style of progressive politics is often anemic, there are efforts currently underway to construct a more culturally robust politics, and these offer hope for the future. In this book, I examine the differing styles of engagement adopted by grassroots activists, looking closely at two major movements—faith-based community organizing and human rights—and more briefly at others. On the basis of the evidence from such groups and an analysis of the arguments made by contemporary social critics, I argue that the potential gains from adopting a more "expansive" mode of politics are greater, and the risks less, than one might imagine.

The work of social movements is the focus of this book. These movements represent an ideal of active citizenship that is an enduring strength of American politics. Furthermore, while political developments in Washington and the state capitals are important, activist movements are equally essential—particularly at times when only a narrow range of options is being articulated in central political venues.

This book is intended not only for people with a personal concern for the direction of American politics but also for a partly overlapping group: students and scholars who wish to understand better the cultural dimension of American politics. I argue that modes of public discourse and styles of political engagement are a factor in public life independent of the content of the political agendas people pursue. Through case studies of the cultural work of grassroots social change organizations, I examine in empirical detail the range of choices progressive activists are currently making about modes of discourse and styles of engagement, the reasons for those choices, and the consequences of making them. This is an especially important task because the cultural dimension of *progressive* political work (except for identity politics) has been almost ignored. These case studies show both the difficulties progressives sometimes have in adopting more expansive political styles and also the ways in which justice and rights activists do construct more expansive modes of politics. The empirical data, and the way of conceptualizing politics developed in this book, shed light on contemporary debates in social criticism concerning individualism, civil society, and the role of cultural forces such as religion in American politics. And finally, these data and concepts contribute to the social-scientific study of political culture, social movements, and religion.

I am persuaded that the political tendencies recently dominant in Washington do not represent the best or only possibilities for our nation. America has always possessed an energetic voluntary sector and a rich and varied set of cultural traditions, religious and secular, many of them with progressive political potentials. We can draw in the future as in the past on these resources, articulating values and ideas that can serve to guide and motivate the work of citizen activists striving for social justice and human rights in the new millennium.

Acknowledgments

My first thanks go to David Roozen, who encouraged me to turn an idea into a research proposal for the Lilly Endowment. The Endowment generously funded the first year of the research, with the Hartford Seminary providing support services. At a later stage, the National Endowment for the Humanities awarded me a fellowship that funded another year, and First Presbyterian Church (Buffalo) provided me with an office. The Center of Theological Inquiry subsequently invited me for an eight-month stay at its lovely facilities in Princeton. And at the end, Frontier Science and Technology Research Foundation allowed me to go on half-time status for seven months to rewrite the manuscript. I am very grateful to William Elgie, Gregory Pavlov, Charles Ranney, and Suzanne Siminski for making this possible.

My greatest debts, however, are to the organizations that allowed me into their midst knowing that what I eventually would write about them might not be entirely favorable, to the staff who spent countless hours assisting my research, and to the participants who shared their thoughts and feelings with me. Among these organizations are MICAH, in Milwaukee; PACT, in San Jose; VOICE, in Buffalo; BUILD, in Baltimore; the Catholic Campaign for Human Development; the Gamaliel Foundation; the Pacific Institute for Community Organizing; Amnesty International–USA; two local Amnesty groups; Interfaith Funders; Citizens for Community Values, in Cincinnati; and the Cincinnati Area Coalition Against U.S. Intervention. I have also drawn on my experiences as part of many other activist groups, and hope my comrades in those groups will tolerate my turning to research use what I observed as a participant. The individuals who granted me the privilege of interviewing them or provided access and materials are mostly found speaking in the pages of the book; three who are not but deserve thanks are Ana Garcia-Ashley of MICAH, Diana Miller of PACT, and Jeri Sundvall of the Workers Organizing Committee.

I also wish to thank the many scholars and activists who read drafts, versions, or proposals related to this research or discussed the ideas that would later become this book. These people have improved it immeasurably. They include John Archer, Robert Bellah, Karen Bloomquist, Gene Burns, José Carrasco, Mary Ann Clawson, Paul DiMaggio, Craig Dykstra, Nina Eliasoph, Cynthia Eller, John Evans, Ward Ewing, David Fergusson, Charles Glock, Niels Gregersen, Benton Johnson, Robert Kanner, Ezra Kopelowitz, Michele Lamont, Michael Lerner, Paul Lichterman, Laura Mangan, David Mann, Bruce McKay, Mike Miller, Jack Murtagh, Richard Peterson, Francesca Polletta, Eric Rambo, David Roozen, Leigh Schmidt, Philip Selznick, Susan Stall, Jeffrey Stout, Heidi Swarts, Ann Swidler, Tamara Thornton, Michael Walzer, R. Stephen Warner, James Weinstein, Rhys Williams, Richard Wood, Robert Wuthnow, and anonymous reviewers.

I was fortunate in having able research assistance at many stages of the project, particularly from Barbara Beck, Tracey Gels, Bruce Hall, Paula Moore, Charlotte Pressler, Anna Reckin, Teresa Reinders, and Cheryl Wiggins. Their skill and commitment greatly surpassed their pay.

At the University of Chicago Press, Douglas Mitchell and Robert Devens have shepherded the project through with great diligence. I was singularly fortunate in having Alan Wolfe as my series editor. His comments greatly assisted in the revisions.

Last but far from least is my wife, Gail Radford, who supported and assisted this enterprise in ways too numerous to list. She read several drafts, improving the book immensely.

Part I: How We Engage in Politics and Why It Matters

Chapter 1

VARYING STYLES OF POLITICAL ACTIVITY

When we become involved in politics, we often disagree on the issues of the day or adopt differing political philosophies. But in addition to these substantive differences, there are differences in *how* we do politics. Some of these have to do with how we talk. Political talk can be full of moral commitment and passion or it can be cool in tone and tightly focused on specific tasks to achieve immediate objectives. Sometimes we relate varied issues to an overall social vision, but at other times issues remain discrete. Within a group with common political objectives, the moral basis of politics can be shared and explicit or private and invisible. Sometimes we link civil-societal cultural traditions—religions and other sources of ethical values and commitment—to the social and political world, while at other times we disconnect them. In addition to these differences in modes of public discourse, there are differences in the cultural dimension of political conduct. Some groups and movements develop a strong expressive life—ceremonies, stories, and practices that are valued for themselves, provide sustenance to participants, and communicate their values to outsiders—while others do not.

Political talk and action, in short, can attend carefully to cultural traditions and the expressive dimension of politics or deal with cultural factors more superficially. This difference crosscuts the divide between progressives and conservatives. In each political camp, one can find groups that pay a great deal of attention to the cultural dimension of their work and others that do not.

Furthermore, styles of discourse and the expressive dimension of political work are not accidental; nor are they merely subjects of aesthetics, public relations, or manipulation. On the contrary, the way we do politics manifests our identity and moral convictions as much as our assessment of what strategy is most likely to result in concrete political victories. Within political and social movements, choices about modes of discourse become deeply ingrained, respected customs.

My purpose in this book is to examine such differences in the cultural dimension of politics—and especially progressive politics. The reason for doing so is that these differences are fateful. A key question about contemporary American political life is why the right has fared so much better in Washington than the left since the 1960s and what potential there is for this to change. Some of the problems of progressive politics, I believe, lie in its cultural work. To diagnose or address these problems one needs to examine the modes of discourse progressives use, the cultural bases they implicitly or explicitly draw upon, and how these can be claimed more effectively. I intend to show how progressive politics often uses modes of discourse that are cautious and constrained to the point of being anemic, and argue that recovering the capacity to express moral outrage, universal claims of justice, and visions of a better society is essential if progressive political initiatives are to prosper—or deserve to prosper.[1]

In addition, a focus on the cultural dimension of politics can clarify topics that frequently arise in social criticism, such as the nature and extent of individualism in America, the state of civil society, and the impact of religion, morality, and cultural movements on American politics. Social critics such as Richard Rorty, Todd Gitlin, Robert Bellah, and Robert Putnam reflect on how American politics has gone wrong and what might be done, particularly by progressives, to remedy the situation. While I share many of the concerns of these authors, my diagnosis and suggestions diverge from theirs. Compared with Rorty and Gitlin, I am less persuaded of the dangers, and more of the advantages, of robustly cultural forms of politics, of moralism and even religious language within public discourse. With regard to individualism, as discussed by Bellah and a slew of critics, in my view the problem is not so much individualism in itself as weakness in the connections between public discourse and the strongly nonindividualistic ways of thinking, speaking, and acting that are still very much alive in America. Therefore, by contrast with thinkers such as Robert Putnam who see our basic problems in terms of weakness in civil society, I believe that what hurts our country the most is the decoupling of a reasonably healthy civil-societal sector from politics. In this book, I ground these arguments in an assessment of the actual state of grassroots public discourse.

Although it has a formal ring to it, the term *public discourse* does not refer only to what politicians, professors, and journalists do. Rather, it is found wherever people talk about our society and the problems and issues we face. Family dinners, office water coolers, churches, and taverns can all be sites for public discourse. The major focus of this book is on the discourse and cultural practices that are found in grassroots social and political action groups. These are where ordinary Americans become personally involved in efforts to improve our society, and they provide an important means by which nonelite Americans can have an impact on public life. Unlike national advocacy groups to which people relate only as contributors, local groups bring participants into interaction with others and provide opportunities to become public actors by organizing other people, speaking in front of the media, writing public statements, and so forth. They have the potential to connect the life of American civil society with politics. Compared with public opinion polls, the political discussions found in grassroots groups provide a more interesting, if less systematic and representative, sense of what is going on outside the Beltway. When responding to a poll, one is talking to a passive listener, what one says makes little practical difference, and the issues under discussion typically have only an indirect impact on one's life; it is rare that one has taken action personally on these issues. By contrast, in local action groups the issues often concern one directly and the group faces practical decisions about what to do. Furthermore, the people one is speaking to are far from passive: they respond to what one says and express their own views. Thus a forum for democratic deliberation takes shape. Furthermore, local groups have been a source of political creativity and change throughout American history—as in civil rights struggles during the 1950s—and may perform the same service again in the future. For all these reasons, the discourse and cultural practices of grassroots activist groups—even though many of them are small—deserve serious study. In examining these groups, the focus in this book is not on their often exciting actions and confrontations, but on their cultural work and their contributions to American political culture.

To provide a first glimpse of how styles of discourse vary, in the section that follows I recount my observations of three groups concerned, respectively, with the Gulf War, pornography, and local economic justice issues. These sketches are not intended to portray what is typical of political work in these three issue areas. In each area there are other groups that operate quite differently from the one reported here. Rather, these groups serve as examples of variation in modes of discourse. The first two, observed at the same time and in the same city, are examples of two dramatically different discursive styles that I term *constrained* and *expansive*. The group with constrained discourse, the one that was working against the Gulf War, was politically progressive, while the antipornography group, which had a more expansive style, was conservative. I observed the third group, which works on economic justice issues, one year later in a similar city. It was progressive but manifested relatively expansive discourse. Thus this set of examples allows us to see how styles of discourse vary independently of the political content of the discourse.

After these examples, I examine the nature of variations in modes of discourse and argue briefly that such variations are important for understanding American politics and the problems of progressive politics.

THUMBNAILS: STYLES OF DISCOURSE IN THREE GRASSROOTS ACTIVIST ORGANIZATIONS

The Cincinnati Area Coalition against U.S. Intervention

After the Iraqi invasion of Kuwait, and continuing after the start of active U.S. military operations in January 1991, a peace movement around the country worked to oppose U.S. policy. In Cincinnati, a loosely structured group with a few dozen active members but no staff met during that period and fielded a few antiwar actions. (It was affiliated with one of the two national anti-Gulf War groups, but was on its own locally. It was not really a coalition but a membership organization.)

At coalition meetings, discussion was entirely on nuts-and-bolts subjects. At a meeting in February 1991, when the ground phase of the war was already underway and it was clear that the war would end within a few days, this became manifest as an explicit choice. Early in the meeting, a draft political statement was brought up but immediately put aside without discussion. In making this choice, the group decided not to try to take a public position beyond the demand that the war end. In addition, it eschewed discussion of the topics that would have arisen while considering the draft statement.

A little later in the meeting, a college student who was a regular participant tried to raise broader questions: What are we as an organization fundamentally about? How do we want to change the United States so that the country will make fewer wars? He argued that the goal of stopping the war made little sense at that time because it was going to be over soon anyway and evidently we weren't going to stop it. So maybe, he said, we should think more about our broader purposes. He was, in a friendly way, immediately ruled out of order. The chair of the meeting told him, without giving any reason, that the group couldn't get into that. And indeed, no such discussion as he proposed took place at that or any other meeting of the organization I observed.

What explains what happened at this meeting? Certainly not lack of time. The remainder of the evening was spent talking about every detail of two elaborate proposals for the group's organizational structure—exactly how many at-large steering committee members to have, for instance. (All this for a structure destined to be obsolete within 72 hours!) This discussion went on well past 10 P.M. and many people left before it ended. The reason for turning down invitations to broader discussions appeared, instead, to be a sentiment that it was dangerous or inappropriate to discuss any larger social visions or grounds for opposition to the Gulf War. The group should stick to an affirmation that the war was wrong.

Another possible explanation for the group's nuts-and-bolts orientation is that diverse opinions among its members meant that the only thing they had in common was opposition to the war and that even talking about anything beyond that would be at best useless, since no agreement would be reached, and at worst divisive and destructive. But this line of argument is not very persuasive in view of the fact that the group was relatively homogeneous politically. Some of the participants were students, but the rest were long-term peace activists (some leftists, others pacifists or people whose political identity focused on peace issues) who had been demonstrating together for years against American policy in Central America and, for the older ones, Indochina. There were certainly differences: the pacifists and the socialists disagreed on some points. But I very much doubt if there was a single participant who opposed the Gulf War alone without feeling that there were underlying reasons why the United States continually got involved in problematic wars.

A third potential explanation is that the group was concerned to make its case effectively among the general public. It is possible that the older participants remembered the flamboyant and perhaps ill-advised rhetoric used by some leftists during the 1960s. This may have been part of the reason not to try to adopt a political statement. The usual argument for issuing a narrowly focused statement on a particular public issue—even if people within a movement have common views on a wider range of questions—is that the movement has a good chance for an important political victory in the near future and that the chance will be reduced if people outside the movement are alienated by broader statements with which they may not agree. Perhaps some people in the antiwar group were thinking in these terms, although it was a somewhat implausible position given that by the time of this meeting the movement had no chance of practical political victory no matter what it did. But in any case, the group elected to constrain not only its external but also its internal discourse. Externally, it declined to adopt a political position statement contextualizing its opposition to the war. But in addition, by not even discussing the draft statement and by ruling the college student out of order, the group failed to take advantage of two opportunities for internal discourse about the broader political or ethical values behind its opposition to the Gulf War. And as we have seen, efficient time use or the likelihood of destructive conflict do not seem plausible explanations. Something deeper and more implicit, some set of customs or rules—learned in the group or brought in from other political experiences—appears to have been in play.

In this group, there seemed to be an implicit rule that people's reasons for belonging and their ethical—let alone religious—sentiments were an entirely private matter. Any discussion of topics beyond nuts and bolts, any effort to talk about values or religion, was effectively embargoed. Connections between the immediate political issues at hand and general social or political visions were not made. Nor were links forged between people's politics and the more general cultural traditions, such as religions, to which they were attached. Furthermore, these activists expressed little passion and transcendence, even though in fact most of them were highly committed to their cause.

Citizens for Community Values

Let us now turn to a group with a much less constrained style of discourse, also active in Cincinnati in 1991. While this organization was more conservative than the one just described, I will focus here not on its goals but on its way of talking about politics and on how it attended to the cultural dimension of public life.

Cincinnati acquired notoriety when the Queen City's contemporary art museum hosted a traveling exhibition of photographs by Robert Mapplethorpe. The show upset every cultural traditionalist in town. It included erotic representations, same-sex relationship themes, and images that some found to violate religious sensibilities. Elsewhere the show aroused some opposition, but in Cincinnati opponents managed to close it down and put the museum officials responsible for organizing it on trial for obscenity. (A jury later acquitted them, however.) A particularly conservative sheriff spearheaded these steps, but his actions were strongly influenced by the presence of a militant and effective grassroots antipornography organization, the Citizens for Community Values (CCV). In Hamilton County—comprising the city of Cincinnati and the inner suburbs—CCV had managed by 1991 to wipe out all adult bookstores, get all X-rated videos removed from video outlets, and ban the showing of X-rated movies in theaters. In the six surrounding counties, adult video stores survived but were close to extinction.

CCV was a local group operating only in the Cincinnati area, although it provided advice to other groups and was part of national coalitions. It was structured as a membership organization. In 1991 CCV had approximately five thousand people on its mailing list, but perhaps more importantly it had a contact network reaching nearly five hundred congregations and a number of local chapters (one based in a congregation, the rest geographic). The contact network meant that there was a person in each church who could quickly disseminate information and requests for action throughout the congregation. For instance, if a crucial legislative issue was coming up, the contact could go to church the next Sunday and organize many fellow congregants to write letters to their representatives. Several dozen volunteers were also involved in committee work. In short, CCV was not a staff-driven organization with a passive constituency dealt with by mail. There was significant personal contact and political activity involved in its work.

CCV defined itself as a nonsectarian organization promoting the observance of Judaeo-Christian morality. In fact, its constituency was largely evangelical Protestant, but there was some Catholic and mainline Protestant involvement. The staff pointed to the presence of nonevangelical faiths as evidence of the group's nonsectarian character and would have been very happy to have Jewish involvement so as to make that case stronger. The reality, however, was that all CCV participants were religious traditionalists and the vast majority were Protestants.

The religious traditionalism of CCV members was linked to their conservative views on pornography politics. However, to understand the ways in which civil-societal cultural traditions can help or hinder progressive politics, we need to be aware that this combination represents an important but hardly representative link between religion and politics. A large body of evidence shows that traditionalist religion supports conservative politics in relation to sexuality but not in other domains of political debate.[2] We will see later that religious traditionalists can easily be progressive on economic justice issues. And in fact, it occasioned no tension in CCV that one of its leaders, an evangelical minister who wrote a column in a local newspaper, took liberal positions when he addressed economic questions.

The organization devoted a large amount of time to the education and formation of members. It was serious about having a practical impact, yet it did not confine its meetings to practical matters. Group activities, in addition to their instrumental purposes, provided a context in which rank-and-file participants were encouraged to become public actors and given training in how to articulate the connections between their politics and their faith and other basic values.

One chapter meeting that I observed started with prayer and song. Then the leader presented information about an adult video store that was renting videos combining sex with violence against women. This led into a lengthy discussion of why this was abhorrent; many of the participants expressed their views. Next, everyone in the room wrote a personal letter to the owner of the store. The leader did not provide any pattern that the letters were to follow—everyone was on their own. Then several members read their letters aloud, precipitating further discussion. The meeting closed with prayer.

Other meetings had strong educational components. At one local chapter meeting, with about twenty people in attendance, a video was shown that presented a revisionist history of the constitutional principles in the First Amendment, arguing that they did not mandate as strict a separation of church and state as contemporary civil libertarians usually thought, and certainly did not bar religious people and organizations from explicitly bringing their values into public life. As at the other meeting, a discussion followed.

A different local chapter had smaller, more informal meetings that were held over lunch in a restaurant. At these meetings members shared their current activities and concerns. At one, a member told of how she was trying to have her mother-in-law's adult video store in the suburbs put out of business. While her husband was supportive, she was evidently in some anguish about the situation. The other members listened with sympathy, talked over what was happening, and offered support.

CCV's case against pornography was linked to broader social issues. It was in part a critique of unbridled markets and individualism. CCV members also bemoaned the loss of traditional moral certainties. Furthermore, like many other Americans, including social critics who focus on deficits in "social capital" or civil society, they were worried about what they saw as a tendency toward social disorganization in our society. I heard little mention of sexuality in the meetings but a lot of worry about divorces and children using drugs. These were problems that members believed to be significantly exacerbated by pornography.

In short, CCV's political proposals were grounded in more basic or general values, that is, values that participants applied to life as a whole, not just politics. These values were mainly religious in CCV, but in other organizations, as we will see, secular values can play the same role. The transcendent quality of CCV's values, plus the universal applicability that people in CCV claimed for them, made a basis for asking people outside the group to support its aims. To be sure, many Americans are not so sure that CCV's moral standards should be applied in full rigor to every situation, and this limits what CCV can accomplish politically by such appeals. But certainly members felt themselves to be urged into action by transcendent claims.

The connection between the particular political issues CCV was addressing and wider social visions was articulated. Even more important, CCV participants became better able to connect their personal commitments and their religious traditions to public policy issues. Through their involvement, they were empowered to operate as actors in public life. They were encouraged to speak in their own words, expressing their own concerns. This was particularly impressive given that most members were people from modest backgrounds who had not previously been engaged with public affairs. In short, CCV members acquired new cultural capacities. One does not have to agree with the organization's political proposals to see the strengths in its cultural practices and the kind of public discourse carried on within the group.

Milwaukee Innercity Congregations Allied for Hope

The antiwar coalition described above illustrates constrained discourse on the left while CCV exemplifies expansive discourse on the right. But progressive politics is not inherently or necessarily more constrained than conservative politics. To see this clearly, let us preview the movement to be examined in depth in part 2 of this book: congregation- or faith-based community organizing. This movement is similar to CCV in the expansiveness of its discourse even though its politics are progressive. The local organizing project in Milwaukee, which I observed from 1991 to 1993, is Milwaukee Innercity Congregations Allied for Hope (MICAH).

Faith-based community organizing is a movement that works for economic justice and radical democracy but at the same time has some of the characteristics of CCV with regard to its political style. This kind of organizing combines a variety of religious social action traditions and the philosophy of community organizing developed by Saul Alinsky—who was a secular Jew—into a distinctive religio-political language.

At MICAH meetings, people are present not as individuals but as representatives of their congregations. In front of me at the table around which the MICAH housing task force met was a manila folder bent into a simple name plate reading, "Steve Hart, St. Andrew's." Faith in such an environment is not a private source of motivation, as it was for the people from the churches that I found in the antiwar organization and other progressive groups in Cincinnati, but a communal identity. (It is for the most part not a limiting identity, however, in that MICAH incorporates varying faith commitments and translates its statements into secular languages as well.)

All meetings begin and end with prayer—frequently lengthy and referring to the group and its members—and some include a reflection period organized by one of the participants, often based on a passage from scripture. From time to time people make references to religious or ethical values underlying the practical work. For instance, at one meeting the housing task force discussed a city initiative to boost inner-city home ownership. Several people argued that MICAH's priority, contrary to the city's, should be on publicly subsidized rental housing, because people with very low incomes could not plausibly benefit from owning homes and the first concern of religious people should be with the poorest of their neighbors. At another meeting, representatives from a Baptist congregation expressed their concern about whether a planned march to the mayor's house would have sufficient dignity to satisfy their sense of decorum and show enough respect for the city's highest official.

But the connection between faith and politics goes deeper than this. In interviews and meetings, MICAH participants continually tell stories about how their lives have been transformed by their involvement in community organizing. Over and over again I heard how they had learned to connect their faith to public life and become effective, engaged actors in the public arena. Far from competing with their spiritual life, this involvement often deepened it. They also reported that their congregations had been affected, becoming at once more connected with the surrounding society and more effective organizations internally.

In addition to business meetings and other task-oriented activities, MICAH devotes an enormous amount of time, energy, and resources to training. Most people who become more than superficially involved attend training, often a lot of it. It plays a major role in how participants are transformed and is a key site for learning and articulating the movement's religio-political language. Training in MICAH is not primarily a matter of learning particular skills (how to run a meeting, for instance) but of developing a systematic perspective on religion and politics. In training, one is challenged to rethink one's connection to public life, the way one's congregation operates, and even the goals for one's personal life. The perspective involves a distinctive set of terms or categories—self-interest, power, relationships, and so on—providing what is explicitly called a "language." Training is a key part of how a richer, more robust discourse, more like CCV's than that of the progressive groups I observed in Cincinnati, has been created within faith-based community organizing.

To draw on the life-affirming values found in religious communities is understood by almost everyone involved in contemporary organizing as the heart of the process. These values are not uniform. There are some very diverse views found within MICAH, given that it includes denominations as different as the Quakers and the Church of God in Christ. But practically everyone agrees that faith has political implications and is comfortable with the kind of things MICAH seeks, such as more resources for inner-city neighborhoods and power for inner-city residents, as part of those implications. To be sure, some members of MICAH congregations do not agree. But most do, and the divisions on these questions do not set whole congregations against each other. Issues that might, such as abortion, are not discussed. This is the most obvious constraining discursive rule that MICAH adopts. Nonetheless, overall the style of political discourse exhibited by MICAH is quite expansive. MICAH persistently and carefully links faith and values—frameworks and commitments found in civil society—to political issues and public policy.

STYLES OF DISCOURSE: CONSTRAINED AND EXPANSIVE

The contrasts among these groups are striking. With regard to political "content"—the kind of political and social change the groups are seeking—CCV is conservative while the other two groups are progressive. But when we consider political discourse from the standpoint of its mode or "style," it is apparent that CCV and MICAH share some important features that distinguish them both from the antiwar coalition. And while I have given only one example of constrained discourse, I observed this style in several other groups, both progressive and conservative, during the research for this book; I have also seen it in dozens of groups I have watched or read about over the years. Neither of these styles of discourse is unique.

Differences in the style of discourse crosscut differences in political agendas. A secular radical, disagreeing fervently with CCV's political stance and its religious basis, could nevertheless admire the care taken in member education and formation, the way the organization empowers ordinary people to enter public life, the attempt it makes to connect specific issues to broader visions, and the encouragement given to members to construct and articulate moral arguments. When I told participants in Amnesty International—an organization in which letter writing is a central activity—how at a CCV meeting people wrote individual letters and then read them aloud to each other, they were amazed and said that they ought to imitate this model but might not be able to do so. On the other side, I have observed conservative groups that operated in much the same way as the Cincinnati antiwar coalition.

As a shorthand for describing these differences in style, I use the terms *constrained* and *expansive*. The former term refers to discourse like that in the antiwar coalition, while the latter applies to CCV and MICAH.[3] What kind of difference does this contrast represent? That is, what kind of choices are people making when they adopt discursive styles?

To begin, note that the constraints adopted by action groups are not *ad hoc*. It isn't as if a group were to do an opinion poll in January and decide to be very constrained, then find in October that public opinion had shifted and a more expansive style would do the job better. In the antiwar coalition and many other groups with constrained discourse I have observed, the degree and kind of constraint have been essentially constant during the period that I observed them. The same is true for groups with more expansive discourse. There, the variation one finds is contextual. MICAH, for instance, uses very expansive discourse in training but a more constrained style in business meetings. Some socialist groups I have observed use expansive discourse internally but constrain themselves significantly when addressing the outside world.

Furthermore, the kinds of constraints on discourse one finds in a particular local group are seldom unique. The groups I have observed that use relatively constrained discourse operate according to rules that, while not identical, are similar enough to suggest that they represent a kind of blueprint for political organizations and public discourse. This blueprint originates outside any particular group and is used as a guide for the construction of discourse in many groups. Groups with relatively expansive discourse, similarly, operate by rules that go beyond the particular group.

The style of discourse in any group develops through its unique history and is in part an unconscious, perhaps even accidental, pattern. But the discourse styles we have been discussing are more than that. They are a set of customary rules—sometimes explicit, sometimes implicit—governing discourse. It was by intention, not accident, in the antiwar coalition, that certain topics did not come up. Nor were these topics absent simply by default; that is, because nobody thought of them. Rather, they were embargoed. The discourse I observed in the antiwar coalition and have seen in many other progressive groups operates as if the following rules were in effect: Don't talk about anything other than the practical steps of achieving the immediate goals the organization is trying for! Don't bring up any basic values (religious or political) that underlie your commitment to the organization! Don't ask anyone to articulate their reasons for participating in the group! Don't talk in terms that engage people's passion! Discuss issues in purely instrumental terms whenever possible! By contrast, CCV and to a large extent MICAH operate under implicit rules like these: Have a single overarching set of values that rules your whole life, personal and political! Talk about these and develop them (through discussions with sympathetic others)! Relate the specific issues of the day to this value system! Engage yourself whole-heartedly in the struggle!

Note that each of these sets of rules is religiously and politically contentless. These ideas are not inherently liberal or conservative, religious or secular. They represent a distinct dimension along which political ideas and practices differ, independent of left–right or religious–secular debates.

But what kind of rules are these? Are they simply instrumental in intent—that is, advice for how to achieve one's purposes more effectively, like the rules for mixing a great martini? To some extent this is surely the case. And to an even greater extent, people in groups with relatively constrained discourse *believe* this to be the case. Numerous leaders in activist groups have told me, at one point or another, something like "If you waste participants' time by endless discussions of first principles, they're liable to desert you." Very frequently, the accounts that group members give for why their groups operate under constraining rules follow this pattern. With regard to the rules governing internal discussions, participants say there is not enough time to loosen the constraints or that destructive conflict would erupt if they were to do so. With regard to external discourse, they say that only with a narrowly focused message can the organization achieve its goals.

These accounts, however, are not always plausible analyses of the group's situation. After all, groups like CCV and MICAH achieve concrete victories and are frequently very task-oriented but also find time for education and values talk. In the antiwar coalition, the relative political homogeneity of the group internally meant that severe conflict was unlikely. Time was not really a problem and achieving the group's immediate objective was impossible, so it is not clear what would have been lost by dealing with broader issues. In this and many groups with highly constrained discourse topics are absent, not just for practical reasons but because they violate norms to which many participants are deeply attached. Observing the antiwar coalition, other progressive Cincinnati groups, plus a conservative one (a group supporting the Gulf War) that used a similar discursive style, I felt myself in the presence of a taboo or prohibition. Certain kinds of discussion were out of bounds for reasons that transcended practical concerns. The fact that constraining rules frequently apply not only to the public statements a group makes, but also to its internal discussions, is another indication that they are more than instrumental advice. Rather, they have the quality of an ethos—an ethically charged way of political life.

In many groups, the accounts for constraint just mentioned are firmly believed and sometimes stated. This attachment to the accounts makes a difference, regardless of how plausible the accounts really are. And there are other accounts we will encounter later, such as the idea that respect for privacy requires group members not to ask each other about the sources of their political views. There are accounts used to explain and justify expansive discourse as well—for instance, the ideal of a life self-consciously unified by a coherent set of values. Such accounts, in short, are themselves part of the cultural life of activist groups.

Thus grassroots social action groups operate according to a set of customary rules governing their style of discourse, and they often articulate justifications for these rules. This combination is parallel to how a political platform might propose new public policies and argue why these would be best for the nation. Choices about how to conduct politics that follow a consistent pattern, implicit or explicit rules manifest in that pattern, and justifying accounts, taken together, constitute what might be called a "cultural structure." This structure is a guide to how one should engage in political talk, without regard to whatever views one holds on particular issues. Ideas about what modes of discourse one should adopt, especially when they become explicit, are a second layer of discourse placed on top of garden-variety political debates.[4] Discursive rules and the grounds for them, in sum, represent a political ethic. They are about the right way to be a citizen activist. And as we have seen, Americans have varied understandings of what that way might be.

As with most contrasts, the difference between constrained and expansive discourse is not a simple dichotomy. In practice there are compromises and syntheses of the two as often as pure instances of either. Furthermore, there are different respects in which discourse can be constrained or expansive. Some of these are shown in the table provided for reference at the end of this chapter.

Religion and Modes of Discourse

The two cases of relatively expansive discourse discussed earlier were groups with a religious identity, and a person might think that for all practical purposes discursive expansiveness and religiosity are the same. But this would be an error. It is quite possible to engage in expansive talk on a secular basis. In *The Search for Political Community,* Paul Lichterman provides a good example of this possibility. He describes in rich detail the life of several activist groups with a broadly environmental focus. One of these is a Green Party chapter in California. The "Seaview Greens," as he calls them, have strong shared commitments. Most obviously, they hold to "Green values" and a "Green perspective"—an ideology mixing ecological and social justice concerns. But in addition, they adopt a mode of political commitment that Lichterman terms "personalism."[5] Theirs is not a life-style enclave or the kind of politics of self-expression and self-development that communitarians love to criticize. It is strongly public spirited and involves willingness to compromise and work collectively. The Seaview Greens seek to win concrete victories in the real political world. Nonetheless, they are deeply committed to the high value and development of the individual activist. As Lichterman puts it, "each individual activist is a locus of personal responsibility and efficacy, outside as well as inside activist organizations."[6] Given this understanding, cutting off discussion or narrowing its scope in order to get something concrete accomplished is almost never done. Also, specific political projects are always discussed in the context of the overarching framework of Green values. These values constitute a whole way of life, an ethical as well as a political framework. In essence, Green values do some of the same things religious commitments do within MICAH or CCV. They provide transcendent commitments and ground particular political choices on the issues of the day. At Green meetings, the moral grounds for politics are manifest. Varied specific issues are bound together into a broader social vision. Issues are addressed with passion and transcendence. And the capacities of participants to relate their most basic commitments to public life are systematically nurtured.

The Greens, and the expansive discourse sometimes found in the human rights movement, to be discussed in part 3, show that it is quite possible to carry on expansive talk on a secular basis. Of course, one could define religion as any framework that asserts transcendent values, and then argue that all expansive discourse is "religious." But if we are talking about religion in the ordinary sense, the connection between religion and discursive styles is contingent.

One key hallmark of expansive discourse is the presence of transcendent talk. By transcendent, I mean using standards of value that are grounded in things outside of normal life in the currently existing world, and giving these standards a morally binding quality such that they trump not just one's personal interests but also the rules and values found in one's social and cultural environment. Thus the biblical injunction that "we must obey God rather than any human authority" (Acts 5:29)[7] manifests transcendence, as does the stance of a journalist who follows strongly held ethical standards and publicly defies the law, going to jail rather than revealing sources. The Seaview Greens clearly believe in transcendent standards, and other examples of transcendence without religion abound.

For instance, I have observed for many years a loose group of ex-communists who are in their seventies and still politically active in various left-of-center groups. They are secular, but they feel that the social world is morally skewed at a basic level. Especially since they stopped appealing to any "actually existing socialism" as a model, they use external, nonempirical bases—hopes and visions for a better society—to assert their stance. They take it that these represent superior principles worthy of being followed. That is, these values have a transcendent, morally binding quality, parallel to the way CCV members conceive of traditional sexual morality. These ex-communists manifest their commitment personally by organizing their lives around a vision of justice and involvement in struggles to achieve it. This commitment has exacted serious risks and costs. One, for instance, was a school teacher who was fired in a procedure ruled illegal only over a decade later, and even then with vastly too little compensation to make up for his economic losses. Nevertheless, they have been able to maintain their worldview over the entire span of their adult lives, and their point of view has sustained them. Having a transcendent worldview does not make these people "religious"—if anything, they tend to be antireligious, although they have mellowed in this regard over the years—but it does give them capacities for expansive discourse.

In fact, transcendent values can lead to an antireligious stance. This was traditionally the case for Marxists. In addition, some human rights activists, while asserting transcendent values about the liberty and dignity of the human individual, see religious faith as one of the great sources of human rights violations.

Conversely, religious groups—especially new or unconventional ones—sometimes deal with public issues in a "cool" way, defining themselves, at least in their external discourse, as just one more cultural grouping. In essence, they want to be treated as interest groups and put forward entirely prudential arguments—we are taxpayers, we are law-abiding, we vote, we are customers—for accepting them and giving them the same rights as any other group. They take an implicitly relativistic stance in their discourse on public issues, even though on religious ones they may be far from relativistic.

To be sure, religious faith offers many possibilities for engaging in expansive discourse. The assertion of transcendent standards against the existing world was something humans first learned how to do within religious frameworks, long before secular worldviews developed this capacity. In the West, as Robert Bellah among others has argued, it was the radical monotheism of ancient Judaism that first decisively relativized worldly standards and authority.[8] Elsewhere, other religious traditions did similar things: witness the Buddhist monks who immolated themselves during the war in Indochina. But this capacity, like other hallmarks of expansive discourse, can now exist independently of religion, or even in opposition to it. It exists among the Greens as analyzed by Lichterman and the ex-communists just described. People who are secular have every right to insist that making a passionate and transcendent commitment to social ideals does not make them less secular or more religious.

WHY STYLES OF DISCOURSE MATTER: CULTURE AND POLITICAL TRENDS

There is a paradox about recent trends in American politics. It is indisputable that public policy and the political discourse found in Washington and many state capitals have shifted dramatically rightward over the last twenty-five years. At a practical level, the shift is evident in national and state legislation, such as the gradual loss of progressivity in income taxes and the offensive against welfare capped by the Personal Responsibility and Work Opportunity Act of 1996. With regard to the tone of debate, there has been a vigorous reassertion of individualistic themes such as self-reliance, and a growth in skepticism about government.

If this rightward trend expressed a sea change in public sentiment, we could explain it straightforwardly. But, in fact, there is no such change. Republicans have done better in elections. But when Americans are asked about issues, no trend to the right is revealed. On the contrary: reliable evidence shows that public opinion in the United States has been largely stable since the 1970s. Leading academic survey researchers have done comprehensive and careful analyses of opinion poll trends, finding little change in grassroots views on most issues.[9] Only on criminal justice is there a clear conservative trend. Opinions on economic equality are essentially unaltered compared with twenty years ago, as are views on abortion and a host of other issues. On a few issues, especially ones about women, the trend is liberal.

Furthermore, Americans today, as in previous generations, regularly manifest in local activities remarkably strong concern for community and the public sphere. Although some commentators worry about Americans bowling alone, nobody denies that civil society is still exceptionally strong in this country compared with other nations.[10] (By "civil society," I mean arenas that are not part of either government or the for-profit business world. An alternate term with nearly the same meaning is "voluntary sector.") People work in soup kitchens, enlist in civic improvement organizations, try to protect the environment, get involved in religious congregations, sing in community choruses, and find solidarity with other parents in soccer leagues. In these and many other contexts, ethical languages are spoken or expressed in action. In grassroots associational life, Americans give practical witness to values that are much less individualistic than those dominant in Washington.

How is that so much has changed in national and state politics while so little has changed in public opinion or civil society? An important part of the answer, documented by Dan Clawson and others, is that the right has organized itself systematically, much more than previously, to use the economic resources of corporate America to advance a conservative agenda.[11]

In addition, however, there is a cultural part of the answer. Progressives, especially in recent decades, have not paid as careful attention to the cultural dimension of politics—and especially to values and religious traditions—as has the right. Progressives often fail to articulate, and sometimes even try to hide, the ethical values that ground their proposals. The right, meanwhile, engaging in discourse that is generally more passionate and transcendent, has seized the discursive high ground. There is sometimes more critique of how capitalism operates in conservative thinking than in what one hears from socialists. Progressives are often appalled by the florid links between faith and politics articulated by the religious right, but have failed to take in the fact that progressive politics has equal need of rooting in cultural traditions to which people are deeply committed. To be sure, progressives want to maintain values of tolerance and diversity sometimes threatened by groups on the religious right, but to do so, as I will argue in part 4, it is not necessary to abjure all connections between religion, morality, or transcendent values and political discourse.

Furthermore, progressives have often pursued politics in ways that disconnect their work from the cultural traditions generated in civil society. This has hurt their chances, since these traditions, at least on economic issues, have more progressive implications, giving a higher value to community and lower one to the market, than the kind of discourse currently dominant in Washington.

In sum, to understand the problems and possibilities of progressive politics, and the role of cultural factors in American politics, we need to examine modes of discourse as well as the content of what people say. To examine political work in this way clearly involves in part a normative analysis in which one makes explicit value judgments. I will go into normative questions in detail in part 4 of this book. For now, I will confine myself to two observations.

First, sound value judgments on social and political issues are based in part on accurate descriptions of what is actually happening. The first task of this book is to describe the modes of discourse that Americans currently use. Only if this is done in a fair and thorough way can we make intelligent judgments. Given the complexity of the judgments to be made, it is crucial to understand in some detail the kind of discursive choices activist groups make and the implicit or explicit moral basis for citizen activism. Accordingly, the major part of this book is devoted to describing and understanding what is happening in grassroots groups. Such understanding can serve as an impetus to improving the cultural work of progressive politics and may help citizens of any political stripe decide how the kind of politics they favor might best be strengthened.

Second, judgments about discursive modes do not follow directly from categorizing them as constrained or expansive. While I do believe that progressive political discourse in America is on average more constrained than ideally it should be, the best mode of discourse in any particular situation depends on the context and the kind of group involved, and there are usually considerations on both sides that need to be weighed. And any group, as we saw with MICAH's implicit rule against discussing abortion, adopts some constraints. The real question is not whether to have constraints but what particular constraints one might adopt and what will be lost or gained by adopting them.

THE ORGANIZATION OF THIS BOOK

The book contains four parts. The first, comprising the current chapter, lays out the issues to be addressed and the approach to be used in the remainder of the book. The next two parts constitute a descriptive account of important cases of cultural work in contemporary progressive politics. Part 2 presents the most extensive case study of the book. It concerns faith-based community organizing—the broader movement that MICAH exemplifies. This movement illustrates ways of constructing a culturally robust politics focused on one of the main agendas of progressive politics, the pursuit of economic equality and democracy. Part 3 deals with a secular case: the human rights movement. This movement is an important expression of a second core progressive agenda, the liberty and dignity of the individual. The language of human rights is also important because its claims to universality—to be valid for people of any religious or cultural tradition—are more widely accepted than those of most other political frameworks. Here, Amnesty International will be the main example. The discourse found in the local Amnesty groups I observed has expansive characteristics but also strong constraints. Amnesty pays unusually close attention to its discursive rules, thus providing insight into discursive constraints that are operative in many other social movements, only less explicitly.

In part 4 the analysis becomes primarily normative. Chapter 7 takes up issues about individualism and civil society that occur frequently in the writings of such American social critics as Robert Bellah, Robert Putnam, and Richard Rorty. In addition, it proposes a way of understanding individualism that integrates concerns about justice and liberty. Chapter 8 deals with the opportunities and perils of integrating culture and politics, taking on social critics such as Richard Rorty and Todd Gitlin and arguing that the need for a richly cultural politics outweighs the dangers. In both chapters, I attempt to clarify the issues conceptually and to bring data about the actual cultural life of activist organizations to bear on them.

Public Discourse: Constrained and Expansive Styles

	Dimensions of Constraint and Expansiveness		
	"Temperature"—Style, Tone, Relationship to Ethical Evaluation	"Issue Links"—Relations amongPolitical Issues	"Civil-Societal Links"—Connections between Politics and Civil-Societal Cultural Traditions
Extremely expansive	All judgments ethical, based on assertedly universal standards. Sacredness, passion, transcendence asserted constantly. *E.g., some utopian or sectarian groups, CCV at times*	All issues merged: organization has position on all. *E.g., Leninist parties*	Politics derived directly from general-purpose cultural traditions (i.e., ones that are not specifically political). *E.g., some in CCV, a little in faith-based organizing*
Extremely constrained	All talk about means, technique. Cool, instrumentalist. Less extreme form: relativism, where no standards clained to be universal. *E.g., antiwar coalition at times*	All issues separate; organization excludes all discourse—internal and external—except on one issue. *E.g., antiwar coalition, Amnesty at times*	No connections made between political issues and civil-societal cultural traditions. *E.g., antiwar coalition, Amnesty at times*
Synthesis or compromise	Both kinds of talk happen; topics can be in one context questions of means and in another questions of ends. *E.g., faith-based organizing, Amnesty, Greens, CCV at times*	Integrated: people work on focused set of issues, don't expect others to have sane view on everything, but talk about connections to broader visions. *E.g., Greens, faith-based organizing and CCV at times*	Integrated: group creates political language and does social analysis but talks about connections to civil-societal traditions. *E.g., faith-based organizing, Amnesty at times*
Dangers of extremely expansive discourse	No good analysis of effective means. Politics easily becomes pure witness. Intolerance, absolutism possible. Hard to cooperate with cultural others	No focus, loss of efficacy; or else issues combined in totalizing way (as in sectarian groups)	Can violate tolerance required in multicultural society. Narrows potential constituency. Hard to do political analysis so proposals may be unrealistic
Dangers of extremely constrained discourse	Passion and energy reduced. Issues of purpose black-boxed. Easy to lose sight of implicit ultimate ends, become opportunist. Only narrow appeals possible outside the group	Reduces available passion and energy. May help achieve organization's immediate goals whil enot advancing broader social change purposes of participants	No way to draw in now-yet-political people Nonindividualistic strands of civil-societal traditions don't help progressive politics. Black-boxes why people really care about political issues

Part II: Congregation-Based Community Organizing

Chapter 2

HOW CONGREGATION-BASED COMMUNITY ORGANIZING WORKS

Congregation-based community organizing is a movement that attends seriously to the cultural dimension of politics. In it, participants wrestle with their basic values and religious traditions, relating them to practical activism addressing concrete local issues. It has constructed an original, systematic religio-political language combining themes from the tradition of community organizing developed by Saul Alinsky with religious social action traditions. The language of the movement is often passionate and transcendent. Overall this is an expansive form of discourse. Furthermore, it pays attention not just to constructing a worldview but also to other forms of cultural work: telling stories, staging dramatic events, and modeling its values in the everyday activities of the movement. While it has some limitations, it is an important example of robust cultural work in relation to progressive politics.

Terms for the movement vary, including "congregation-based community organizing," "faith-based organizing," and "broad-based organizing." These phrases, in my view, do not point to organizing approaches that differ in any major way, and I will use them interchangeably.[1] This movement is somewhat different, however, from other kinds of organizing, such as the work of labor unions or the Association of Community Organizations for Reform Now (ACORN). Since I will not be discussing these other species of organizing, in this book the terms *community organizing* and *organizing* will be used to refer to faith-based organizing.

The main focus here will be on the cultural side of organizing rather than its political strategy and impact. I will not try to provide a full portrait of the movement or a broad evaluation of its contributions to social change—this book is about the cultural dimension of politics, not community organizing. Many people with progressive politics would not choose to participate in congregation-based organizing either because they are not involved in any religious body or because they find other avenues for political change more promising. But those same persons can still gain from examining the strengths and weaknesses of the cultural practices of faith-based organizing. These strengths and weaknesses have implications for other kinds of progressive politics, where analogous cultural strategies—not necessarily ones involving religion—are possible. Organizing, in short, can help us understand the potential cultural bases for changing American politics.

These implications, however, would be much weaker and less interesting—much less plausibly generalizable—if this were a narrow and sectarian movement that involved only elite Americans, that operated only on a small scale, or that by doing expansive cultural work condemned itself to having no practical impact. But congregation-based organizing may be the largest coherent contemporary movement for economic justice—either secular or religious—that engages grassroots Americans locally in face-to-face political activity.[2] By spring 2000, when the most recent national survey of congregation-based organizing was completed, there were 133 local organizations located in thirty-three different states plus the District of Columbia. These had enrolled over thirty-five hundred congregations, with nearly 3 million adherents, as official, dues-paying members. Faith-based organizing operates on a vastly larger scale and recruits a much more varied array of participants than other religiously based progressive movements. It involves not elites but ordinary Americans, giving them opportunities to be articulate leaders in their local organizations. It engages major secular institutions such as corporations and local governments. While there is room for debate about the efficacy of the political strategies faith-based organizing has evolved, it clearly takes practical objectives very seriously, and few would deny that it has significantly influenced public debate and practical outcomes in many of the cities in which it operates. Furthermore, it is theologically, denominationally, racially, and ethnically diverse. And it manages to be explicitly religious while connecting its claims to secular ethical and political languages many Americans care about, such as those concerning human rights, democracy, and civil rights.

In this chapter we will see how one such congregation-based community organization, Milwaukee Innercity Congregations Allied for Hope (MICAH), developed and how it works, and then we will briefly examine faith-based organizing as a national movement. That is, I will largely be describing organizational arrangements and practical activities. These form the context for the cultural work of the movement. They also have a cultural element themselves, expressing in action many of the core values of faith-based organizing. Furthermore, the practical character of the movement—the kind of people it enlists and so on—is something we need to know when considering how its cultural work might relate to other forms of progressive politics. The following two chapters will focus on the movement's cultural work. In chapter 3, I will describe the main features of the religious and political perspective it has constructed. Chapter 4 looks at the narratives and public events that emerge from organizing, and a conclusion to this part of the book sums up the ways in which its cultural work is both expansive and constrained.

AN ORGANIZER AND HER ORGANIZATION: CHERYL SPIVEY-PERRY AND MICAH

Let us start with the intertwined stories of MICAH and the organizer who played the primary role in building it, Cheryl Spivey-Perry.[3] These stories exemplify patterns found in many congregation-based community organizations and in the development of many people who become involved with organizing. The work that eventually evolved into MICAH began in 1988. There had been previous organizing in Milwaukee, including an Industrial Areas Foundation project in the late 1970s. But these precursors do not appear to have had much, if any, influence on the development of MICAH. Rather, MICAH had two roots.

First, the Catholic archdiocese had promoted the formation of a coalition of inner-city parishes. Many of these parishes were suffering from membership declines and financial woes as inner-city neighborhoods became poorer and members of traditional Catholic ethnic groups moved to more affluent neighborhoods. The coalition was intended to take up joint planning and social action in hopes of alleviating such problems. This work started in 1986, and Paul Bormann, who is white, was hired to lead it. Bormann was aware of faith-based organizing models and interested in applying them.

Second, a city-wide hunger task force was experimenting with new directions. It had been an effective but traditional feeding program that provided twenty-seven thousand meals a month and involved nearly two hundred Milwaukee congregations, both black and white. In 1988 this project received a grant from the Catholic Campaign for Human Development (CCHD), which is the social action and antipoverty arm of the National Conference of Catholic Bishops. The grant was awarded to allow the task force to add a new dimension to its work: organizing.

The distinction between organizing and service provision is critical to community organizing. Congregation-based community organizations are primarily involved in what might be called political or social action, rather than in providing social services or running economic development initiatives. They aim to bring people together into an organization that can exert power. Typically they do *not,* except as a sideline or through a spin-off, build housing, operate food pantries, or open credit unions or recreation centers. Instead they typically pressure governments and corporations to bring more resources into communities that need them. This focus reflects and expresses one of the basic concepts of community organizing, "power"—a concept that is understood in this movement to have religious as well as political dimensions.

People involved in community organizing also contrast their work with "advocacy." In advocacy, groups put forward public policy positions in a disinterested voice, presenting themselves as speaking on behalf of others or for the general good. For instance, church groups with largely middle-class constituencies sometimes fight cuts in welfare that will hurt the poor. By contrast, organizing is intended to create vehicles for people to speak *for themselves,* advocating their own needs, agendas, and concerns through organizations *they* control. The idea of "self-interest" is central to this approach, and is interpreted within organizing in a way that is not inimical to religious ethics or a strong focus on community and the common good.

The contrast between organizing and either service provision or advocacy also helps explain the heightened concern with cultural work in faith-based organizing. Consider an example of service work: running a community-based housing development corporation. To do this requires, above all, a small cadre of people with a high level of what might be called "middle-class" skills: technical, legal, and financial expertise. Organizing, on the other hand, requires the involvement of a large number of people, and they must come from the indigenous community. To be sure, organizing participants are often committed and effective people, but their skills need to be honed as part of the organizing process. As for advocacy, those who do this kind of work, seeking to advance what they take to be the needs of others, are typically experienced in writing and speaking in public, and are accustomed to having their views be taken seriously. Here again, organizing differs in that many of the people who come to be the most important leaders are not articulate at the outset. To involve only people who are would defeat the whole purpose of organizing. If the agents and beneficiaries of change are to be the same, people who are *not* used to being articulate public leaders will need to become so. Organizing is often taken to be politically populist, and this may be so, but it is certainly culturally populist in the sense of aspiring to dramatically widen the range of people with the kind of cultural capital useful in politics.

CCHD staff strongly encouraged the hunger task force to engage the Gamaliel Foundation, headquartered in Chicago, as a consultant for this new direction of work. Gamaliel, which was relatively new at that time, was primarily interested in promoting the development of congregation-based organizing projects. It brought that orientation to its work in Milwaukee, presenting a model for how to relate faith to politics.

An early step, overseen jointly by Greg Galluzzo, the director of Gamaliel, and task force leaders, was to hire an organizer. That organizer was Cheryl Spivey-Perry. Often organizers are newcomers to the cities in which they work—it helps to have a fresh perspective and not to be fazed by the likelihood of making enemies—but Spivey-Perry was a native of Milwaukee. Born in 1954, she went to tough inner-city schools. Then her life took a different direction when she entered Marquette University. This, Spivey-Perry reported in an interview, was "a drastic, drastic change. [It] took some adjusting to, that type of life versus what I was coming from."[4] She became pregnant, had a child as a single mother, and went on welfare. Fortunately, in the early 1970s there were federal job-training programs that allowed her to finish her degree with public support, find a job, and get off welfare. She ended up working at Shalom High School, an alternative school in the inner city, where she ran various programs and ultimately became the second in command. Spivey-Perry was recommended to Galluzzo and the hunger task force by people she had met at Shalom.

From their first meeting, Galluzzo told me in an interview a few years later, he thought she had great potential. "She came to the table with intelligence, commitment, [and] anger. She was very receptive to ideas, wasn't afraid of being challenged."[5] She ultimately became, in Galluzzo's view, the best female African American organizer in the country. Spivey-Perry described the hiring process from her perspective: "They called me over for an interview and I tried to get a sense of what they [wanted]. They were talking about something that really scared me. You know, it was very political, what they were talking about, and it sounded a lot like what Martin Luther King did. So I was like, I don't think I can do this, this isn't me. [But] for some reason, a higher spirit sort of guided me, this was something that I should try, that

I should do. And I talked it over with my husband, and so we decided that we would try it. Plus they had offered to buy my contract and I was getting quite a bit of a raise. So you know the money is always important. So I accepted the position and I went to the hunger task force."

Spivey-Perry's first task was to develop a cadre of African American pastors committed to developing a congregation-based community organization. Efforts in this direction were already being made but were ineffective. As she described it, "About twenty days after I was hired at the hunger task force they had already organized what they called a meeting of black pastors. And I went to the meeting. [Various pastors were there, including hers,] and Greg Galluzzo, and then the staff from the hunger task force was there. And really the white people outnumbered the black people. And it struck me that this is *not* a black pastors' meeting." A lot of the pastors were looking on passively, "and my pastor, he was like, 'yeah, this is good,' and everybody else just sort of looked and said 'yeah,' you know, but I could tell that there was no honesty in the meeting. Those pastors were clammed up. They just sort of said, this is another white folks' organization trying to tell us what to do. There was a definite aura in the room."

After attending a second meeting where no more was accomplished, "I started observing that something else had to be done. That people weren't hitting the mark. So I decided I would go out and try all these interviews. And so I went out and I started meeting with black pastors and talking to them about what this could be. I [talked with them] about what they could do. Why do we take [the injustices in the inner city] for granted? And what is the role of the church? What would they like to see their church do more of in the community?"

Over a period of months Spivey-Perry met with dozens of black pastors, usually several times each, before finally setting up her own meeting. In adopting this strategy, she was partly influenced by what she was absorbing from training, readings, and mentoring in congregation-based community organizing. Contemporary organizing is highly systematic and relies heavily on building an infrastructure of relationships. One does laborious work up front, as in these months of individual meetings, so that an enduring, stable, coherent organization can be built. This organizational strategy is cause and consequence of the strong cultural work done in community organizing. A permanent congregation-based community organization is an institution—some have existed for nearly thirty years. To build an enduring institution one must take cultural concerns much more seriously than if one is constructing a coalition that is only expected to last a few months. Looking at it the other way round, a short-lived group has a hard time doing cultural work. If members of an organization have no solidarity based on shared experience and no long-term commitment to working together, it is difficult to take time away from immediate tasks in order to cultivate shared understandings, construct ceremonies, or tell stories.

When she was ready to hold a meeting, Spivey-Perry organized it as blacks-only. She had a premeeting with Galluzzo and Bormann to plan strategy and had them return for an evaluation afterward. To help her run the meeting itself she enlisted the help of a black organizer connected with Gamaliel. As she reported, "Of course, I was terrified. But I did it anyway. I did it anyway. So, you know, it was about this time that I started realizing that I was going [to] be just fine, [with] what I can get other people to do. These twenty-four ministers came, all different denominations, all in their suits, you know. It was just incredible. And it took off from there because then I had a group to work with. That group of twenty-four and I started meeting once a month."

The evaluation following the meeting is something that almost always happens after an important event. It allows the people who planned or helped run the event (most of whom are present at the evaluation) a chance to understand and explain their victories or defeats—to place what happened within a broader narrative and view of the world. It also manifests what the "new institutionalism" in organizational theory terms the "ritual" aspect of organizational practices.[6] This means in part that many practices, in addition to fulfilling practical functions, *express* things about the organization. This is true even for highly goal-oriented organizations and those that think of themselves as entirely modern and rational. For example, most corporations have an affirmative action office. This unit makes a practical difference: for individuals, by righting particular wrongs; for the corporation, by avoiding lawsuits. But its existence also says to employees and the world—not just as public relations but as something believed by participants—something like: "This is a company that values diversity and wants to help America move beyond the legacies of slavery and xenophobia." The evaluation process in community organizing, correspondingly, is a way of saying, "We're committed to holding ourselves accountable and learning from our mistakes. We're a rational and modern organization, working systematically for social change. If we haven't fulfilled our goals yet, we will soon—watch out!"

With regard to the meeting she organized, I observed to Spivey-Perry, "It sounds like [they] made commitments to each other which they really meant." She replied, "They put it all on the table, Steve. And they talked honestly of what was in their hearts, not only about white people but about each other, because they all had apprehensions about Methodists, apprehensions about the Church of God in Christ and [so on], even though they were all [black]. There were black Lutherans there, black Catholics there, but it was just all black and they put it out on the table and hashed it all through. I had a vision I wanted to catch on, [for] something spectacular. It was a vision to see them all and the power of their churches stand up for things. That was my vision, that we don't have to have all this disaster in the community. If somebody says something about it, and says it forcefully enough, people will have to listen to us and deal with us on a whole different level."

Although the work before the meeting was important, the mutual influences that happened once she got the pastors together was equally so. "I did the ground work to get them into a place where they could hear about it and talk with one another. I talked about it with them individually. But what good does that do unless they see that there are sixty other pastors that have been talked to and are interested in this, too? And it was incredible to me to see how they all just sort of walked into the room and took their seats. And the black pastors were always impressive to me, because they would put on their good suits and come and see whose suit looked the best."

All this and more had to happen *before* an interracial organization could be formed. Paul Bormann (the archdiocesan organizer) and various white pastors wanted to form a faith-based community organization. Spivey-Perry had to deal with the diocesan group, which "had even gone to training" run by Gamaliel, "so they were a lot ahead of us." At this point Bormann was laid off because of funding problems, "which was a blessing because it gave me a chance to let my group catch up. And I went out and visited those white ministers and shared with them what I was doing and how I needed them to almost stop, to let this group catch up with where they are, and let them feel like they can take ownership. [They] agreed to put everything on hold for a minute. [This] gave us a chance to catch up and the black pastors a chance to feel like this was their project. And then we brought them all together. At the first [interracial] meeting they formed a steering committee, made up of black and white pastors." Thus Spivey-Perry's all-black organizing tactics at the outset had nothing to do with racial exclusivism and everything to do with building a strong interracial organization in which black and white participants related on a genuine basis of equality.

At this point the new organization—MICAH—was formed with sixteen congregations as members. Spivey-Perry moved from the hunger task force staff to the position of lead organizer for MICAH.

In small or medium-sized cities, community organizations typically operate throughout the whole city or sometimes even a larger area, but Milwaukee was large enough that the decision was made to define a specific set of neighborhoods, somewhat loosely termed the "inner city," as MICAH's territory. Thus a rectangular region with specified borders north, south, east, and west was defined. This territory comprised about one-third the land area of the city, with one-half of its population, and included the predominantly black and Hispanic neighborhoods as well as some white ones. Very few of the neighborhoods in this territory were prosperous. The purpose of this geographic restriction was in part to give focus—a manageable scope—to the organizing process and in part to work in an area that had more in common in terms of neighborhood needs than if one worked in the entire city.

This decision manifests one of the hallmarks of congregation-based community organizing: it focuses on a particular local place. That differentiates community organizing from kinds of activism that focus on shared issue concerns (as in environmentalism), or shared ethnicity or cultural identity (as in Hispanic organizing or gay rights work), or shared economic situation (as in union organizing). Organizing operates in a geographic space, and while the size varies—it is bigger in rural areas—the territory is never larger than a few contiguous counties.

This is significant in two ways. First, it relates to the idea embedded in the traditional conception of a parish (found especially in Catholicism, Episcopalianism, and Lutheranism) that a congregation is called to serve God in a particular *place*. That is, it has a geographic ministry that includes responsibility for people who are not part of the faith community. In theory, especially in Catholicism, individual believers are expected to belong to the parish in which they live. The congregation, then, is not an elective affinity group composed of like-minded individuals or people who like a particular kind of church. There is an isomorphism between this religious ideal and the idea of "community" embedded in community organizing (along with other forms of neighborhood activism and betterment), and that isomorphism is one basis for the convergence of religious social activism and community organizing over the past generation.

Second, the area is always small enough that everyone who is involved can gather face-to-face as needed, whether in meetings of work groups or assemblies of the entire organization. People participate personally and form relationships.[7] This builds solidarity and allows for a level of cultural work that would be difficult at long distance. People in MICAH largely enjoy their meetings and are not resistant to attending. Furthermore, community organizing regularly involves large—often extremely large—gatherings. These events or meetings, involving hundreds or thousands of people, generate enormous energy and enthusiasm, in part simply because of the experience of so many people coming together under one roof in the name of one cause. This helps sustain the more mundane work that goes on at other times. (Sociologist Emile Durkheim has shown how this operates in religious rituals but also implies that the same processes can work in secular contexts.)[8] The scale of these events also impresses outsiders with the ability of the organization to mobilize large numbers of people.

MICAH has always been a congregation-based project. That means that its structure, like that of all such projects, is that of an enduring community of organizations (of which most or all are religious congregations). MICAH and similar organizations are much more than coalitions set up to achieve a specific purpose. But their membership is *not* based on individuals. The "members" of MICAH are congregations, not persons.[9] One cannot join the organization as an individual but only through being a participant in one of the member congregations. The boards and even the work committees of the community organization are conceptualized as being composed of representatives from the member organizations (although in practice congregation members can easily get themselves appointed to work committees). There are, of course, organizational advantages to this arrangement. Culturally, as we saw in chapter 1, it means that religious allegiance is not something that individuals privately, almost accidentally, bring into the political organization—as was the case for the antiwar coalition in Cincinnati—but rather is something to be talked about and attended to.

At this early stage, the core of people involved with MICAH apart from pastors was minimal, and so Spivey-Perry started recruiting, training, and interviewing. "We kicked it off officially October 1st of 1989. And it began by me going out and interviewing all the pastors that were a part of MICAH. And the pastors gave me people to interview. I went into each church and I would spend two nights, three nights, whatever I needed, at their church. And so, from October until January I interviewed five or six hundred people. It was a lot of people, my God. Sometimes I think about that and [say] I must have been crazy, to do all of those interviews. So I did all those and out of [them] I would go back and [describe] what happened [to] the pastors: This is what I heard about your church; this is what I heard about what's going on in the community of your church and what's going on in the people's lives that I interviewed; and these are the three people, I think, you should bring into the training to train as core leaders."

The interviews Spivey-Perry did were only the beginning. "We trained three people from each congregation about the concepts of church-based organizing and how to conduct interviews. And their challenge was to go back and do their interviews and build a team to do interviews in their congregation, to interview every member of their congregation. And they went back and everybody started getting excited about how for us to be talking with one another, this was really something God would be wanting us to do. And then we had this whole worship service where all these people, all different faiths, came together [to be commissioned for interviewing], it was just really nice. And then, it was so well orchestrated and everything that people were excited about it and they understood, it wasn't complicated, you know, you just talk to people. And they went out and they did over 3,100 interviews in the community. And that was when the lay folks got involved in it, understood it and took it on. It just started spreading like wildfire."

The imagery of wildfire is strongly reminiscent of recurring patterns in American evangelicalism. And this is not an accident; there is a lot of revivalism involved in faith-based community organizing, at least as practiced by MICAH. This is apparent in the stress on transforming people and the attention given to methods for bringing this about, in the development of energy and excitement through mass meetings, in the witnessing many participants in community organizing do—telling the story of how their lives have been changed through involvement in organizing—and in the focus on personal relationships. And we can see in the commissioning service another hallmark of contemporary organizing: the effort put into the ritual or dramaturgical life of the organization, with carefully constructed, often dramatic ceremonies.

The kind of interviewing that Spivey-Perry did and trained others to do is a basic process found in every congregation-based community organizing project. It is done early in the organization's development and is then repeated every couple of years, especially at points when the organization is about to make major new decisions.

It is helpful to hear how the interviewing process was experienced from the perspective of a rank-and-file participant—Joan Hauser, a lay member of Gesu, a large Catholic parish near downtown Milwaukee. Joan was first recruited as an interviewer and later became a key leader in MICAH. As she tells it, "We were given a list of a number of parishioners and we called them up to set up an interview. So I called them up, went to their home, and I sat and talked [with] them about their lives, where they came from, who they were, their families, their expectations, what things they liked about Gesu, what things they didn't, what they wanted to see changed about the community where they lived, Milwaukee, and just got to know them, basically. And from that [we] wrote a little bit on a piece of paper so that we could give it back to the congregation and they could figure out what the concerns of our congregational members were."

This had gains for Joan personally. Among the people she interviewed, there were three "that I know for sure that I really, truly built a relationship with, and [the] relationship has really grown since those interviews. So it was really a good process, because like I said, [we] made good friends in our parish from that process." I asked whether she recorded the concerns people expressed about the parish, as well as the concerns about the community. She said, "Oh yes. Absolutely. One of the neat things that came out of it was at the time I felt the need for some sort of support [coping with her three] young children in church. So we started a childcare co-op from [some] of the people I found out were in the same situation [from interviewing them]. They were looking for the same thing. So from there I called all sorts of other people in our congregation and started our childcare co-op which has worked just so wonderfully for those who wanted to participate in it. So that came out of the interviewing."

From this story one can see the multiple purposes served by interviewing. It provides information to the organizer; input to congregational leaders who will later be representing their congregation's perspective on what issues the community organization should pursue; information for internal use by the congregation about the needs, concerns, and capacities of its members; an opportunity for the person being interviewed to clarify and articulate his or her values and "self-interest"; and a context in which relationships within the congregation are built and strengthened. The interviews enriched the inner life of Joan's church through originating a new programmatic structure (the childcare co-op) and also through building new relationships among members. As Joan puts it, "a lot of us know each other a lot better. You know, the community aspect is building." For the persons being interviewed, the experience probably built commitment to both Gesu and MICAH, since this kind of conversation is usually interesting and clarifying, and makes one feel listened and attended to.

The kind of interviews Joan did are termed "one-on-one's" in congregation-based community organizing and are a pervasive practice within the movement. Organizers talk of how many one-on-one's they do per week—twenty, thirty, forty, or even more. Pastors, during training, are told that one-on-one's should be the biggest part of their jobs.

These interviews fulfill important practical purposes. But in addition, the one-on-one is taken to be a strong expression of respect and regard for the interviewee, who is implied by the process to be a fascinating, unique, and self-determining person, a child of God whose views deserve to be listened to with care and sympathy and whose personal purposes deserve to be treated seriously. Thus one-on-one's are quite intentionally and explicitly a way of expressing or acting out core values of faith-based organizing, in addition to their practical utility for building the organization. They express the central focus of this movement on the sacredness of every human person, regardless of race, class, gender, or status. They are, in the sense described a few pages ago, a "ritual" within congregation-based community organizing.

As we saw, the interviewing process was intended to help the member churches as much as MICAH. Faith-based organizing normally takes seriously the task of building the member churches. Church social service and action is usually seen by both congregants and outsiders as altruism: contributions to the world at the expense of the congregation. By contrast, organizing is supposed to help congregations function better and achieve their *own* purposes more effectively. Rather than competing with other congregational priorities for scarce volunteers and money, involvement in organizing, it is hoped, will leave congregations with more energy and funds than they had before. Naturally the actual returns to congregations vary. The majority of MICAH pastors report significant gains for their congregation, such as improved leadership skills in their members, stemming from their involvement with MICAH. Some even see improvements in such concrete indicators of congregational performance as membership and giving.[10] Dennis Jacobsen, a Lutheran pastor in inner-city Milwaukee, reports that since his congregation joined MICAH its stewardship campaigns have gone better.[11]

The reasons for this commitment are in part practical: to keep congregations involved. In addition, this bespeaks the same ideology behind the contrast to advocacy, and the same cultural populism that ideology manifests. And of course, if one is serious about doing faith-based organizing, one will not kill the congregational geese that lay the golden eggs—the faith traditions and values that are fundamental to organizing.

The experience of being trained for and then carrying out the interviews built Joan's skills and self-confidence, leading to deeper involvement in MICAH and also enhancing her usefulness to her parish. Her story follows a pattern found repeatedly, telling of how she has become a more powerful and effective person, with a more interesting and fulfilled (if more stressful) life, through her involvement in organizing. Organizers frequently say, correspondingly, that the development of the capacities of participants is a very important goal. Some say that it is the most important aim of organizing. After staff salaries, the biggest budget item in MICAH, and probably most faith-based community organizations, is training. This expresses not only the movement's focus on the individual but also its cultural populism and focus on doing cultural work. Training is the most important context in which the characteristic concepts and ideas of the movement are transmitted to—and sometimes debated or modified by—participants. Training has the goal of making every person into an articulate, powerful leader.

Throughout MICAH's organizing process, new congregations were recruited. By 1993, thirty-five congregations had joined. Organizing, as we can see, is a process-heavy enterprise that expends enormous effort on building an institutional infrastructure, and this work was done very effectively in Milwaukee. But, in addition, there naturally has to be something this structure *does*—issues it deals with and actions it takes directed to the outside world. Congregation-based community organizing describes itself as "multi-issue," and in practice this means that it starts out with *no* issues. In fact, issues, while certainly important, are not nearly as important to most organizers as building an organization and developing the participants (people like Joan). MICAH did not ask congregations to sign on to working on any particular issue or package of issues. Rather they were asked to make a commitment to working collaboratively with other congregations on whatever local concerns emerged from a broadly participative process in which issues were discerned and defined.[12]

The way this process worked was that each congregation processed internally the concerns surfaced by the one-on-one's and then delegations from the member congregations came together in a lengthy Issues Assembly in 1990. Out of that came four priority issue areas: housing, economic development, education, and crime/drugs. For each issue area, a task force composed of representatives of the member congregations was formed. The task forces typically meet twice a month. In practice, not every congregation is represented; but the meetings of MICAH task forces I observed almost always had representatives present from at least half, and often three-quarters, of the member congregations. These task forces are where MICAH's day-to-day work on particular issues gets originated and planned.

The great attention given to the process of determining issues, and the fact that each congregation is involved in making decisions not only about which issues to address but also how to address them, has benefited MICAH organizationally. Not a single congregation has left the organization because of disagreements with the choice of issues or the stances taken on them. This is a striking contrast to the conflicts within congregations and denominations that sometimes resulted from the religious social activism of the 1960s and 1970s. Culturally, the issue determination process bespeaks the value faith-based organizing gives to democracy and (with some qualifications) how it puts a strong, deliberative "process" of decision making ahead of the "substantive" decisions that are made.

A few months after the Issues Assembly the organization was ready to pull together a large public event, with more than one thousand people from member churches present. As Spivey-Perry remembers it, "it was phenomenal. I watched the politicians' faces as they walked in the door." One of them arrived, and "saw the building overflowing, and said, 'Holy Shit!' And I chuckled and walked away, and I [thought], she knows what can happen here. And that's really what I wanted them to see. I felt like my job was not only to do the issues. The issues were important, but something I thought more important was to get the organization recognized. That they have to know that this is a viable organization that they have to deal with. So more than the issues, what I really wanted was that [the politicians and media and everybody in the community] had to recognize MICAH's power."

In October 1991, MICAH's official founding convention was held in a packed college auditorium with over sixteen hundred people in attendance. By 1993 it had become a major presence in city life. In terms of practical work, by this time MICAH had successfully lobbied the Common Council to pass an ordinance committing the city to converting fifty abandoned buildings annually into scattered-site public housing; had won an employment provision for local public contracts requiring that a certain proportion of jobs go to unemployed inner-city residents; had pressured a number of banks into making commitments to increased small-business, mortgage, and home improvement loans in the inner city; had supported an unsuccessful ballot initiative to allocate additional funds to the Milwaukee public schools; and had won an increase in the number of state-funded drug treatment beds in the county. What practical results these accomplishments have had for the lives of inner-city residents is a complex issue, but the scope of the work and its impact on public debate is indisputably quite significant.

One sign of MICAH's cultural success is that it has put the mayor of Milwaukee on the defensive. Mayor John Norquist is fairly liberal but is frequently pushed by MICAH toward taking more progressive actions than he had in mind. He does not always *do* what MICAH wants. But in my time in Milwaukee I never heard him contest the goals of MICAH's proposals. Rather his stance was usually something that might be paraphrased in roughly these terms: "What MICAH proposes is good, but we don't have the funds to do it right now" or "I agree with MICAH's ends, but there are better means for achieving them." We will see in chapter 4, for example, that when MICAH pursued a line of housing policy that the city administration did not like, the mayor never felt able to publicly disagree with MICAH's philosophy and was forced to take refuge instead in arguments about lacking the resources required to implement it. In short, MICAH has significantly managed to define the terms of debate and to occupy the discursive high ground. This is an important achievement and is particularly impressive since the combined membership of MICAH congregations constitutes only about 3 percent of the city's population.

Let us review a few practical facts about how MICAH works. Organizationally, MICAH has been governed since the founding convention by a board with one representative (lay or clergy) from each member congregation. Each congregation pays annual dues that in 1993 ranged from eight hundred dollars to about twice that, as well as committing significant energy to MICAH. The combined membership of the thirty-five congregations was around twenty thousand. Ethnically, twenty-five of the congregations were predominantly African American. Religiously, about one-third were Catholic and one-third "mainline" Protestant (Lutheran, Presbyterian, Episcopal, etc.). In each of these groups, about half of the churches were predominantly European American and the rest African American. The final third of the member congregations were from predominantly black denominations, such as the National Baptist Convention, Missionary Baptist Church, and Church of God in Christ. Most of the members of these black churches were theologically more traditionalistic than the mainline Protestants or Catholics.

Thus in 1993 the organization had considerable theological and racial diversity. However, white evangelicals, non-Christian groups, and minority groups other than blacks were largely missing. The last of these gaps has been addressed since 1993, to the extent possible given Milwaukee's ethnic composition, by the arrival of several Hispanic congregations. Religiously, there has been informal participation from a black Muslim temple that wants to be involved but not to join officially. One Jewish congregation has joined. The multiracial character of the organization is quite impressive; at meetings there are often heated arguments but they never involve or seem to encode race. Theological differences do show up occasionally, although not very frequently or with much divisive force given that the issues discussed are almost entirely concerned with inner-city economic justice.

MICAH is not just a coalition built on top of congregations, as we have seen, but strives to contribute to the congregations' own development and to establish an intimate relationship with them. Each member congregation is supposed to have (and most of them do) what are called "core teams" consisting of the pastor, the congregation's board representative, its representatives to each of the task forces, and anyone else who is involved with MICAH. This structural arrangement allows sharing of information and coordination of the various ways in which the congregation relates to MICAH. It also means that each congregation has a specific body responsible for MICAH work. The core teams replicate in miniature the structure of MICAH and place each participant in a dual role. A member of the MICAH housing task force, for instance, works in that task force with people from other congregations on a shared issue, but is also in the core team, working there with fellow congregants across issue lines. Thus the core teams are an important means for weaving together MICAH and the congregations. Other community organizations have ways of fulfilling this same function, although how they do it varies considerably.

So far, we have not dealt much with the influence of other organizations on MICAH. It is an independent nonprofit corporation, governed by its own board of directors. It fiercely guards its independence. But it does have enduring relationships with other organizations, and these have an impact on its life.

The most important such organization is the Gamaliel Foundation, MICAH's consultant. MICAH has a contract (which it can terminate at any time) with Gamaliel, paying it (in 1993) about ten thousand dollars a year for a broad range of services. This relationship with Gamaliel was especially close in the early days of the organization, but the expectation on both sides is that it will continue permanently. From the time Cheryl Spivey-Perry was hired until after the founding convention, Greg Galluzzo (who lives in Chicago) spent one day almost every week in Milwaukee, and in 1993 he was still spending about two days a month on site. The organizational design of MICAH is similar to that of other Gamaliel-affiliated community organizations, and this is not an accident. The sequence of steps that MICAH and Spivey-Perry went through was worked out in collaboration with Galluzzo, and many of the strategies were ones successfully used before in other cities where

Gamaliel had been the consultant. Galluzzo was Spivey-Perry's mentor, a person with whom she could discuss the perplexities that arose in the organizing process. Neither Spivey-Perry nor Galluzzo talk much about their interactions, but from observing them I would judge that Galluzzo had a significant influence but that Spivey-Perry ultimately made the key decisions and by no means always took Galluzzo's advice.

In addition, Gamaliel staff run week-long, intensive, residential training programs at least three times a year. These have been attended by dozens of MICAH participants, along with people from other Gamaliel affiliates. Gamaliel staff also come into town several times a year, providing one-day on-site training events to broader groups of people. The relationship with Gamaliel, furthermore, makes MICAH part of the Gamaliel "network." Organizations and organizers in the network share ideas and provide mutual support at key points. For instance, staff and key leaders from many other Gamaliel affiliates came to MICAH's founding convention. And increasingly affiliates are developing collaborative projects. The ones in Wisconsin, for instance, are working together on statewide issues.

The other organizational relationship that has been important for MICAH is with the Catholic Campaign for Human Development (CCHD), which as we noted earlier brokered MICAH's relationship with Gamaliel. CCHD itself provides MICAH with advice and information, and its staff visit Milwaukee regularly. It is a vital relationship financially; CCHD was still providing about one-quarter of MICAH's budget in 1994 and had provided a higher proportion earlier. There are a set of expectations and limitations that go along with the funds CCHD provides. MICAH is expected to have a reasonable system of financial accountability and a democratic internal governance structure, to make reports regularly, and to work on issues dealing with the poor. CCHD would not fund a group working for abortion rights or one that consistently and publicly worked at cross-purposes to the local Catholic bishop. CCHD is strongly committed to local self-determination, however, and imposes only these general principles.

These organizational relations and their importance are typical of faith-based organizing. Almost all local projects, and certainly all the ones funded by CCHD, have a consultant, and the majority of congregation-based organizing projects receive funds from CCHD at least at the outset.

Let us wrap up our account of MICAH by returning to Spivey-Perry's story. Near the end of an interview I asked how the organizing experience had changed her thinking and that of others involved in MICAH. In response she told a story of how a new way of connecting faith to politics had developed and won out. She spoke first about MICAH participants: "Well, I think that there are a lot of people of faith that understood this and had a vision for it and realized that this is really what God wants us to do, and that we are His vehicles to do whatever's going to be done here on earth. And every time somebody tells us to just pray—yeah, we have to pray but then we have to act. And I think a lot of people started trying to live that out, that's what I saw."

A few moments later I asked how her own relationship with God had changed. "It's all been the grace of God, Steve. Because you have to think, I didn't know anything about organizing, I never heard these concepts before—nothing. But it's all on faith. And I believe God led me into this, that's my own personal belief about it. And it has strengthened my faith, because so many things came up that I had never [seen]. I had never really been in a Catholic church, I had never been in a Lutheran or Episcopal [church]. To be able to deal with them, to go to their churches and understand and have them understand me and to talk and find we have a lot in common, and we meet together on a common ground to do things, I think was all the grace of God. When I gave my farewell speech at the last MICAH meeting I tried to say that to them, I said, I stand here today a witness to the grace of God, because I don't really want to take any credit, because I never knew anything about what I was really doing, Steve. I believe it was all His direction. I used to pray every day. I still pray a lot, a lot every day. And I just always asked for strength and guidance. And I really believe that MICAH was a miracle. I really do."

If this was a miracle, Spivey-Perry was part of how God brought it about. And she herself has been transformed not just politically but also personally and spiritually by her experiences. She tells of how she can now read and handle any situation, of how she has become more effective, and even of how she is a more equal partner in her marriage. The story of her empowerment parallels her story of MICAH's growth, and both stories are powerful and persuasive. Similar stories are told by others who have been strongly involved in faith-based community organizing. The creation of such narratives is an important part of the cultural work of this movement.

Although Spivey-Perry is certainly a shrewd organizer, faith is central to her life. In her work, religion is not something manipulated for political purposes but constitutive of those purposes. And the growth of her political consciousness has if anything further deepened her faith rather than competing with it. Critics of the activism that developed in many denominations during the 1960s and 1970s, often around the civil rights movement or opposition to the war in Indochina, saw this activism as reflecting a hollow faith or leading to a hollowing out of faith. This line of criticism may have been unjust, but the rhetoric and practices of the activists of the time sometimes created tempting targets. With regard to contemporary faith-based organizing, by contrast, it is hard to imagine how such criticism would ever occur to a person who spent any time observing or participating in an organizing project.

FAITH-BASED ORGANIZING AS A NATIONAL MOVEMENT

MICAH is reasonably typical of congregation-based community organizing, although it is stronger and larger than average. Let us now look very briefly at the movement nationally to understand the context within which it creates its distinctive cultural forms. More details, based on two national surveys of faith-based community organizations, can be found in appendix A. (I conducted the first survey in 1994 and served as consultant and analyst for the second, conducted in 1999–2000 by Interfaith Funders.) The most important findings from the two surveys are that

- as of March 2000, there were 133 organizations of this kind in the United States, with an estimated 3,515 member congregations, comprising 2.99 million adherents;
- the organizations also had an estimated 494 member institutions of other kinds, predominantly school groups, labor union locals, and neighborhood associations;
- the movement has been growing significantly, with the present number of local organizations up 48 percent and the number of member congregations up 95 percent in the six years between the earlier survey and the most recent one;
- the movement was highly diverse ethnically and racially: 35 percent of the congregations were predominantly black, 21 percent Hispanic, 2 percent Asian or Native American, 6 percent interracial, and 36 percent European American;
- and the movement was fairly diverse religiously, with broad representation from all kinds of Christians except white evangelicals, a Jewish presence at about the level found in the American population, and a sprinkling of congregations from non-Judaeo-Christian faiths; the presence of non-Christian religions increased somewhat from 1994 to 2000.

The vast majority of the groups share a set of "family resemblances"—the hallmarks of organizing noted in MICAH's story. Even though the local organizing projects are independent, they are fairly similar in their structure, organizational principles, strategy, and even political theology. In short, they all follow a common blueprint. There are, for instance, a number of terms that are regularly used in practically all these organizations but only occasionally in other kinds of social change organizations. The issues dealt with in different cities are fairly similar.

These commonalities have three sources. First, they are based on the spread, through imitation, of a model that appears to succeed. Many clergy and members of religious congregations want their congregations to assist in improving their communities but have been frustrated by what they see as the failures of traditional social service and advocacy efforts. Often they read or hear about faith-based organizing projects in other cities and follow these inspiring models. One example of this kind of imitation is the appeal of fair wage proposals since the concept was successfully pioneered by Baltimoreans United in Leadership Development (BUILD), a congregation-based organizing project. By November 1999 fair wage laws had been passed in forty-two cities and counties around the United States.[13] The second source of similarities is environmental. The issues addressed by organizing are much the same from city to city in part because American inner cities face common problems.

These two factors could explain the kind of family resemblance that one often sees in social change organizations—for example, among local peace centers in various cities. Faith-based organizing projects, however, have much more in common than peace centers. They are almost as much alike as congregations of the same denomination, which are constrained by denominational rules, or as local chapters chartered by a nationwide organization such as Amnesty International. The factor responsible for this high degree of commonality is the work of institutions like the Gamaliel Foundation.

Almost every local organizing project has a consultant, and in most cases this is one of four training and consulting organizations, or "networks." The largest and best-known of these is the Industrial Areas Foundation (IAF) founded by Saul Alinsky. As of March 2000 it had forty-eight affiliates among the 133 groups existing at that time. These were mostly in Texas and the Northeast Corridor. BUILD is an IAF affiliate, as is Communities Organized for Public Service (COPS) in San Antonio, which was developed by Ernie Cortes. Gamaliel, MICAH's consultant, had twenty-seven affiliates; it is strongest in the Midwest and the Plains. The Pacific Institute for Community Organizing (PICO) had twenty-nine affiliates, mostly in California. Direct Action Research and Training

(DART), which is concentrated in the South, had twelve. Fourteen organizations, mostly in the Northeast, used small-scale consultants, and three had no consultant.[14]

Within a network there are common training procedures, staff who circulate from city to city, and opportunities to interact with people from other communities. For the organizers, the network provides professional career tracks. Increasingly the networks are also pioneering common initiatives, such as attempts to influence statewide politics in Texas (IAF), California (PICO), or Wisconsin (Gamaliel). This is intended to break out of the localism that often characterizes community organizing. The networks add organizational coherence to the movement. They provide institutional memory and connect the local groups to other locales.

The networks are a source of similarity among their affiliates, but they are also alike in many respects—the basic themes in their training, for instance, are very similar—and their influence therefore makes groups similar across as well as within networks. Each network makes claims of distinctiveness and often superiority—they are intensely competitive. And there are certainly differences among them. But well-informed, impartial observers such as CCHD staff and long-time organizing guru Mike Miller argue that these differences are not enormous, that they are in fact smaller than the differences among the projects *within* each network.[15] Even more important, the differences among the networks and even the individual projects are small compared with the differences between this kind of organizing and other forms of activism in the United States today.

In sum, congregation-based community organizing is a movement that engages large numbers of Americans, many of them not previously active, in public life, and works hard on building their personal capacities for leadership and for connecting their faith to the social and political world. Let us now examine the religious and political perspective this movement has developed.

Chapter 3

THE RELIGIOUS AND POLITICAL PERSPECTIVE OF COMMUNITY ORGANIZING

The ideas that underlie and inform faith-based community organizing are a creative although sometimes uneasy melding of concepts from various Christian social action traditions and the philosophy of community organizing articulated by Saul Alinsky. To introduce this perspective, I will briefly review its religious and political sources and then recount the story of a thoughtful priest who is a core participant in Milwaukee Innercity Congregations Allied for Hope (MICAH). The balance of the chapter will describe four key concepts that largely define the perspective: power, self-interest, relationships, and values.

SOURCES FOR COMMUNITY ORGANIZING

Five Religious Traditions

The most important religious tradition providing a basis for contemporary faith-based organizing is the stream of modern Catholic teachings about the economic order, beginning with Pope Leo XIII's encyclical *Rerum Novarum* (1891). Catholic economic teachings today carry a political outlook close to that of European social democracy, upholding private property but pushing for public intervention in economic life and egalitarian corrections to market outcomes. They favor a "moral economy," that is, one governed by ethical principles rather than market forces. In 1986 the U.S. Catholic bishops' conference issued a pastoral letter on the economy reflecting these principles. On the tenth anniversary of this pastoral, the bishops articulated a brief "Catholic Framework for Economic Life." This statement, reprinted in this book as appendix B, proposes among other things that "all economic life should be shaped by moral principles. . . . A fundamental moral measure of any economy is how the poor and vulnerable are faring. . . . Society has a moral obligation, including governmental action where necessary, to assure opportunity, meet basic human needs, and pursue justice in economic life."[1]

The Catholic influence on community organizing was evident even in Alinsky's lifetime. Alinsky maintained a close friendship, lasting three decades and including an extensive correspondence that has now been published, with the French lay Catholic philosopher and social thinker Jacques Maritain.[2] Bishop Bernard Sheil was an important early ally, and Monsignor John Egan worked with him closely on many projects. Today the lines of influence are if anything stronger. John Baumann, who heads the Pacific Institute for Community Organizing (PICO), is an active member of the Society of Jesus. His organizing work has the enthusiastic blessing of his order, which also provides substantial financial and infrastructural support. Greg Galluzzo of Gamaliel is a practicing Catholic and former Jesuit, and Ed Chambers of the Industrial Areas Foundation (IAF) was a Catholic seminarian in his youth. The national survey reported in appendix A indicates that 42 percent of the organizers and 33 percent of the congregations are Catholic. Further, as the major funder of community organizing, the influence of the Catholic Campaign for Human Development (CCHD) should not be underestimated. While the support of CCHD is not conditioned on Catholic content in what a community organization says, its involvement gives Catholic themes and figures a certain prominence. For example, at organizing events one often finds bumper stickers produced by CCHD and with its name on them. These quote Pope Paul VI saying, "If you want peace, work for justice!"

African American Christian social action traditions constitute a second strong and clear influence on organizing. African American Protestantism is highly biblical, drawing fluently on scriptural resources and emphasizing, as prominent black theologian James Cone describes it, themes of "love, justice, liberation, hope, and redemptive suffering"—themes that have social as well as spiritual meaning.[3] In chapter 2 we saw these influences in MICAH organizer Cheryl Spivey-Perry's reference to Martin Luther King, Jr., and they are implicit in the constant use of stories from Exodus. A senior PICO organizer, David Mann, pointed out in an interview that African American pastors are on average the most biblically literate and articulate group of people involved in organizing. Therefore, he said, organizers are "constantly inviting their African American pastors into their actions because they can talk about Moses and the Exodus in terms of the pain and the changes needed just like that [snaps his fingers]."[4] These pastors and the social action traditions they bring with them have a major influence on the discourse of congregation-based community organizing.

A third important tradition is liberation theology, which is best known in the United States from the writings of Latin American theologians such as the Peruvian Gustavo Gutiérrez. This is a primarily Catholic social justice theology taking a more radical position than mainstream church teachings. It understands scripture as telling intertwined stories of salvation and human liberation. An often-used concept coming out of the development of liberation theology is that of the "preferential option for the poor." In addition to its theological contributions, this tradition has made a contribution to religio-political practice by developing base church communities: small groups of church members that combine Bible study and theological reflection with social and political action. In PICO, Gutiérrez's writings are regularly used in retreats.[5] Another sign of influence is that biblical texts are used to reflect on practical problems in very much the way that occurs in base communities.

A fourth strand is the Social Gospel tradition within American Protestantism, which emerged near the turn of the twentieth century. Social gospelers ranged from moderate reformers to socialists, but they had in common, as historian Sydney Ahlstrom puts it, "the idea that the doctrine of laissez faire required Christian modifications."[6] The core aspiration of this tradition is to bring gospel principles—the ethics of Christian love—to bear on economic life, modifying capitalism and the market system to institutionalize a higher degree of human solidarity. The Social Gospel movement influenced the development of urban ministries around the country, and many participants in community organizing were involved in these prior to their encounter with organizing. Dan Weir, an Episcopal priest who is a core leader in VOICE, the Buffalo affiliate of Gamaliel, spontaneously cited the Social Gospel as a major influence within organizing, and other participants have spoken to me about their involvement in urban ministries. David Mann of PICO worked in urban ministry but came to see it as "patronizing" and also "frustrating" because it lacked the "methods and principles" by which to make change. Typically, when people like Weir and Mann come to community organizing they bring unchanged most of their goals for reforming economic life, but decide that organizing offers more hope than traditional forms of urban ministry for achieving these purposes.[7]

A final influence is Christian realism, a way of thinking for which Reinhold Niebuhr's work might serve as paradigm. This is a perspective that takes a more pessimistic view of human nature and the malleability of the world than the four influences just discussed, but nevertheless remains socially engaged and progressive. The pessimism is grounded in the traditional idea that humans are radically sinful and in the disheartening historical experiences (World War I, totalitarianism, the Holocaust) of the twentieth century. Christian realism's pessimism regarding human nature leads not to withdrawal from but affirmation of politics, since if humans are not likely to create a good society out of their spontaneous nature there is all the more need for laws and public institutions to ensure some degree of social justice. The influence of Christian realism is more diffuse than that of the other traditions identified above, but it would be hard to understand the full range of assumptions in organizing without taking realism into account. That is, while one finds few explicit references to Christian realism, it is not unusual to hear within community organizing the expression of ideas that manifest a spirit closer to this tradition than to the other four. Among these are the emphasis one often hears from organizers on assessing actual outcomes rather than intentions; the separation between personal and public relationships constantly urged upon participants in organizing; the great attention given to power and self-interest; the suspicion organizers constantly express about forming permanent alliances; and the frequent emphasis on understanding how public policies really get formed rather than believing civics-class accounts. Lutheranism is the strand of Christianity in which pessimistic theological currents are strongest, and the principal U.S. Lutheran body has provided more grants and organizational support for organizing, from its national and synod offices, than any other Protestant denomination.

A final sign of the influence of Christian realism is that residential training programs in community organizing almost always include a role-play, near the outset, of a bleakly realist story from Thucydides' *History of the Peloponnesian War*. The story tells of Melos, an island city that was more or less neutral in the struggles between Athens and Sparta. The Athenians wanted to absorb it into their empire, but the Melians tried to persuade them, on the basis of justice and fairness, to allow their city to retain its independence. However, the Melians developed no strategy for dealing with the actual power and interests of the Athenians, simply refusing Athens what it demanded. In the end, the Athenians took the city, killed the men, sold the women and children as slaves, and sent their own people to inhabit it. The moral of the story, in training, is that organizing deals with real life and death issues, and that witnessing to high ethical values and relying on moral persuasion are at best inadequate, often useless, and sometimes harmful.

Although one can see influences from these five traditions, the pedigree of *particular* religious ideas expressed in organizing is often unclear.

Biblical references and explicit theological claims are frequently made. However, what wider theological tradition these particular references and claims are supposed to manifest is seldom stated. Which tradition is in play at any moment, and which has most influence, is hard to tell. Jim Dammier, the priest of a Catholic parish that belongs to MICAH, has his own view: "It's Catholic theology [that the Gamaliel Foundation is] doing. They took a little bit of the optimism out of the Catholic stuff so that it is acceptable to the Lutherans, and threw in some biblical approaches to cover the Baptists. But it is downright 'Church in the Modern World' Vatican II [thinking]." (The reference to the Lutherans has to do with the above-mentioned strength of pessimism in some Lutheran theology. "Church in the Modern World" refers to a key Vatican II document, *Gaudium et Spes*.)[8] But Episcopal priest Dan Weir disagrees. As we saw, he believes the Social Gospel tradition has a significant influence. Weir feels that the input from Catholic social teachings consists only of ideas that have nothing specifically Catholic about them and are in the area of overlap among various Christian social action traditions.[9]

Weir is wrong, I believe, in downplaying the role of Catholic social teachings. But he is absolutely right about the overlap. MICAH's position that the housing policy of the Milwaukee city government needs to give more priority to the needs of the poorest residents could easily be justified by *any* of the five traditions we have considered. The area of overlap is so large that except when people make specific reference to the sources of their theological statements—which happens, but not very often—the positions they stake out could usually be plausibly attributed to any of them. Furthermore, these traditions have been disseminated so widely, for so long, and in such varied ways that they now live in the air, so to speak. A person can easily encounter an idea coming out of one of these traditions in a magazine, a radio show, a sermon, or a conversation—but get no sense of where the idea came from. The particular religious ideas are known, but their sources and the frameworks they fit into are often unknown or at least unspoken. Participants in community organizing can and do pull ideas eclectically out of all five of these traditions (and sometimes others) rather than being limited to any single tradition's way of connecting faith to politics. This in no way diminishes the importance of religious traditions: they are to a large extent the sources of the particular religious ideas that organizing participants express. Catholic social teachings, the Social Gospel, and the others are perspectives that clergy have been hearing and reading about at least since their seminary years and that have also affected lay participants, if less systematically. Nor does eclecticism in the use of religious traditions diminish the authority of faith or its importance in orienting people involved in organizing. For most participants, their faith and congregations are far higher priorities than organizing. For example, it was clear to me while observing and talking to participants that if they felt that the organization's purposes were contrary to their faith, that it was bad for their congregations, or that MICAH used religious language manipulatively, they would desert it instantly. The ideas people find in religious traditions are transcendent sources of guidance, models, and inspiration as they go about work they consider to be in the service of social justice, democracy, and the Kingdom of God.

Saul Alinsky: A Secular Source for Community Organizing

Most people involved in any kind of community organizing today regard Saul Alinsky (1909–72) as its modern originator. Alinsky's work and thinking came out of and sought to develop the American tradition of radical democracy, the dominant form of indigenous American radicalism at most points in our history. This tradition includes populism, working-class republicanism, the New Left of the 1960s and 70s, and many American versions of socialism. It has been drawn upon by most progressive movements in this country, including, over the past half-century, the civil rights and labor movements, economic democracy initiatives, environmentalism, feminism, and the many varieties of community organizing. Radical democrats usually work to enhance the political and economic resources of ordinary Americans as over against elites, privileged sectors, and established institutions. They want more democracy: citizens should have continuous channels for engaging in politics rather than only the opportunity of voting every two or four years, and there should be an end to arrangements by which many of the most important decisions are made in settings such as corporate boardrooms that are not accountable to ordinary people. Radical democrats are perfectly willing to restrict market forces or take to the streets, and have no great respect for experts or authorities—their spirit is iconoclastic. As Alinsky put it, democracy is not "neat and orderly."[10] Many radical democrats, certainly including Alinsky, also tend toward a pragmatic mode of thinking, rejecting highly structured political perspectives—which they often pejoratively call "ideologies"—whether of the right or the left.

That Alinsky worked in this tradition is obvious in page after page of his most influential book, *Reveille for Radicals,* published in 1946. In this book, the most frequently mentioned hero was Tom Paine, a paradigmatic figure for radical democracy. In addition, Alinsky referred to other American radicals like John Altgeld, Edward Bellamy, John Brown,

William Jennings Bryan, Henry George, A. Philip Randolph, and Upton Sinclair. Alinsky continually used language that bespoke a transcendent commitment to the ideal of democracy, speaking of "sacred" values" and "our democratic faith." "The issue of democracy," he wrote, "transcends [all others and requires] every ounce of our energy, our faith, and our hope." Over and over, Alinsky's language manifested populist sympathies. This is evident in the term he used for community organizations—"People's Organizations"—and also in his frequent references to what "little Joes" or "John Smith" can do. And the purpose of the political methodology he advocated, the creation of community organizing projects, was to bring more people into active citizenship and also redress the material injustices experienced by under-resourced communities.[11]

Compared with religious traditions, Alinsky's influence is less authoritative within contemporary faith-based organizing. People sometimes argue against it and always use it selectively. But it is used more systematically than religious traditions and with a clearer realization that it represents a particular tradition of political thought. This higher degree of continuity and explicitness is the result of the history of community organizing.

Alinsky developed the methodology we now call community organizing in the late 1930s. His first and most famous project was the Back of the Yards Neighborhood Council in Chicago, which emerged publicly in 1939. This came to serve as an exemplar to be followed in future organizing work. After World War II, he spearheaded the creation of a number of well-known and controversial projects, notably in Rochester and the Woodlawn area of Chicago. In addition, Alinsky tirelessly spread his ideas about community organizing, most obviously through books such as *Reveille for Radicals* (1946) and *Rules for Radicals* (1971), but also through speeches, training programs, and personal contacts with younger radicals.[12]

The Industrial Areas Foundation (IAF), which Alinsky founded, has been directed since his death by Ed Chambers. Chambers has made the IAF into an important vehicle for both maintaining and revising Alinsky's tradition. Alinsky's own projects were brilliant and exciting but short-lived, falling apart or changing into forms Alinsky would not have endorsed within a few years after their founding. Things that Alinsky did *ad hoc,* such as training and working with local organizers, IAF started to do systematically. But the approach to organizing also changed. In the decade after his death in 1972, contemporary congregation-based (or broad-based) community organizing—a strategy of institution-building for the long haul, deeply enmeshed with religion—began to develop. Two milestones were the work of Ernie Cortes, who pioneered new kinds of organizing in San Antonio, and a widely influential position paper, "Organizing for Families and Congregations" (1978), written by Chambers. Further important developments were the emergence of the other three major networks—Gamaliel, PICO, and Direct Action Training and Research (DART)—and the increasingly important role played by CCHD. Starting in the 1980s, congregation-based community organizing spread quickly and became independent of IAF, with each network contributing to the methodology and perspective and developing it in new directions.[13]

As community organizing has developed over the years, a fairly high degree of continuity from one generation to the next has been maintained, preserving as a coherent perspective the source tradition from which its ideas come. Few community organizers have learned their craft in school or from books, or have practiced it in isolation. Rather, they were trained by organizers of the previous generation in a lineage—a kind of apostolic succession—that almost always leads back to Alinsky.[14] In particular, the key leaders in all four networks were formed, if not by Alinsky himself, then by his disciples and coworkers, and many of them have had connections to IAF at some point in their lives. The result is a significant cultural continuity, although Alinsky's ideas are certainly not accepted uncritically. Chambers expresses ideas that derive from Alinsky's, albeit with significant changes. The organizers in IAF affiliates, all of whom have been influenced if not trained by Chambers, continue to use Chambers's ideas, gradually modifying them. Leaders and organizers in other networks have made greater modifications, but they started from the same base. Thus many of the basic concepts of faith-based community organizing continue to be ones originally articulated by Alinsky. Furthermore, contemporary organizers are aware of this connection and mention Alinsky explicitly. Alinsky's ideas, however, have been greatly altered in their encounter with religious faith and new concepts have been developed. The outcome is a new religio-political language, distinct from both Alinsky's thinking and the religious sources of community organizing.

PHIL REIFENBERG'S STORY

Father Phil Reifenberg, who told me his story in an interview in 1991, had what the Catholic Church calls a "delayed vocation." That means that he had an earlier career, in his case as an Army officer. Born in 1948, Reifenberg went to the military academy at West Point, the traditional point of entry into a high-powered military career. After graduation and further training, he was sent to Vietnam. At this point, as Reifenberg describes it, almost everyone knew that the war had been lost but the pretense had to be maintained that U.S. forces were still fighting to win. The particular postings to which he was assigned often left him with long stretches of free time—often at night or out in the field—which he filled by reading widely in history, philosophy, current events, and literature.[15]

Reifenberg returned from Vietnam with a severe leg injury that cut short his military career, and in 1975 he entered seminary. There for the most part he read and learned standard contemporary theology, although he also encountered liberation theology. After ordination, he took advanced training in canon law and worked in the Milwaukee archdiocesan tribunal (the internal judicial body that deals with marriage annulments and the like). He became interested in inner-city ministry almost by accident during his period with the tribunal when he took up residence with a priest in the city who needed a colleague to help occupy the parish rectory and preside at weekend masses. Reifenberg loved the environment and parish, and here his readings expanded into urban and sociological work, much of it concerned with African American issues. He described this as the period in his life when his perspective really changed, especially because of encountering black culture through practical experiences in the parish and extensive readings of African American literature and social commentary. Later he went into parish ministry, ending up at St. Ann's Roman Catholic Church in Milwaukee, where he was serving as administrator when I interviewed him in 1993. St. Ann's is a characteristic example of the situation of inner-city parishes. The parish had twenty-four hundred members in the late 1960s. By 1993 its membership had shrunk to four hundred, yet it continues a vibrant presence in the city and lovingly, if with financial difficulty, maintains a beautiful church.

Reifenberg was involved in a wide range of social service and social justice work before MICAH arrived on the scene. Perhaps his strongest involvement was in the St. Vincent de Paul Society, which does social ministry, helping people who are in serious material need. When MICAH was formed, he became active in the fledgling organization. Although some organizers want to emphasize the gap between social service work and community organizing, Reifenberg seemed to experience no discontinuity and continued his involvement in service work alongside organizing. His MICAH activities have been varied and important: he has became a core member of the housing task force and the pastor's caucus, has been called upon regularly to speak at public events, and has served as MICAH's financial secretary.

He explained that after his inner-city experiences, "when I was exposed to the kinds of possibilities that church-based organizing presents, I wasn't uncomfortable with them at all. It seemed to me that this offered as realistic a possibility as I had seen yet for people actually taking control of their own lives and making a difference. Are we going to have a perfect solution through MICAH or through church-based organizing? Of course not. It's not a panacea. But [there] seem to be so many possibilities." He was deeply impressed with the ecumenical dimension of organizing, its multi-ethnic quality, and the commitments it has been able to elicit from regional denominational bodies. But he also gained a lot personally from his involvement in community organizing, and he has incorporated its central political and religious ideas into his worldview.

Reifenberg attended the seven-day residential training offered by Gamaliel and the parallel ten-day training from IAF. He found these different in method but not in substance: they "covered a lot of the same material" and the basic concepts were the same. "They got to the same point but perhaps by means of a different methodology. They are both going in the same direction." Both training processes were transformative, he reported. "It is fascinating to be in an environment with kindred souls. With people who are angry and frustrated, and who all of a sudden see a new possibility. People come together out of a deep sense of commitment. Frustrated with things that didn't work in the past, [but] not ready to give up. And they see a glimmer of hope, and just an inkling of possibility. You get people like that coming from Milwaukee and East St. Louis, and from Chicago and Peoria and Gary and Detroit, and you get all of these different people from all around the region together in one complex, and it is tremendously uplifting spiritually. [Through this you discover that] we don't [operate in a] vacuum, but there are people who feel like we feel, and talk like we talk, and who are angry like we are angry and want to change like we want to change, and yeah, it can be a very, very revivalistic kind of experience."

For him personally, one key result of the training was to build for the first time strong bonds and a sense of solidarity with clergy beyond the Catholic matrix. Another result was a much stronger sense of the importance and potentialities of lay ministry. "To see the other people, and to feel the excitement, especially in the nonordained church people, and how they want to use [organizing] as a way of living out their faith commitments, that was perhaps the greatest thrill of the training experience. I still think that it's the greatest thrill I get out of MICAH."

Reifenberg is thoroughly conversant and comfortable with the basic concepts of community organizing. Self-interest, for example, is an idea that to some seems antithetical to Christian values, but Reifenberg has come to understand it in a way that is congruent with his faith. He described how Gamaliel explains self-interest in terms of the etymology of "interest": a word that conjoins "*inter*" (which means among or between) and "*esse*" (being). Reifenberg interprets this to mean that the idea is rooted in "being among others"—that is, interests are relational. By contrast, "selfishness" is concern for oneself alone. Thus "my interests are never mine alone. They are tied up with a whole lot of other people at various levels. When I think of self-interest, I see a whole lot of interrelatedness that goes on, and how my self-interest is intimately and intriguingly linked with the self-interest of different people and different aspects of the community."

Another key organizing concept is power, and again Reifenberg, unlike some church people, is comfortable with this idea. He is against the "presumption that it's a limited commodity"—that is, that if someone gains power someone else must have lost it. Power, he says, is "the ability to act, the ability to produce, the ability to tolerate, the ability to express oneself. [But] a vast majority of people do not see power as relational." Instead, they see it as "dominational." In his parish and "all over, I think that there are people who react negatively to power as healthy. Who don't like to talk about self-interest because they're confusing [it] with selfishness."

The ideas Reifenberg has appropriated from community organizing are not in discontinuity with his past. He has not had a conversion or changed his sense of what kind of person he is, and his activities also represent continuity, with social service work continuing alongside organizing. But concepts such as self-interest and power have come into his life through organizing, and have "had an effect on me." He uses these ideas regularly, trying to build them into his sermons on occasion.

Reifenberg explained that his involvement in MICAH has brought many gains to him personally. For one thing, it has given him a "sense of satisfaction [in] seeing concrete accomplishments." Also, as he put it, "being involved with MICAH allows me to live with myself. This is a chance to take my faith commitments and actually draw some connections and act more [in a way] that is consistent with what I am feeling [and] believing." In addition, he reported enjoying the continual encounter with new ideas — new things to read, new speakers to hear — that has come from involvement in MICAH. "It certainly serves my interests. And it's fun. MICAH is exciting. It gets me out of this professional stuff, and moves it around, doing things, meeting people, just having fun."

In addition to the story he told about his own experiences, Reifenberg chronicled the relationship between MICAH and his parish. Combining personal and congregational narratives in this way is typical, especially for ministers. St. Ann's, Reifenberg reported, was one of the founding members of MICAH and one of the group of parishes Paul Bormann had been working with in the late 1980s, before Cheryl Spivey-Perry started work. All this meant that the parish had a long time to get used to the ideas of community organizing. Furthermore, there were "days of reflection and workshops" in which the parish council familiarized itself with organizing and thought through what it would mean to join MICAH. The result was that there was no opposition or skepticism within the parish council when the time came to make the actual decision. Even outside the council, only one family has ever voiced objections to MICAH or the social action perspectives, such as Catholic social teachings, that undergird it.

Reifenberg had high hopes for what MICAH could do for his parish. He encountered pastors in other cities who described the value their parishes had gotten out of involvement with faith-based organizing: "That new leaders were being surfaced. That people who had thought the churches were wrong were coming back. That it breathed a whole new kind of vitality into the church. I said, hey, if MICAH can do that for St. Ann's, great. So that was the kind of expectation that I had. That it would surface new [leaders] and establish a relevance that people could see. That it would make a difference in the physical community around St. Ann's."

The parish went through an interviewing process like that described in chapter 2, in which twenty interviewers did one-on-one's with 170 other parishioners. While Reifenberg did not assert that involvement in MICAH had led to significant growth in giving or membership for the parish, he saw the interviewing process as building important relationships, improving teamwork, and helping the leadership make decisions. He also saw major gains for his parish in terms of developing leadership skills and improving how well members understand local issues. And he felt that MICAH had had a strong positive effect on his own skills, sermons, and knowledge, and thus his work as a pastor. He told a story, in short, of intertwined personal and parish development resulting from involvement in faith-based community organizing.

CENTRAL CONCEPTS IN ORGANIZING

To speak of the religio-political "language" of community organizing is not just to use a metaphor. The worldview of organizing is largely shaped by a set of *words* that are given distinctive meanings and used on a daily basis within organizing. These words serve as both concepts and values. They are defined explicitly, repeatedly, and in some detail, and their meaning within organizing is not the same as in everyday language. Simultaneously, they express value judgments about how to do politics and what religious faith should mean for one's life. The terms that serve these functions within organizing and that one encounters most frequently are *power, self-interest, relationships,* and *values.*

The meaning and implications of these concepts are communicated to participants in a variety of settings. Training processes, which are ubiquitous in community organizing, are a key context in which this communication takes place. All the networks conduct half-day and one-day on-site sessions for the local organizing projects and also offer multi-day residential trainings. (I will draw on a seven-day residential training offered by Gamaliel that I attended in November 1991 for many examples of how the central concepts in organizing are defined.) Local projects also conduct training on their own. At training events, immediate tasks are put aside and attention is focused on developing the thinking, and the religious and political capacities, of participants. Here is where the religious and political language of community organizing becomes most explicit and systematic.[16]

The terms in this language are familiar, but within organizing they are used with new and unfamiliar meanings, taking people into uncharted territory. Language use is an explicit issue in training. At one point in the Gamaliel residential training, reacting to a trainee's comment, an organizer told a trainee to recast the idea he had just expressed "in the language we're using this week." At another point, a trainer talked about how our language has been "corrupted" by politicians and at still another argued that trainees should "unclutter" their language.

Underlying all the specific assertions of the organizing perspective is a challenge to thinking of religious life as a matter of private spirituality. Over and over again, organizers and network staff, who together make up the cadre of trainers, argue that the Bible is largely a story about *public* life. It tells about kings and judges; wars and the life of nations; and struggles over resources, the accountability of leaders, and the meaning of justice. The trainees, of course, are the kind of church people predisposed to agree with this interpretation of scripture. But the major reason this understanding is presented so frequently and strongly is not to convince the trainees of it but to better equip them for convincing others in their congregations. There, a significant proportion of adherents think of faith as having little to do with material life or as concerning only the private relationship between each believer and God. Organizing works constantly to put forward a contrary view.

Power

The idea of power serves to define a good deal of what organizing is about. In particular, this concept, in the view of people involved in faith-based organizing, differentiates what they are doing from standard politics, social service, advocacy, and also the ways churches and their members usually organize their activities. Power is explicitly contrasted to the kind of service churches have traditionally provided. According to a recurrent aphorism, if Moses had responded like many churches today, he would have set up a health clinic for the Israelites rather than leading them out of Egypt. Here scripture serves to indicate the superiority of political action and empowerment.

Community organizing defines the concept of power in a particular way. As we saw in Phil Reifenberg's story, power is understood in terms of the capacity to act effectively. This can be contrasted to traditional, zero-sum ideas of power, such as the sociologist Max Weber's classic definition of power as "the chance of a man or of a number of men to realize their own will in a communal action even against the resistance of others who are participating in the action."[17] To use Reifenberg's formulation, power is understood in organizing as "relational" rather than "dominational." In PICO, a central principle is that "power is in the relationship." And the Gamaliel training emphasizes the proposition that powerful people are highly relational—they get their power largely by establishing a rich network of relationships. Alinsky himself, in a more eclectic formulation, repeatedly said that power comes from "organized money" or "organized people." The dualism implicit in this formulation is that community organizing, having a lot less money than its opponents, will resort to organizing people and thus not only serve the interests of its participants but also promote democracy.

Similarly, the focus on relationships (rather than economic resources or access to the means of violence) as the basis for power is a way of focusing on the tools for power actually likely to be available to grassroots social action groups. In all the networks, the organizing process relies heavily on relationship building. Later we will examine why building relationships is valued as an end in itself. Here, however, the key point is its instrumental value: that careful attention to relationships is regarded by participants in community organizing as the best means for generating long-term popular power.

Power is also discussed in more traditional senses. Community organizations strive for "victories," and these are what the community organization achieves when it assembles and uses its power in ways that overcome resistance to the changes the organization seeks. That is, victories manifest power in Weber's sense. Another context in which one can observe a more traditional conception of power is what organizers call a "power analysis" of the city in which the organization is operating. In such an analysis, one identifies the people currently in control of decision making and the levers they use to exercise that control. The kind of power analyzed in a power analysis or in planning how to achieve victories may not be entirely zero-sum, but organizers often say that current political arrangements to some degree intentionally disempower the communities in which they are working, and community organizations intend to reduce the capacity of current elites to control what happens, thus reducing their power.[18]

An important tenet of community organizing is its positive view of power. Organizers argue that from a biblical standpoint power is not negative, not even neutral (as in Weber's view), but rather is something to be valued and sought. The most important goal of the movement is to give power to people who have not had it before. We are, said Greg Galluzzo at Gamaliel's residential training, "trying to sanctify the word 'power.' Power is a sign of God's presence. Where it is absent, evil will be perpetrated on someone." Trainers and organizers wage a never-ceasing battle against ideas of humility, servanthood, and meekness that they believe the churches tend to understand in ways that undermine the ability of churches and church members to act purposefully. (This claim might be less persuasive with regard to synagogues.) The church, a trainer said at one point, encourages us *not* to have power; in particular, "women in the church are encouraged to be powerless people." Statements repeating these sentiments, in varied forms, occurred dozens of times during the training.

Gamaliel's trainees did not take this assault lying down. In an angry exchange, one pastor accused the trainers of "church-bashing" and walked out. The trainer told the remaining trainees that he loved the church but "must speak the truth": that a lot of the churches "do absolutely nothing." Another trainee said, "Let's move on. We've heard over and over that the church is useless and we agree. Now let's get on with how to change it." Yet another participant told the trainer that he and his colleagues needed "more sensitivity."

One could argue about whether the trainers were bashing congregations. But what is hard to dispute is that they were calling for changing them. To a very large extent, congregations fulfill traditional functions for their members and in some cases people in the neighborhood. Organizers challenge them, instead, to emphasize proactive and outward-looking goals, working to bring outsiders in as new members and to affect the neighborhoods in which they are located.

Some women have complained of macho overtones in this conception of power and congregational life. In fact, an informal women's caucus developed during a Gamaliel training I attended. On the other hand, many women give testimonials about how they have felt empowered by their involvement in congregation-based community organizing. Cheryl Spivey-Perry's story is a clear case of such personal growth, as is Joan Hauser's, and we will encounter others later. It is in fact women, not men, who tell the most dramatic stories about the gains in power they have experienced. Outside observers notice the same thing. Here is a description of a MICAH public meeting in 1993, with nine hundred people in attendance, from a person who had not previously encountered community organizing: "All the speakers were articulate, well-prepared, and easy to understand. I was particularly impressed with the women who addressed the crowd. They appeared much more relaxed and self-confident than the men."[19]

Whatever differing views there may be with regard to how organizing relates to the roles of women and men, everyone involved with organizing agrees that many church people are uncomfortable with having power, taking responsibility, and being leaders. This is seen as an obstacle to churches' operating as a positive force in the community. Consider, for example, the testimony of Nathan Johnson, chair of the education task force and a lay member of MICAH's largest congregation, Greater Galilee Baptist Church: "The experience [at training] to me was that as Christians we really don't understand what power is all about. We've been so conditioned to always turn the other cheek and not take on the powers that be, [thinking that] as Christians we should not be going to the political side of the world to demand what is [just]. The book of Micah was telling the people who are in charge: do what is just. And see, we don't get that. Church people historically have always [said] well, I'll just take what you give us and be satisfied. So, it was a rethinking for me that people can have — do have — the right to demand things which would make our community better."[20]

Local organizing projects work to acquire power, as organizations, and to make the member congregations more powerful. They also make a major commitment to empowering individual participants. One reason for this focus is that individual empowerment helps build the organization's power. But there are more important reasons: empowered individuals are a permanent resource for the nation and the local community, and the dignity and well-being of each participant is enhanced by acquiring more power.

There are many signs of this focus. One is the enormous amount of money and time devoted to training programs. But formal training is only one tool for empowerment. Organizers think daily about how to develop and empower the participants in their organizations. They almost never speak in public or deal with public officials themselves; instead they prepare volunteer participants for these roles. Another sign of the focus on empowerment is that "leader" is the term used in the movement to describe anybody from a congregation who gets involved. (The Green Party groups described by Paul Lichterman, discussed briefly in chapter 1, have the same terminological convention and for the same reason: a strong commitment to the development of the political capacities of the individual activist.)[21] Furthermore, one finds organizers articulating the development of individuals—their capacity to act in the public sphere—as the central goal. One example comes from Pat Speer, an IAF organizer in New Haven and a lay Catholic who has had some theological training. Speer maintained, in remarks at a 1994 conference on faith-based organizing, that the key purpose of organizing is "the creation of primary leaders," whom he also defined theologically as "apostles." In his view "the issues don't matter," and equally "organizations don't matter," if these leaders can be developed. Some people might stress organizations more, but in other respects Speer's sentiments are typical. In a 1993 interview, Ed Chambers of IAF told me that the development of individuals is "the more important thing," compared with concrete victories. And David Mann, a PICO organizer who had gone from the San Jose to the San Mateo project shortly before I interviewed him in 1997, reported that at the party in honor of his departure "the part that brought tears to my eyes was testimonies. People stood up and talked about what I had taught them, in different forms. And that's the part that's most meaningful to me: to have people realize that they've learned how to become powerful agents of change, community leaders, through this process."[22] Mann speaks here of his personal feelings, but he expresses in a nutshell a sense of priorities that is pervasive in congregation-based community organizing and derives from this movement's distinctive thinking about power.

Self-Interest

The concept of self-interest, within the language of faith-based community organizing, has a very different—almost opposite—meaning from the one found in ordinary language. Let us take a look at this specialized meaning, and then at how participants accept, reject, modify, and supplement the idea of self-interest.

Organizers and trainers repeatedly stress the difference between self-interest and selfishness, as we earlier learned in Phil Reifenberg's account. Self-interest does not mean looking out for number one in disregard of others, but is rather an empowering clarity and focus on one's needs, values, and purposes. A person's most fundamental interest, trainers repeatedly say, is what one hopes will be written on one's tombstone. Or more generally, one's self-interest is really one's agenda, whether economic, social, or spiritual. This might be narrowly self-concerned: to get a higher salary, for instance. But it could equally well have to do with one's role in the world: to have one's congregation grow and prosper, or to become the mayor of one's city, for example. The important thing is that there is a strong "me" when one talks of one's self-interest. One lay leader in Buffalo returned from training and decided to assert his self-interest by ceasing to wear ties and renegotiating household duties. For Cheryl Spivey-Perry, as we saw in chapter 2, a central self-interest is to be economically independent, never to go on welfare again. Reifenberg finds MICAH meeting his self-interest through the fun he has in it, the intellectual stimulation it provides, and the clear conscience he obtains.

The concept of self-interest is understood in faith-based organizing theologically, and specifically in relation to Christ. It is based not only in an affirmation of oneself as made in the image of God but also in the idea that Christ died for humans and called them to new life as distinct, unique individuals. This is characteristic of Catholic social philosophy, as for example in the personalist tradition best known in the United States from Dorothy Day's Catholic Worker movement, and of many Protestant theologies as well.[23] There is even a kind of imitation of Christ embedded in the idea. Christ, trainers say, eschewed money, coercion, and manipulation in recruiting people to his movement, challenging them instead to seek abundant life—which the trainers take as equivalent to pursuing self-interest—by following him. One way in which trainers make this argument is through an exposition of the meaning of the biblical story of Jesus' temptations in the wilderness (Luke 4:1–13). In this passage, the devil, playing on Jesus' hunger, first suggests that he turn a stone to bread. Trainers equate this with using money to buy people's agreement to follow one's agenda instead of their own. In the next temptation, Jesus is promised that he can be the ruler of all the kingdoms of the world if he will worship the devil. That is interpreted as offering Jesus the chance to use coercive power to make people do his will. And finally the devil suggests that Jesus throw himself from the pinnacle of the temple so that God would perform a miracle to save him. This would be the path of getting followers by showing magical powers—a kind of manipulation.[24] The moral of the story is that we, like Jesus, are tempted to use tools for action that do not respect others. Instead we should motivate people through appeals to their own self-interest.

Thus self-interest is a concept not just about what kind of life to live as an individual but also about the basis for relationships with others. In Galluzzo's formulation, people need to know what they want and to understand and respect what others want because each person is "a center of activity and power," "a child of God." Dominance, and the kind of persuasion that tries to shape another person in accord with "my" agenda, are attempts to "usurp God's work." Such efforts constitute idolatry, since the other is "created in *God's* image," not one's own. That does not mean one is passive or that people are aware from the outset of their self-interest. What trainers call "agitation" consists of challenging others to become conscious of and act upon their own self-interest. In practice, this involves a hope that they will find their self-interest advanced by participation in the community organization. The training itself includes considerable time spent clarifying each participant's self-interest.

The counterpart of celebrating one's individuality as a child of God is to recognize the particularity implied in being only one of many such children. Pat Speer articulated this dimension of self-interest in the talk mentioned earlier: "If you say to me, there is a show on public TV tonight of Lithuanian dances, do you want to watch it, I will say no. But if you say the Chieftains [an Irish musical group] are on, I'll say, what channel? I can't like every culture and understand every issue. I can't; I am limited; I am who I am. We build a notion of humility into our training. Self-interest is an acknowledgment of our own [limits], our indebtedness." This means giving up the claim that one's political proposals are universal rather than based in the particularities of one's situation. This is an important statement, sharing one of the thrusts of postmodernism and pointing toward a stance that takes the diversity of American culture more seriously than did some progressive politics in the past.

In addition, this understanding of self-interest contradicts the way it is usually understood, in which it is a concept embedded in individualistic ideologies. Speer went on, immediately after the statement just quoted, to say that his work "has an underlying ideology: what church-based organizing is doing around America is a relentless frontal, total assault on the philosophical and epistemological individualism [in our country]. That doesn't mean that we are Marxist. But the underlying ideology which says that you stand where you stand alone, you got there through your own effort, [and] you are indebted to no one, is a fundamental lie." In his perspective, which he describes as "primarily theological," self-interest points to our limits, which in turn points to our interdependence with others. Thus in the end the concept takes on an almost communitarian cast, quite at odds with the kind of utilitarian individualism criticized by communitarians or Robert Bellah and the coauthors of *Habits of the Heart.*[25]

To be sure, some elements of more common meanings of self-interest persist. The geographic boundaries set by a community organization are intended not just to make the organizing task feasible but also to define a community of interest. MICAH, for example, works in a territory defined as inner-city Milwaukee; the issues with which it is concerned are those of that part of the city and its residents. These are the recurring problems of low-income urban neighborhoods in America: poor schools, dilapidated housing, crime and drugs, too few decent jobs, and so on. Whereas people from outside the inner city might be interested in the needs of low-income people out of altruism, one might say that MICAH people are acting out of self-interest.

Even here, however, the kind of self-interest is more than utilitarian individualism. Very few active participants are poor. Practically all come to meetings in cars. They can afford a baby sitter or have stable family lives where someone will reliably take care of the kids on meeting nights. In fact, many do not themselves reside in the inner city, even though they belong to inner-city churches. This is true for members of the African American churches that make up three-fourths of the organization as well as for members of European American congregations. Many of these are middle-class churches with members who have moved out to more affluent neighborhoods in the city. Nonetheless, MICAH participants have a stake in the inner city. Even if they do not live in inner-city neighborhoods, the value of their houses goes down and their tax burden for sustaining municipal services goes up when center-city conditions worsen or spread. The state of the schools affects them. Their congregations are hurt by inner-city blight. Those who do not live in the core city usually have friends or relatives who do. For the participants who do live in the inner city, even if they themselves are not poor, these impacts are even stronger. The self-interest of MICAH participants, in short, is practical and in part material, although it has to do with their embeddedness in the urban fabric rather than their situation as isolated individuals. As Reifenberg would say, it is relational.

Furthermore, self-interest, like power, is in some respects an individualistic concept, encouraging people to focus single-mindedly—in a sense ruthlessly—on an agenda *they* define, rather than getting deflected by the desires or even the needs of the people they encounter. Organizers apply this message over and over again to pastors, and also to women in the church. In doing so, they explicitly or implicitly compare self-interest to altruism or selflessness. That is, self-interest is contrasted, and preferred, on the one hand to selfishness and on the other to altruism. Speer argued that "it is important to realize that we have people who do not love themselves. I mean pastors and [others] who are so big into responding to every phone call that they have never figured out what their self-interest is. They don't know how to say no." One Gamaliel trainer cautioned, "If pastors act like suffering servants their churches and [they] themselves will not survive." The term *suffering servants* refers to passages in Isaiah 53, traditionally understood by Christians as pointing to Jesus, about one who suffers and thereby redeems the community. A lot of suffering, this trainer was arguing, doesn't redeem anybody. Articulating the goal of personal transformation found in the training, another trainer said that "this whole week [the training] is about people deciding they're going to take control of their lives" rather than letting life be organized by events around them or the demands of others. Repeatedly, participants in organizing are challenged to clarify their personal agenda and then pursue it.

Participants react in varying ways to the concept of self-interest. Some people, like Reifenberg, seem totally in tune with the idea. But there is some opposition. At a PICO training, one trainee was heard to comment that it was "such a *limited* idea." Others, thinking about being a "concerned citizen," wanted to assert that there could be legitimacy in an altruistic motivation for doing politics. Some MICAH participants feel that the idea of self-interest is not really compatible with gospel ethics. And trainees sometimes criticize trainers for what they believe to be an excessive focus on self-interest. At a Gamaliel training I observed, a woman who described her "self-interest" in terms of contributing to social change was criticized by the trainer for the absence of any "me" in her statement. Another trainee observing the exchange said she felt it was a typical male–female interchange and that the trainer's perspective "feels foreign to me."

However, in interviews with people who have been active in community organizing for some time, the typical story is that the speaker was originally uncomfortable with the concept of self-interest but later decided that it was helpful and not anti-Christian. An example is the account of David Boyd, an Episcopal priest serving a MICAH congregation. Boyd had no prior experience in inner cities or multiracial contexts but was open to learning. In a 1993 interview, he said, "The self-interest concept was [troubling] to me in the beginning because it sounds [contrary to] Christianity. I am coming from a very white middle class background and it's only after three years here that I am really beginning to relate to and with the oppressed. So the self-interest thing took me a while to warm up to. I think it's absolutely important now." In terms of defining it, he continued, "I guess I would put it in gospel terms of claiming [the] rights of the individual who is a child of God. I like that. We have certain rights. Self-interest [involves] speaking up [for them]. We used it at a MICAH march: housing is a right, not a privilege. Medical care. Adequate food. Decent jobs. I wouldn't have said these things before. That's how I describe self-interest: claiming the rights that are ours as a child of God. I am not a political person, but I see the need for systemic change. There is nothing wrong with us claiming that abundant life and working together to ensure that everybody has that."[26]

Thus few participants in community organizing reject the idea of self-interest. Most, however, continue to use altruistic language in ways that would seem to contradict the message conveyed in training. For example, notwithstanding his endorsement of self-interest, Boyd in fact frequently used altruistic language. He said, for instance, that "the way that I am being changed now is that I need to be an advocate for people who don't have a voice." This sounds very much like the kind of altruistic advocacy that organizing sets itself against. Another example is Pastor Samuel Jones of Greater Galilee Church, an important figure in MICAH. Jones had been to the Gamaliel training and therefore heard trainers inveighing against self-sacrificial churches and pastors. Aware of the language of self-interest and power, he could use it in the meaning intended by organizers. Yet when interviewed about his experiences in MICAH, he spoke of being "sacrificial," and said "I don't have any self-interest" in relation to his involvement in MICAH.[27]

Even in training, such sentiments were expressed as a kind of resistance to the language of self-interest. I saw trainees hear about self-interest, nominally accept the idea, and then talk in ways quite at odds with the principles embedded in the concept. At a one-day training in Milwaukee, held in 1993, the idea of self-interest was presented early on. Later in the day, a participant was asked why she and the other people from her church were involved with MICAH, and she answered "we want to do something for the people."[28]

This mixture of languages, where expressions of altruism persist alongside the assertions of self-interest, continues in the daily life of faith-based organizing. In MICAH, one frequently hears blatant references to abstract principles of justice, expressions of desire to act on an altruistic basis, and hope that city officials and even bankers will react affirmatively to appeals to conscience. At a meeting of the housing task force dealing with the failure of the mayor to fulfill a commitment the city had made to MICAH, several task force members spoke of how the mayor needed some "good ideas" about ways to do what the task force wanted. As an experiment, I suggested that perhaps the problem wasn't that he didn't know how to do it but that we hadn't generated enough power for him to decide that it was in his self-interest to do so. Therefore maybe we needed to focus not on what we could say to him now but on how to develop more power so that he would listen later. In essence, I was suggesting using the ideas about power and self-interest communicated in training. Everyone listened politely, but nobody picked up on this suggestion and the tenor of the meeting did not change. As they discussed the next steps to be taken in pursuit of MICAH's goals, people continued talking about the appeals the task force could make to the mayor and the ideas it could give him.

Still, the perspective on self-interest put forward at the training does have an important impact on many trainees. They are more willing to speak about their own agendas and to describe these as something positive, rather than as an obstacle to Christian action, than they were before their encounter with organizing. "We are gathered here," said one lay participant during the opening prayer for a MICAH drugs and crime task force meeting, "in our self-interest"—a parallel to the customary ". . . in Christ's name."[29] In congregation-based community organizing, self-interest is given a meaning very different from how it is commonly understood. This new meaning is closely tied to theological ideas and is largely accepted by participants in organizing. But participants also modify and reinterpret the concept of self-interest as they go about their work. They create a discourse that mixes the language of self-interest with altruistic talk and claims for justice in a rich if not always systematic blend.

Commentary: Alinsky and the Democratic Meaning of Self-Interest

Stereotyped descriptions of community organizing abound, and many of these originated as misunderstandings of Alinsky. In particular, people have often regarded his focus on self-interest as bleakly utilitarian and anticommunitarian. The full meaning of the concept of self-interest will be clearer if we put it in the context of Alinsky's thinking and correct these misunderstandings.

In fact, Alinsky's writings are far from putting the needs of each individual or particular group first. Even before the religious modifications made to the idea of self-interest by contemporary faith-based organizing, it was first and foremost a *democratic* concept. This is evident when we look at Alinsky's polemics against liberal, middle-class, "outside do-gooders" such as social workers or university professors. These are people who are fluent in the language of disinterested altruism—who can talk easily and articulately about the needs of the residents of low-income neighborhoods. They put themselves forward as advocates for the poor. They do so using expertise or by making moral claims that they assume to be universal rather than expressions of a particular perspective. They claim to speak for the common good rather than for any particular interest. As one of them put it, speaking (in Alinsky's account) to representatives of a community organization: "You people are really isolationists, [while] we represent the [whole] City of Chicago."[30]

One problem, from Alinsky's perspective, is that such do-gooders, living elsewhere, do not themselves experience or fully understand the problems neighborhood residents encounter. Furthermore, from a democratic point of view they have no right to speak for residents: they have no following or accountability. And their moral universalism, their supposed disinterest, is in part a form of imperialism. It uses what sociologist Pierre Bourdieu calls "cultural capital"—their command of rhetoric and abstract moral theories, their superior education and experience at public self-presentation—as a source of power over the less advantaged.[31] They impose their own agenda on people who are quite different from them, further disempowering people who already have too little power. As Alinsky put it, they "evaluate what is good or bad in the community according to *their own* . . . code or standards."[32]

Self-interest, both for Alinsky and for present-day community organizing, is first and foremost a way of asserting a radically democratic alternative to the do-gooder's approach. The residents of low-income neighborhoods are to define their concerns and needs, and the injustices they experience, *themselves*. They *themselves* are to be the primary agents in bringing about change. An important organizing principle is that the agents and beneficiaries of change should be the same. This is a model of participatory democracy. To put Alinsky's views in language close to Pat Speer's, when one does not expect anyone (especially not the do-gooders) to produce political proposals that are truly universal rather than based in the particularities of their situation, the way is opened for everybody—even those of the most modest status—to participate as equal citizens. It was for the sake of democracy, not because of a utilitarian view of human nature, that Alinsky wanted to focus on interests experienced and articulated by neighborhood residents. Reliance on appeals to self-interest narrowly understood, said Alinsky, would be needed only at the outset. As he put it, "after the organization is soundly built, [participants] will work cooperatively for reasons of social good rather than individual interest."[33] The reworking of the concept of self-interest in contemporary faith-based organizing makes explicit this anti-utilitarian assessment of human potential, and further develops the democratic core of the concept already present in Alinsky's thought.

Relationships

"Relationship" as understood in community organizing does not carry the same meaning as in American popular culture. The term does not necessarily imply anything romantic, intimate, or emotional. Relationships are not tools of individual self-expression and development. To get a sense of what this concept *does* mean, we will consider a sermon given in February 1992 by James Leary.[34] Pastor Leary served Calvary Baptist Church in Milwaukee and was MICAH's first president. He also became a part-time staff person for Gamaliel and a prime theological resource for that network. The sermon was delivered on a Sunday devoted specifically to celebrating the family. The church was large and packed, and for this occasion many people had invited family members who were not church members. The visitors were all introduced in the course of the singing and prayer that formed the first half of the service, before the sermon. In the sermon, entitled "The Glue that Holds Families Together," Leary first criticized an individualistic, humanistic view of marriage, which he saw as the outcome of the 1960s and 1970s. This view, he said, devalues family life and is not biblical. In essence, his analysis was that this has tended to remake marriage into a purely contractual relationship valid only while and insofar as it advances the separate interests of both parties.

One might—especially given the occasion—have expected this to lead into celebration of "traditional" family life, but it didn't. Instead, the pastor went on to criticize the older conception of marriage as "an institution." To focus on the rules of traditional marriage, he said, was "legalism"—a term with pejorative connotations in a Baptist context, where grace, not law, is the path to salvation. It is a mistake, he said, to understand the traditional family as the biblical family. He then offered several Bible verses and an interpretation of them to back this view. He talked, for instance, of how every human is created in the image of God and how God gave us dominion over nature but not over each other; only after the Fall does man dominate woman. He also argued that while families "are the basic unit of society" they vary from one society to another. While the language of the sermon was highly biblical and used no radical or feminist rhetoric, he criticized traditional family life for rigidity and male dominance leading to oppression and suffering.

What we need, he argued, is a third path. He put forward the idea of "relationship" as that path: an egalitarian and flexible alternative to individualism. Relationships are structures valid and important in themselves, but they have to be molded to be life-affirming for the individuals relating to each other. As they are talked about within the Gamaliel training, relationships can involve an enduring commitment that goes beyond the contractual, yet does fulfill the self-interest (understood in the broad sense described earlier) of both parties. In the kind of relationships that faith-based organizing seeks to build, the other is not (as in a purely contractual relationship) a means, but an end—another child of God, just as sacred as oneself. Relationships need not be intimate, but ones worth having involve at least mutual respect and some degree of trust. Relationships are the basis for most of the other activities in organizing. It is only legitimate to challenge others—to clarify their self-interest (what Galluzzo calls "agitation") or to hold them accountable—if one has first established a relationship.

Thus building relationships is a central part of the community organizing process. This focus is a strategy for gaining power, as we have seen. But it is more: building relationships is considered a valuable end in itself. One source of concern for relationships is a desire to enrich or restore the fabric of civil society in the United States. Alinsky, writing in *Reveille for Radicals,* was very concerned about "social disorganization" and an "urban anonymity" that "erodes the foundations of democracy."[35] Community organizing, in his view, was not only a tool for social justice and democracy but also a corrective for these deficits in civil society. Organizing would establish a rich network of relationships and involve individuals in organizations within their communities. In the same vein, a 1994 statement from Gamaliel stated that "community is as vital to human beings as water is to fish, and community in our country is under attack." In a 1993 funding proposal, Gamaliel argued that the main source of urban problems is "a radical breakdown of community." Local bonds and institutions are too weak to stave off drug trade or provide safety for inner-city residents. "Hopelessness and isolation" are characteristic mental states; "mediating institutions that used to connect the individual and the neighborhood with major political and economic resources are no longer capable of performing this function adequately." Thus community organizing is presented as a way to restore what are considered to be lost structures of community.[36]

Many of the activities of community organizing aim to address this problem. The interviewing process described in chapter 2 is intended to strengthen bonds within the parish. In PICO affiliates, congregation teams make a similar interviewing effort oriented toward people in the immediate neighborhood of the congregation, which presumably could strengthen civil society beyond the church. Conducting one-on-one's is a relationship- and community-building enterprise for the community organization, its member congregations, and potentially also for the community outside the organization.

Building community—within the organization, within congregations, and within neighborhoods—is a major goal of contemporary congregation-based community organizing. Earlier we saw communitarian strands in the ideas of power and self-interest. The concept of relationships is even more focused on community, and the same is true for the idea of "values," discussed below. These more communal concepts, while arguably present in Alinsky's thinking, were not articulated by him as clearly as were power and self-interest. They have become pivotal more recently, largely as a result of community organizing's encounter with religious faith.

Values

A final core concept that helps define the perspective of organizing is values. This idea is found in all the networks, but PICO puts even more stress on values than the other networks, placing them at the center of the organizing process: organizing should be "value-driven." José Carrasco of PICO articulated the concept of values more clearly than anyone else I spoke with. In his interview, he also connected the other core concepts we have been examining, showing their links to values. Carrasco's thinking is therefore a good basis for understanding the role of values in faith-based community organizing.[37]

Carrasco is a professor of Chicano Studies at California State University, San Jose, rather than a full-time staff member in PICO, but he is the person who more than anyone else gives direction to PICO's training process. After John Baumann, who had founded PICO several years earlier, became interested in pursuing a church-based approach to organizing, Carrasco became his collaborator. While Baumann runs the organization, Carrasco carefully and systematically delineates its philosophy. He does so on the basis of a great deal of practical organizing experience, paid and unpaid. He has worked for IAF, and during that period of his life saw Ernie Cortes, the leader of IAF's efforts in Texas, "break open this new paradigm" of congregation-based community organizing.[38] He has frequently participated in or served as consultant to organizing initiatives in schools and colleges, neighborhoods, and workplaces. At the same time he is a well-read and thoughtful intellectual.

In the interview, Carrasco argued that one needs to get away from what he called "neighborhood-based" organizing, where one "worked with anyone who came forth, usually activists—good people, beautiful people, a lot of heart, a lot of stamina, often quite bright." Such people "did some good things." Their activism wasn't bad, but it was "issue-driven [and therefore] not capable of tapping deeply." That is, it could not elicit strong commitments or engage people at the level of what they most cared about. He went on: "The adhesive, the human cohesiveness that is necessary for long-term [work] is absent in those kinds of settings." This missing glue "is basically the relational, the value foundations" of organizing.

Training, as Carrasco described it, should focus on values. Here is how he spoke of the concept: "I don't see values as something that you just put out there and say these are your values. They *don't* exist [in that sense. The] values that we have are for the most part ideologically cemented in our psyche. That doesn't mean that we understand them, they're just ideologically there. And they're very powerful." In other words, we often don't know our values; they are not phrases we might give to a sociological interviewer who came to our door, but the things that really undergird our core concerns. We need to "put our values out there and reflect on them and raise questions about where we are exercising them [and how real they are]. We can't be held accountable for them until we reembrace them."

This process of reembracing our values is central to organizing. In Carrasco's view, it should be "value-driven, not issue-driven. Organizing is about people; they set up the issues. If you're interested in dealing with an issue you are organizing for your interests, not the people's; [you are] using people as a means. Other approaches may do great things, but not what I want to do; [they're] not empowering." In other words, in value-driven organizing one begins by helping people to own their values, and the issues follow as relatively unimportant corollaries, whereas issue-driven work starts with the *organizer's* priorities and enlists others to advance those. Thus "action for us is not viewed simply as winning the issue. In PICO the central principle is 'the power is in the relationship'; [that is,] power is a product of relationships." Power, he said at another point, comes from the "breathing of life." It is "an awakening of the spirit" that comes out of relationships. "The power—the emotional, spiritual feeling—generates enthusiasm that requires some kind of manifestation in action."

Carrasco spoke of how "self-interest shifts from concrete to relational" in the course of organizing. This somewhat cryptic statement means that participants become less attached to winning gains for themselves and their specific groups, and more attached to the people they work with and the solidarity generated there. Here Carrasco's analysis was very close to that of Alinsky, talking about the shift from the outset of organizing, where one relies on self-interest narrowly understood, to a more mature phase in which people are motivated by broader concerns. Carrasco saw this shift as a strength but also a danger, since it can separate deeply involved participants from their local constituencies.

Values and self-interest, as one explores Carrasco's thinking, turn out to be two sides of the same coin. It is self-interest more than values that "opens the door" in organizing, he said, but "for us, self-interest is not separate from [values]; self-interest exists in the social domain but it's basically the value inverted, if you will. Values are being expounded through the pain that [people] are expressing. That pain is linked with self-interest, physically; it is a social phenomenon. When you start moving into the 'why' it moves you right back into the values." In other words, self-interest—the desire to alleviate the pain—is a good way to connect to one's true sense of values, to see what they really are rather than to parrot ideological slogans that have only a superficial meaning.

Carrasco does not assume that "values are already conscious and operative." Rather, they have to be "massaged, challenged, and intellectually stimulated." But he rejected the idea that they could or needed to be significantly changed. "I believe that they are dormant, atrophied if you will for lack of exercise, and require stimulation. They have to be surfaced. People have to surface them themselves, and examine them. I don't believe they need to be reformed. I believe the values are still very, very functional. They still have tremendous capacity, and aren't necessarily in any way inconsistent with what a free society requires. We may need to hermeneutically examine them, but that doesn't mean that we discard them." In a sense, the values, like power, emerge from a dormant state through a spiritual awakening. At another point, he said that the values to be surfaced are "very conservative in general. I don't think that's bad; [being] conservative isn't bad *per se*." This is different, he argued, from the meaning of being "conservative" in American politics, where the term serves mainly as a form of "political manipulation."

In Carrasco's way of thinking self-interest and values are not at opposite poles—as they are commonly perceived to be when people contrast "materialist" and "idealist" perspectives—but are two different ways of looking at who one is, what one cares about, and what kind of community one is embedded in. The gap between "is" and "ought" is manifest on the one hand in the pain that energizes self-interest and on the other in the discoveries about values that are made when one examines and appropriates them as a standard by which to evaluate one's own life, the life of our society, and the performance of its institutions and leaders. One has to get personal and real about the values, which is difficult unless one clarifies one's self-interest. But the self-interest is unlikely to go anywhere interesting or sustainable politically, or to become a focus for truly public engagement (as opposed to manipulating public institutions for private or narrow group gains), unless the "why" is addressed—which brings one into the realm of values. Power and relationship, parallel to values and self-interest, are two sides of a single coin: on one side, the ability to have a practical effect on the world, and on the other the solidarity and community that are simultaneously preconditions and results of effective practical action. Power and self-interest are the practical, material, more individual sides of these two coins. Relationships and values are the more communal and in a sense spiritual sides.

Keeping all these factors in balance and in proper connection with one another, Carrasco thinks, is a difficult task that requires great alertness and "discipline." It is hard to see how this task could even be attempted except in a local context where people meet face-to-face, develop sustained relationships, and are personally trained and challenged. Religious congregations, with an explicit basis of shared values and an organizational structure providing intimate local settings that frequently manifest considerable solidarity and sense of community, are essential parts of a process that intends to cut as deep as Carrasco intends. Thus congregations are the best site for value-driven organizing. As he put it, "the church has a whole lot more going for it than what you even know." When one moves even to the citywide community organization—the level of the "federation," in PICO's terminology—value-driven organizing is less possible. This provides a strong reason for one of PICO's distinctive organizational characteristics: it emphasizes "local organizing committees" that are most often based in single congregations and engaged in organizing within the immediate neighborhood to deal with highly localized issues. Thus the relational and value-based character of organizing, in Carrasco's view, implies a strongly local focus as well as the centrality of congregations.

I have quoted Carrasco at such length because he articulates the values basis of organizing so clearly. He also brings together in an elegant and moving way all the central themes of church-based community organizing. In his statements one finds self-interest, power, relationship, and value, all enunciated and linked. His is perhaps the most systematic exposition of the philosophy of faith-based organizing. While he speaks only for PICO, in practice the leaders of all the networks would affirm the views just described. That is, the philosophy he articulates is in my view not fundamentally different from that of the other networks (although Carrasco would not agree). It is the common language of contemporary faith-based community organizing.

The language of faith-based community organizing—articulated largely through the core concepts we have considered in this chapter—is a rich and complex one. It cannot plausibly be described as politics with a religious veneer, nor as religion imposed on politics. Rather, this type of community organizing takes ideas from Christian social action traditions and from secular political thought—primarily Alinsky's version of radical democracy—and weaves them together into a language that is irreducibly both religious and political. While this system of ideas manifests some constraints, which will be discussed later, overall it is quite expansive in the style of discourse it implies.

Community organizing shows that it is very possible for progressive politics to be expressed in richer forms of discourse than are currently customary. Expansive discourse is not the exclusive property of the right. To be sure, faith-based organizing is a religious movement, and we will have to consider later the degree to which similar styles of discourse are possible on a secular basis. What should be clear at this point is that the religious quality is a not a narrow or sectarian one. Consider as a contrast the Hutterites, an Anabaptist group that lives in communities, each called a "Bruderhof," located in various countries throughout the world including the United States. These communities are intensely communal, following the example of the early church apostles as described in Acts 4:32: "Now the whole group of those who believed were of one heart and soul, and no one claimed private ownership of any possessions, but everything they owned was held in common." The

Hutterites manifest a highly expansive mixture of religious and social thinking, and their communal values are consonant with core principles grounding economic justice politics. But their story is not very interesting if one is trying to understand the potentials for progressive politics in the United States, since this group's historical background and religious identity are so specialized. It is hard to imagine a scenario in which any significant proportion of Americans would adopt the way of life of the Hutterites.

The same is true, although not in such an extreme way, of many other forms of religious left politics in America, such as the Sojourners Community founded by Jim Wallis or the pacifist groups found in many denominations. Faith-based community organizing, by contrast, is highly diverse religiously, extending in some cities even beyond Christianity and representing a religious spectrum within which most Americans can be found. This breadth makes congregation-based organizing politically significant in a way the Hutterites and other marginal groups are not. In addition, the movement's religious diversity is one reason why the dangers often ascribed to religiously based politics—intolerance, absolutism, inability to compromise, black and white thinking, and so forth—are notably absent from congregation-based community organizing.

Two other aspects of the language of community organizing deserve mention before we move, in the next chapter, to a consideration of its practices, rituals, and stories.

One is the centrality of language use. We might say that the terminology encodes the conclusions. That is, learning to express the concepts in the ways suggested by those who are strongly committed to organizing means accepting a good part of the perspective they advocate. Furthermore, appropriating concepts arguably cuts deeper into consciousness than simply accepting propositions. Thus the focus on language is a powerful way to form participants' ideas.

The other key point about the organizing perspective is the importance of the active appropriation, modification, and use of organizing ideas by rank and file participants. Systems of ideas do not have an iron logic that the people who use them cannot affect. As it turns out, participants use organizing ideas in a more eclectic way than movement leaders appear to wish. That eclecticism has advantages. It allows participants to draw upon a range of religious ideas, as a basis for talking about social and political issues, that is wider than they could access if they strictly followed the discursive rules represented by concepts such as self-interest. In particular, the use of the discouraged language of altruism, while not without its problems, adds important dimensions to the language of congregation-based community organizing. In combining the language patterns taught by trainers and organizers with other religious and political traditions, grassroots participants show their self-determination. They creatively construct a rich web of connections between the civil-societal cultural traditions they are most committed to and the public issues of contemporary life.

Chapter 4

STORIES AND PRACTICES OF COMMUNITY ORGANIZING

In addition to articulating a religio-political language, faith-based community organizing has created other distinctive cultural forms. This chapter describes some of these, especially the stories and practices generated by this movement. First, we will examine a recurrent form of story telling in which participants interpret their lives in the light of organizing principles. Second, we will look at one example of the unconventional, special-purpose "actions" that community organizations sometimes mount, studying the ways in which practical action and discourse combined to communicate the organization's political proposals and principles. Third, we will consider a standardized dramaturgical form central to congregation-based community organizing: the large public meeting. And finally, we will assess how even the most routine activities, such as business meetings, serve not only to accomplish practical purposes but also to enact and reinforce organizing values. Such practices and stories give faith-based organizing a much richer cultural life than it would have were it solely a system of ideas.[1]

ORGANIZING TALES: NARRATIVES OF EMPOWERMENT

We have already heard the stories of Cheryl Spivey-Perry and Phil Reifenberg, as well as some of what other participants have to say about their experiences in faith-based organizing. Now we will hear one more story and consider the genre they represent.

Pearl Cabanilla's Story

Cabanilla is a key volunteer leader in People Acting in Community Together (PACT), the San Jose affiliate of the Pacific Institute for Community Organizing (PICO). She is what theorists of organizing call a natural leader: a person who before becoming involved in organizing was already highly relational and effective. Cabanilla is a part-time nurse, has been married for twenty-five years, and has two children. She belongs to Santa Maria Goretti, a large Catholic parish with a pastor who is active in PACT. The parish is multicultural, with Filipino/as, Vietnamese, Latino/as, and others. She values this diversity, saying "we should try to live together, [and] we worship together *first*."[2]

At the start of the interview, I explained in a few words the purpose of my visit to PACT. Before I said anything about what I hoped we might accomplish, or was even able to ask her one question, she took over and started executing her plan for the conversation, which was to tell me a personal narrative. This experience was frequently repeated when I went to interview participants in community organizing. The speed with which people jump into this kind of narrative is an indication of how powerful and pervasive a genre it is.

Cabanilla explained that after her kids were born, she stayed home. "I was playing the 2.5 kids, [station wagon], shaggy dog kind of thing, and I was enjoying that." She was volunteering and became president of local PTAs in "I can't even remember how many schools." Everything was going fine until her daughter, now twenty-three years old, began to have problems (Cabanilla did not specify the exact kind). Two months after starting high school, the daughter "came to me and said 'mommy, I'm in trouble, I need help.'" Cabanilla and her husband sought desperately, persistently, and resourcefully for solutions, discovering a nightmarish situation in terms of the number of phone calls and level of doggedness required to find appropriate sources of help. They sold their house to raise eighteen thousand dollars for a twenty-eight-day stay at a rehabilitation center for their daughter. "We went through hell, literally, for three years to get her back." And it seemed to Cabanilla that a piece of the hell was gratuitous: the difficulty of finding resources. Her anger about this later became a source for part of her political agenda, as she worked on reforming the social service referral process in San Jose.

Two years into this period, David Mann (who was the organizer for PACT at that time) came to her on the recommendation of her pastor and tried to recruit her to become active in PACT. But Cabanilla "said I wasn't ready, and so he waited until I got my daughter back. He was very persistent. A few months later he came back and I was ready. At that time I got my daughter back and I didn't know how to say thank you. Of course I was praying [all along], but somehow just to pray and say thank you wasn't enough for me, and I started looking for things, and I said to David, now I'm going to do something. Because I want parents that have more trouble than I do [to be able to get help]. I mean how many parents have a house to sell? Or speak enough English to [penetrate the bureaucratic maze of the agencies]? So David said, OK, if that's what you want, then this is your avenue." Thus, as Cabanilla described it, all of her work in PACT has been an extended thank-you prayer to God for the gift she has received. She used the word *amen* at several points in the interview to symbolize the prospective end of this prayer and thus of her work in PACT.

The first organizing work she did was to recruit parish members and neighborhood residents into what PICO calls a "local organizing committee." At this point the committee, which deals with issues of the immediate neighborhood around the church, has fourteen members, and it can turn out 200–250 people for actions. "The relationships," she says, "are [what] bring the people out." This work was only the beginning. She works two days a week as a nurse and the other five days on "PACT kind of stuff," which includes, in addition to PACT itself, several city commissions and task forces on which she has been invited to serve because of her work in PACT. She has been active in the "federation" (that is, PACT beyond her parish) but last year "I took a step back because I wanted to work more on the local side," dealing with micro concerns such as their particular neighborhood schools. But she still does some federation-level work, and believes in going "back and forth." She has also continued to work on her original issue: to make social services more accessible. "Right now, in the city of San Jose, you can call one number—one number alone can get you all the services you want if you have a child in trouble, I guarantee that."

The end of her thank-you prayer for the return of her daughter had not been reached, when I interviewed her, because she found "there are a lot of problems—and it's a fulfilling thing for me" to do. She speaks of how this work has helped and changed her: "I would like to say to you that I would have been just as happy not to get involved with PACT, but I probably would have been very bored. And actually the training that I got in PACT is very valuable because without those trainings I wouldn't be as productive. I've learned how to fight, and to fight constructively."

Her account of the training, with no prompting at all, surfaced in classical form the issues about power and self-interest discussed in the last chapter. "Coming from a church-based, church values [background], at first I was debating on the self-interest issue. And oddly enough I was feeling guilty about the self-interest: I'm not really doing PACT work because I was a good person or wanted to be good, it was because I wanted to finish my [prayer]. Is that self-interest or isn't it? At that five-day [training] that was answered for me, that it was OK. I think it gave me the permission, at least from people that were there and said, 'that's the way I joined, too.' Just hearing this from people who are realistic, saying 'I didn't do this because I was good either, I did it for self-interest, for me, for myself.'" As with most organizing participants, Cabanilla's interpretation of "self-interest" is clearly not a utilitarian one.

She also confronted the idea of power. "And then I had a power issue—power corrupts, it's ingrained in you—and I didn't know how to make that OK from my values base. And I didn't really want to be powerful; I was afraid to be powerful. And surprisingly enough that's very hard for people to talk about, it was hard for *me*. [However,] the reality is that power doesn't come from you but from the people behind [that you're representing], and if you learn that concept then you [can get over reluctance to be powerful]. I hear people even in this church say, you're too political, if you become that powerful it's no good, that's not what you're supposed to do. The reality is, the people we talk to, especially from this parish, [have trouble with this]. We're trying to teach people that it's their right to get the whole pie if they want to, when what they're used to—coming, say, from the Philippines, *I'm* used to—is getting a quarter of the pie, or sometimes none at all, and that's the way I've been raised. So we come to the United States and they hand us a half a pie, and we say, that's great, even if we're not satisfied, even if we're not making do. [And then comes someone] saying you can have the whole pie—and that's the job that we're trying to do really in empowering the community—if you want to, if you work for it, because it's your right, in America. Not only is this difficult to teach, but when you do, some of the people get angry." This understanding of power is relational, like Reifenberg's, but it also involves a strong assertion of rights.

Her story about the difficulties members of minority groups often have in asserting their rights was very similar to the one Nathan Johnson told in the last chapter. This is particularly striking because their context and backgrounds are so different: Johnson is a black Baptist man in a rust-belt city, involved with a Gamaliel affiliate, while Cabanilla is an Asian Catholic woman in the Silicon Valley who participates in a PICO affiliate. Yet Johnson and Cabanilla reported confronting the same issues about power and about church people being politically involved, and they came to the same conclusions. What both of these people said constitutes a recurring theme in organizing stories, especially when told by people of color or women. The story line goes something like this: "I didn't know that it was all right or possible to engage in politics or fight for justice, and a lot of women (or blacks, or immigrants) don't either, and traditional understandings of faith were an obstacle. But organizing overcame all this for me personally and it's doing the same for others. We're becoming powerful people."

For Cabanilla the links among faith, public involvement, and spirituality were strong and explicit. Near the end of the interview, summing up what I had been hearing, I asked her, "So you came into this with your self-interest being to pray—it was a form of prayer? She said, "That's right, a form of praying." To the follow-up question "So what's been God's answer? What has changed between you and God as a result of praying in this way?" Cabanilla answered, "I think God is my friend, really. I got responded to because of my praying, and [received love from God]. Whereas I [was] doing religion before, to me it's now faith, it's a more personal thing with God."

This aspect of her story is similar to the account Cheryl Spivey-Perry, the MICAH organizer, gave of how her faith has been deepened by her organizing experiences. Both of these women told a story of how organizing has made their faith less abstract, more vivid, and more personal. The outcome they described is reminiscent of the personal encounter with Jesus Christ that many evangelical Protestants in America regard as a necessary part of becoming a Christian. Cabanilla's account is even more in this evangelical mode than Spivey-Perry's—and since Cabanilla is a Catholic, this mode is less expected. Some religious traditionalists believe that social action is a distraction from faith, while many secularists hold that faith is a distraction from social action. In a sense, these two views agree: they both see faith and social action as opposed to each other. Organizing stories such as Spivey-Perry's and Cabanilla's challenge this assumption.

Cabanilla ended the narrative by describing her future: "So I'll probably be forever with PACT. My daughter is fine, my son is fine, my family is very supportive, even if they have to make an appointment to see me once a month. I keep saying to myself, perhaps next year I will say amen, I will be finished with PACT but next year comes another issue and I get riled up all over again and I say no, this is not justice, this is not the way God wants it to be. I guess, when people no longer have to work for justice then I can [say amen]." Thus her organizing work remains part of her prayer life. Her spirituality and work for social justice reinforce each other.

Narratives of Empowerment and Growth

The stories related by Pearl Cabanilla and Cheryl Spivey-Perry are only two instances of a recurring type of story that might be called "empowerment narratives." These are stories of how one's life was transformed by involvement in organizing—how one became a powerful person engaged in public life. These stories are told over and over again by organizers, clergy, and lay leaders. They are found in every city where organizing is taking place. They are not only sincere but believable—the individuals who tell them do indeed appear to have developed major new capacities. I call them "narratives" not to express incredulity but to emphasize their structured, cultural quality. They are tales with a definite, replicated, stylized story line—they constitute a genre. Also, they do not just transmit raw biographical material and life experience to the listener but interpret them from a particular standpoint—that of the concepts and value commitments in faith-based organizing. These narratives take abstract ideas like power and relationship and give them flesh and blood in accounts of one's own life and events seen firsthand. They often have the quality of conversion stories. Sometimes, as with Cabanilla's and Spivey-Perry's stories, they have an explicitly religious dimension, telling of how one's religious life has deepened. In other cases (we will see an example shortly in Joe Marino's story) they describe a major personal transformation that is secular, but do this in much the same way people describe religious conversions. Whether religious or not, the narratives generally give a major role to something like what Christians call "grace": an event or person (in a religious context thought of as an instrument of God) that sends one off in a life-affirming new direction without one's having planned or willed the transformation in advance. The tradition of the conversion story is strongest in evangelical Protestantism and black Protestant churches. But stories of the transformation of one's life through organizing are told by people with all kinds of faith. Using narrative models drawn from various religious traditions, such stories enrich the cultural life of congregation-based community organizing.

The most poignant narratives tend to come from women, and especially women who are not European American or do not have a privileged background. These are frequently stories of individuation: of discovering, claiming, and asserting an agenda of one's own. We have seen this in Cabanilla's story and in Cheryl Spivey-Perry's as well. Within congregation-based community organizing, one continually hears such accounts. A lay Catholic leader in a Gamaliel affiliate in Chicago's south suburbs told of how when she first became involved she was told "my role would be to assist my pastor."[3] But instead she became empowered on her own. She is now leading a housing development corporation, spun off by the organizing project, that has received national attention. Betty Smith, MICAH's president and a lay African American Baptist, told of how she used to be "quiet" but now was "noisy" and felt powerful. This was not without its costs: her marriage suffered and she reported that whereas before she had been "liked," now she was "tolerated." But she had no regrets, and seemed to be enjoying her life greatly.[4]

White males tell stories as well. Often their stories also tell of growing powerful. But sometimes they emphasize different kinds of growth, and when they do talk of empowerment they often highlight routes other than individuation. Phil Reifenberg's story was of learning new ideas, stepping into an exciting new world of activity, and becoming more effective by using new methods of action. His development happened by gradual evolution rather than a conversion. But men can also tell conversion stories. Joe Marino, a Gamaliel organizer who conducted part of a training I attended, gave an account of how he become more relational, and therefore more effective and powerful. The session he conducted was about leadership, and he said he had plenty of personal experiences of "nonleadership." These constituted his "before" story. He told of how as a young adult, in a public sector job, he had bucked the system all by himself, having made a personal decision that what he saw around him was wrong. This was ineffective. In those days he was, as he put it, a "lone ranger." The "after" story was of becoming a good organizer, working in ways that were accountable to others and in which power came from relationships.[5] The contrast between before and after was a kind of conversion story, although of a different kind than Spivey-Perry's or Cabanilla's. His account, like theirs, was not unique. Rather, it manifested a kind of subgenre within the wider genre of organizing narratives. It was a story about overcoming some of the deficits that typically stem from male socialization, whereas the stories from women often deal with what are taken to be unfortunate effects of female socialization.

To hear such stories is both inspiring and comforting. They tell the listeners that power can be attained, that others have blazed the path before them. They say that the doubts and weaknesses newcomers experience are not unique and can be overcome; that ordinary people, male and female, can affect the world and have power; and that personal lives and communities can be dramatically changed. Many stories describe how the narrator's faith was enhanced and he or she experienced a closer relationship with God. They are always stories focused on community, in which one works with others and solidarity develops. Community, the stories implicitly say, is both a precondition for effective action and a reward, a kind of home, a source of belonging that may be especially valuable and needed in the contemporary world. And finally, these are stories of entertainment. One learns during training that to become an organizer is to make a decision to have an interesting life. Saul Alinsky wrote in *Reveille for Radicals* about the "dull" life a person has when not publicly engaged and the exciting, brilliant life of the citizen-activist working through a "people's organization."[6] All of the stories we have seen in one way or another express that same sense of stimulation, of exploring new universes.

Narratives are an important part of the life of any community. They are especially important for people who seek social change, helping them sustain an unconventional perspective and be persuasive when talking to people who do not yet share their views. The tales told in organizing fulfill these purposes and enhance the richness of the cultural life of faith-based community organizing.

COMMUNICATION THROUGH UNCONVENTIONAL ACTION: MICAH MARCHES FOR BETTER HOUSING

Now we turn to a characteristic genre of action in community organizing: carefully planned and staged, often dramatic protests designed to pressure their targets and bring public attention to issues and grievances. The story of MICAH's struggle for the implementation of a housing ordinance, which culminated in such an action, is an example of how community organizing becomes a culturally rich practice. In addition to its practical value, the action was a discursive and symbolic event. It put forward ideas through statements and also communicated the organization's perspective and values nonverbally, through the action itself.

Housing was identified as a priority issue area early in MICAH's life, and a housing task force was established. Its first major issue concerned boarded-up houses, often seized by the city because of failure to pay property taxes or by the U.S. Department of Housing and Urban Development (HUD) or banks because of foreclosures. In the view of the task force, these were an eyesore and a symbol of neighborhood deterioration, hurting local morale and making banks more likely to disinvest from the inner city. They were also targets for scavengers and havens for drug dealers. At the same time, the task force was concerned about the shortage of decent and affordable housing in inner-city Milwaukee. Members pored over figures showing that many low-income residents were paying more than half their income in rent, and that the waiting list for public housing and rental assistance contained well over ten thousand families. It was an affront to members' sense of rationality and justice that potential housing should be sitting vacant and causing problems when housing was so badly needed by so many.

Out of this thinking came an initiative from the housing task force to get the city to convert boarded-up residential buildings into scattered-site public housing.[7] After many compromises and much negotiation, the Milwaukee Common Council finally passed an ordinance, in October 1990, that committed the city to transfer to the municipal housing authority fifty city-owned properties annually and provided for these to be rehabilitated and run as subsidized rental units. The ordinance, read literally, says that all outside sources of funds (housing authority bonds, the state, HUD, etc.) are to be sought before general city funds are used, but does not exclude the use of city funds. The city administration, however, maintained that such use *was* excluded. By early 1992, something over fifty units of housing ought to have been created under this ordinance. In fact, only two had been completed. Throughout the end of 1991 and early 1992, task force representatives met with the city to try to get action. They obtained occasional promises. More often, they got explanations, usually blaming HUD, the State Division of Housing, or suburban communities for the problem. But nothing actually changed. In essence the city government was unwilling to spend any of its own money to implement the ordinance and was waiting for outside funds to materialize.[8]

Eventually MICAH's housing task force, feeling that other means had failed, decided to stage a march to the mayor's private residence. One task force member reported that her congregation was uncomfortable with this plan, feeling that the mayor needed to be treated with more respect. Nobody else took this position, but everyone agreed that going to his private home was a strong action and needed to be handled with care. The solution the task force decided upon was to operate under a rule of silence and prayerfulness. The march itself would be conducted silently, with the message conveyed by signs and leaflets. At the mayor's house, there would be a vigil, again silent. A single speaker would read a brief message.

The event was carefully planned, incorporating marshals and training. There were clear decisions about who would speak, when and where, and what would be said. Petitions from MICAH congregations, asking fulfillment of the ordinance, were completed in advance for delivery to the mayor's wife (the mayor was out of town) during the march. Vans from MICAH churches provided transportation to the staging point, which was a church near the mayor's residence. There the participants gathered to receive orientation, instruction, and inspiration. Given the rule of silence, the visual element of the march was crucial. Most of the MICAH churches were represented, and each brought large banners—the kind used in church processions. Some brought crucifixes. The participating pastors donned full clerical garb and regalia. As might be expected, the Episcopalians put on a particularly good show. Some of the laity carried posters with greatly enlarged photographs of particularly ugly boarded-up homes located near MICAH churches. Other posters displayed housing slogans.

A leaflet was prepared that was intended for both observers and participants. It is reproduced on pages 92–93 (first showing the back and front covers, then the inside of the leaflet).

The flyer resembled the worship bulletin one gets at a Protestant church. The front cover, which is what anyone would be most likely to notice, accomplished two things. First, it identified MICAH, showing its full name, acronym, logo (a scale representing justice), and slogan ("To do what is just!"—a reference to a biblical passage, Micah 6:8, emphasizing God's command that we do justice). Second, it enunciated a philosophy in three affirmations—also used on the posters carried in the march—each representing a principle underlying the more specific statements made inside the flyer:

1. "Housing is a civil right."
2. "Housing is a human right."
3. "For us, people of faith, housing is a divine right."

All three statements speak of "rights." Thus they are moral claims, not arguments about what would maximize anyone's self-interest, and are an attempt to seize the discursive high ground. But they do so on differing bases. The first has overtones of the civil rights movement and of appeals to the U.S. Constitution. It is within the ambit of American civic discourse and is not religious. It appeals to its audience as U.S. citizens and to the national political tradition, without distinctions having to do with interests or cultural particularity. This kind of language is often used to procure and protect the rights of minorities, such as African Americans or ill-housed Americans. The second ground is more universal (by use of the term "human") and makes claims similar to those espoused by the human rights movement. Human rights are things people deserve not because they belong to a particular national community but by virtue of their humanity. The basis for the claim is in what are taken to be universal moral truths, not laws, the Constitution, or specifically American traditions. The phrase is secular, as it must be for human rights discourse, since people want to redress human rights violations

PURPOSE

To bring congregations together, to address social issues concerning the central city residents of Milwaukee. The organization will address a variety of local issues through a process of education, dialogue and action.

GOALS

- To identify basic, unmet human needs in our community and to respond with concern and action.
- To enable low and moderate income people to act on their own behalf.
- To raise the community's level of social awareness and social morality through education, dialogue and action.
- To be a strong advocacy force for and with the poor and powerless in our community.
- To support and strengthen member congregations.
- To stimulate new and different kinds of community efforts as needed to change our community for the better.
- To develop a democratic and participatory structure with a sound funding base and full-time, professional staff.

TO DO WHAT IS JUST!

M.I.C.A.H

MILWAUKEE INNERCITY CONGREGATIONS ALLIED FOR HOPE

4011 W. CAPITOL DRIVE, MILWAUKEE, WISCONSIN 53216, (414) 449-0805

M I C A H

H O U S I N G

- Housing is a civil right.

- Housing is a human right.

- For us, people of faith, housing is a divine right.

Back and front covers of flyer, MICAH action, July 15, 1992 (back cover is on left)

in countries with very different religious traditions than their own. At the same time, human rights concepts are part of the language of Catholic social teachings. Therefore this phrase may be interpreted by some readers as a religious statement, addressing Christians in their specific religious identity as well as in their universal human one. Episcopal priest David Boyd, for example, thought of self-interest as asserting the rights of every person as a child of God, and referred to the housing march as an instance of doing this. Thus he linked faith to human rights language explicitly.[9]

The language of the third affirmation is somewhat different. Unlike the first two it starts with a qualifying phrase: "For us, people of faith, . . ." The difference in the phrasing is significant. While the first two statements present themselves as speaking authoritatively to all, the qualifying clause gives the third a more narrow focus. It acknowl-

JULY 15, 1992

A RESPONSE TO GOD'S CALL IN SILENT PRAYER

6:15pm	All congregations meet at St. Ann's. Briefing for marshals and banner carriers.
6:30pm	Instructions to congregations on silence and prayer. Load up.
6:55pm	Arrival and Prayer.
7:00pm	Walk and vigil begins.
7:10pm	Deliver Petitions.
	Silent prayer on each corner within the boundaries. Head bowed and hands in spiritual symbol.
7:30pm	Return to St. Ann's.

MILWAUKEE INNER CITY CONGREGATIONS ALLIED FOR FOR HOPE - MICAH

1. Ordinance Number 900641 was adopted by the Common Council and signed by the Mayor in October 1990, that 50 city owned houses be rehabbed each year for subsidized rental units. One and one-half years later the city has not met its obligation legally or in good faith.

2. We applaud the City's efforts toward home ownership as its first goal, but our ordinance calls for affordable rental housing. The City cannot escape its responsibility to all its citizens; it can no longer refuse to look at alternative sources to fund public housing; it can no longer allow its citizens to live in substandard housing; nor can it any longer allow its citizens to be sleeping in the streets.

3. This action is for the voiceless people who do not have decent housing, and who have been forgotten by our civic leaders. There are 13,000 people on the waiting list for public housing, or rental assistance who are unable to get decent housing without rental subsidy. The city is directly responsible for these citizens - not the community based or non-profit organizations - but the city of Milwaukee.

4. We are going to continue to advocate for adequate affordable housing for the poor, and are going to hold the City of Milwaukee accountable for the timely fulfillment of our ordinance.

Mr. Mayor, the City is behind in meeting the requirements of our ordinance, and we insist that you find additional funds to rehab the remaining 30 units due by the end of this year according to the ordinance.

Inside of flyer for MICAH action, July 15, 1992

edges cultural particularity and therefore that the claim is *not* universal. In the terminology of French philosopher Jean-François Lyotard, a pioneering exponent of the idea of postmodernism, the third claim is given only a "local" legitimation rather than one constructed according to an account that claims universality.[10] And this is the one explicitly religious claim. That religious claim, in other words, is made with a certain modesty—almost a kind of relativism. The bystander who is not part of a MICAH church is invited by this phrasing to understand this statement mainly as an explanation of where the demonstrators are coming from rather than a claim for universal authority or a demand for the bystander's assent. By contrast, the first affirmation is meant to direct the conscience of any American, and the second of any person.

It should be noted that talking about rights is not unique to MICAH or the Gamaliel network. In the PICO training, there were references to people's rights along with related terms such as "human dignity" and "development of the whole person."[11] Such discourse seems likely to have come to congregation-based community organizing not only from contemporary Catholic social teachings but also from secular rights languages—which, as communitarians lament, are widespread in America.

The statement inside the flyer, describing MICAH's position about the ordinance, is where one finds discourse about actual public policy. One important characteristic of this policy argument is that its grounding is quite indeterminate. One could ground it either in entirely secular principles or in religious ones. *Any* of the three basic principles articulated on the front cover could be invoked as the basis for MICAH's policy position. Those three affirmations come out of different domains of discourse, but they all lead to the same conclusions on the issues at hand. Therefore, the front cover manifests correspondences between religious and secular discourse and between local and universal ways of making political claims. It is like a traveler's phrase book, showing the practical equivalence of statements from different languages. It refers to the specific language of faith as something explaining and motivating its political commitment, but then translates this into national and universal languages.

This kind of translation is important in relating religion to public discourse, allowing connections to be drawn while the legitimacy of different faiths, and of secular perspectives, is acknowledged. Such translation is made easier by the strong Catholic influence on organizing. Catholicism has a tradition of "natural theology," teaching that most of the things believers know by revelation can also be known by carefully observing the world and using one's natural intellectual and moral capacities. Thus the kind of translation manifest in the MICAH flyer is a legitimate and logical move for Catholics.

Also inside the flyer is a schedule for the event and directions for participants, and then a brief statement of the particulars of MICAH's case against the city. The schedule very much resembles the order for worship frequently found in a church bulletin and is full of religious references (God, call, prayer, congregation, vigil, head bowed, etc.). The statement against the city is entirely secular. The arguments that make up this statement, however, are ethical and in fact have an altruistic tone. "We are going to continue to advocate for adequate affordable housing for the poor," it says. The impression this gives is that "we" (implicitly, the members of MICAH congregations, or more directly, of the task force) are *not* mostly poor and are not the people who are going to live in the housing. Or again, the flyer says: "This action is for the voiceless. . . ." The marchers carrying out the action were perhaps literally voiceless, given the rule of silence, but are not of course the "voiceless" referred to here. Thus the agents and beneficiaries of the changes in public policy the march sought are *not* the same. Actually, the only part of the language that sounds like what one learns in training is the idea of holding the mayor "accountable."

To return from discourse to the course of events, the action went as planned and was described in uniformly positive terms by participants in postaction evaluations. The spiritual quality of the march, with its silence, robes, and banners, was particularly satisfying to task force members. The event was visually striking and appealing, and the silence focused attention on the visual elements. (Since the action took place on quiet residential streets, the main noise came from feet hitting concrete.) Communicating by visual images more than talk probably contributed to the excellent television coverage the march received. Newspaper coverage was also good. In Milwaukee's public discourse, the action raised issues about the need for affordable rental housing in addition to home ownership, the importance of government action to complement private initiatives, and the ethical priority of addressing the needs of the poorest segment of Milwaukee's population. What Catholic social teachings call the "preferential option for the poor" was put forward as a plausible choice.

The many meetings on this issue with the mayor and senior city staff, both before and after the action, mostly had a moralistic tone. They consisted of MICAH's ethical arguments for city action and, more technically, discussions about how MICAH's goals might be achieved without using city funds. The preparation and debriefings from these meetings, in the task force, had the same quality. In chapter 3, we saw how task force members in their internal discussions used altruistic languages in preference to—or at least to complement—the language of power and self-interest. But in other ways the work of the task force expressed in action core organizing principles. The representatives to the task force were enough in communication and accord with their congregations—to put it in organizing terminology, "accountable" and "relational" enough—that most could get their pastors and a number of co-congregants to participate in the action at the mayor's house. The move from private meetings to a public action, and therefore a more explicit struggle with the city administration, was not an easy step, but it constituted a concrete striving for power and democracy.

The end of the story is ambiguous. The city was eventually able to get outside money to convert one hundred or so abandoned buildings into various forms of subsidized housing (not necessarily public housing units run by the local housing authority). MICAH leaders were willing to accept this as fulfillment of the ordinance, wanting in any case to move on to new issues. From an off-the-record account by a city official, it appears that pressure from MICAH, while not sufficient to get the mayor to fulfill the ordinance literally, gave the stronger liberals within his administration (which was moderately liberal) some leverage in intra-administration debates about priorities. They were able, in essence, to define themselves as the sensible middle between the "extremes" of MICAH on one side and more conservative city officials on the other.[12] While the city never committed significant general revenue funds, it did make a large investment of staff time and probably took out political IOUs in the process of finding the outside (primarily federal) money used to expand affordable rental housing. And this was undoubtedly more effort than the city would have made in the absence of pressure from MICAH's housing task force.

MICAH's march on the mayor's house, like organizing stories, drew on religious traditions, especially the rich deposit of experience that religious communities have in staging colorful and dramatic processions. The action helped "move the issue," as organizers put it. But in addition to its practical impact, it symbolically expressed such organizing values as the religious basis of organizing, the maintenance of relationships (in this case with the mayor), but at the same time the assertion of power by ordinary people through unconventional tactics when conventional ones prove ineffectual. The leaflet for the march took seriously both the particularity of faith and the necessity of translating its claims about housing into secular languages. This same combination was also expressed nonverbally. The profusion and variety of sacred clothing and symbols in the march gave a sense of religiosity but also diversity. The silence left the message a little undefined, something that observers could to some extent define for themselves from within their own perspectives. And finally, the march was an enjoyable and solidarity-building experience for the participants, most of whom were not members of MICAH's housing task force.

PUBLIC MEETINGS: POLITICAL ACTION AS DRAMATURGY

Much of congregation-based community organizing takes place in the back room: one-on-one's, business meetings, informational and negotiation sessions with public and corporate officials, and all the other mundane but important activities required to build and maintain an organization with internal solidarity and external power. This work is punctuated, however, by public events or "actions," such as the MICAH march just described. These can vary greatly in kind and size. But there is one kind of event that more than any other serves as a hallmark of community organizing. This is the large public meeting. Such assemblies are mounted by every local organization, usually twice a year or more. These meetings serve many practical purposes for organizing, but they also constitute a structured, recurring cultural form. First we will examine a characteristic example of this form. This was a meeting staged by PACT in which it met with Susan Hammer, the mayor of San Jose. Then we will consider the nature of such meetings more generally.

PACT Meets with the Mayor

This meeting was held in April 1997 at Most Holy Trinity Roman Catholic Church, a large parish located in a modest neighborhood on San Jose's east side. The packed church had standing room only as more than one thousand people from PACT's member congregations were in attendance. The room was hopping with energy and remained so to the end. The meeting had been prepared with great care and ran like clockwork, finishing, as scheduled, precisely ninety minutes after it started. All the speakers were well prepared, and even the exchanges with the mayor were scripted in that Mayor Hammer knew what PACT would ask and the meeting planners knew which of their demands she would accede to. Most of the presentations were in English, with translation following, although one was in Spanish first. About two-thirds of the speakers were women, and a similar proportion were Hispanic.[13]

The first part of the meeting set the stage for the confrontation with the mayor. There was an introductory presentation by Jeff LaBell, a Catholic priest who served as the meeting chair. He previewed the evening and gave some background on PACT and its dealings with the mayor. He spoke of how PACT had seventeen member congregations, with thirty-five thousand families, and had conducted over one thousand interviews during the past year, more than five hundred of them in the past five months and implicitly in preparation for this meeting. Next came prayer, followed by a "faith reflection." The roll of PACT congregations was then called, with the delegation from each standing up in turn and greeted by loud applause.

The most important element in this part of the meeting was the faith reflection, given by PACT's president, Aurora Solis. This was based on a well-known passage, Luke 11:5–10. Solis started by saying, "Your response to our humble invitation tells us that you are listening to our concerns. I will illustrate to you through our scriptures the reasons we are here today." She then read and interpreted the scripture, which tells of how Jesus asks his disciples to imagine that one of them goes to a friend's house at midnight and says, "Friend, let me borrow three loaves of bread. A friend of mine who is an expatriate has just come to my house, and I don't have any food for him." The response from inside is: "Don't bother me. The door's already locked. . . . I can't get up and give you anything." Jesus reassures his disciples that this is not the end of the story. "Even if he will not get up and give you the bread because you are his friend, yet he *will* get up and give you everything you need because you are not ashamed to keep on asking. And so I say to you, ask and you *will* receive; seek and you will find; knock, and the door will be opened to you. For those who ask will receive, and those who seek will find, and the door will be opened to *anyone* who knocks." (The text and emphases are as Solis read the text.)

Solis is an example of the kind of personal growth engendered by community organizing. An immigrant from a low-income background now working at a public school, she has become a forceful and articulate public speaker. Her talk was frequently interrupted by lengthy applause or laughter, especially in its Spanish version. As Solis went over the story from Luke, it became one about the urgency of the need—the request for bread, the most basic human food—and about the persistence and forcefulness of the asking. The asker's self-interest is addressed not on the basis of friendship but because of the power implicit in how the asking—one might almost say demanding—is done. Solis reminded the mayor that "in May 1993 we knocked and you didn't open. Will you open the door for PACT this time?" She said that actually PACT wasn't asking for an entire loaf, not "the whole tortilla," but only a piece of bread, in that the demands being presented represented less than 1 percent of the city's general operating expenditures. The things PACT was demanding, she said, had to do with protecting families and communities, things "we love." What PACT members wanted were streets where their parents could walk in safety, and places where their children could play and learn. Thus the human goods, based in scriptural values, that PACT spoke for were implicitly contrasted to other priorities. As the meeting continued, themes in this reflection were picked up on time after time. Speakers repeatedly—showing the persistence described in Scripture—asked the mayor to "open the door." They spoke of how the city was providing "caviar" to satisfy business interests or those of the most affluent segments of the city, rather than the "bread" PACT sought.

Solis's thinking was not only egalitarian but democratic: the way she told the story emphasized how "anyone" can and should knock, and will be admitted. This is, of course, a theme about empowerment.

The second major part of the meeting consisted of laying out challenges for the mayor and hearing her responses. First, a youth leader in PACT presented a "research report" outlining PACT's analysis and evaluation of the city's budget priorities. The presenter found the sentiments stated by the city—about the importance of investing in youth—admirable. But in his view the city's actual allocation of resources was wrong. It needed to put a great deal more emphasis on education and youth programs rather than funding downtown development or amenities for the upper middle class. The mayor responded in general terms, explicitly deferring her comments on specific programs until later. Next, representatives of eight local organizing committees, parallel to the one Pearl Cabanilla organized, spoke for the needs and concerns of their neighborhoods. Some of them referred to the many interviews with neighborhood residents each committee had carried out. Each speaker demanded particular actions the city needed to make to deal with local needs, and some of them named a particular price tag for doing so. Some also pointed out the large sums the city had spent for other purposes. A final speaker presented an overview, mentioning the $4.5 million total cost of meeting these demands, and called on the mayor to respond.

At this point the mayor said, "I'll tell you what I will do. The answer is no to 4.5 million, but I'll tell you what I *will* do." Then she proceeded to list things she was willing to commit herself and the city to, which appeared to total somewhat over $1 million. In her response, the mayor tried to seize the discursive high ground by saying that she was responsible for the entire city, with ten council districts and over eight hundred thousand residents. Thus she implied that PACT was an interest group confined to one part of the city. PACT speakers replied that member churches were located in eight of the ten districts. Although they did not say so, clearly they do not think of themselves as an interest group. While many speakers mentioned the pain found in their neighborhoods—crime, drugs, kids with no future, and so on—the tone of their speeches was that they were addressing broad social problems more than their personal needs or the self-interest of their neighborhoods, and making moral claims on public policy in addition to expecting response on the basis of their own numbers and power. After the mayor's responses, various youth and school principals gave testimonials about the transformative effect of homework centers and other youth programs. Here, too, the claims were moral. Self-interest was clearly involved in PACT's work in that participants spoke of concrete wrongs they cared about personally; but their self-interest, like that of the MICAH housing task force, was relational. That is, it had to do with their embeddedness in the city around them, not the advantages they might get as isolated individuals.

In the final part of the meeting, the chair summed up what had happened, concluding, "I think we consider this a win tonight." The meeting closed with a prayer that operated like the dismissal in a Christian eucharist, telling the assemblage to return to the ordinary world with renewed strength and blessing, to love, serve, and bring justice.

Public Meetings as a Cultural Form

Gatherings like PACT's meeting with Mayor Hammer are a replicated structure. The mayor commented early in the meeting that such gatherings in San Jose have "become an annual event"—in other words, a kind of ritual. She knew, in considerable detail, how the meeting would unfold. Meetings I have observed in Milwaukee and Buffalo followed almost exactly the same pattern as in San Jose, and had the same high turnout and level of energy. They similarly got their focus from a set of specific demands presented to public or corporate officials. In all these cities, much of the actual (if not always full) agreement to these demands had been worked out in advance. Public meetings by community organizing groups always have opening and closing prayers and usually some kind of scriptural or religious reflection. They usually give center stage to many and diverse leaders. The organizers themselves, however, almost never speak. The events usually follow a precisely worked out meeting agenda—timed down to the last minute. They are immediately followed by an evaluation session involving all the people who participated in planning or running the event.

The standardized character of public meetings is not an accident. In the PICO residential training leaders are presented with a suggested plan for such meetings consisting of eleven steps: (1) welcome; (2) prayer; (3) credential and background; (4) focus; (5) research report; (6) testimony; (7) response; (8) question and answer; (9) summary; (10) adjourn; and (11) evaluation.[14] It is apparent that the meeting with Mayor Hammer followed this plan, with the local organizing committee presentations—which described the pain in their neighborhoods and demanded response—a form of testimony. And there is a logic to this blueprint, one shared with the Christian eucharist and many other rituals. The meeting starts with fairly "cool" steps. The emotional intensity builds, leading to the confrontation that constitutes the climax of the event. This is followed by a brief celebratory ending, a lowering of tension, after which people are sent back into the ordinary world with renewed purpose and energy.

Gatherings like this serve many purposes. At a practical level, a public meeting as an isolated event does not necessarily result in any new concessions. But concessions *are* won by the negotiation process leading up to the meeting, which receives its focus, on both sides, from the upcoming public event. Furthermore, the meeting makes commitments hard to get out of. One PACT speaker, while expressing dissatisfaction with the amount of funds the mayor put on the table, noted with appreciation that Hammer had never reneged on a promise. Also, the size and energy of the meeting demonstrates the strength of the organization's constituency to public officials and the media, making future concessions more likely. Mayor Hammer said she was "overwhelmed" by the turnout, and she did commit about $1 million in new city funds to purposes defined by PACT.

Within the organization, these occasions can be extraordinarily energizing. People go home from them renewed to do the unglamorous daily work of the organization. In this way, such events serve functions parallel to those of religious gatherings and holy days. Public meetings are exciting and generate a feeling of solidarity with the organization and one's coparticipants. They give people a sense of the organization's power and efficacy, especially since concrete victories are won through the process that culminates in the meeting. They also show the empowerment that is happening within the organization. At the PACT meeting, for instance, it was impressive to see people as young as high schoolers as well as those with foreign accents and dark skins give poised, articulate, and often moving presentations in front of a very large audience.

In addition, both internally and externally these events serve to express the organization's self-understanding. The careful research done for the meeting, the thoroughness of its preparation, and the precise timing used in working out the flow of its agenda say to participants and the world: "We are rational, modern, and systematic." The huge turnout (in organizations larger than PACT, two or even three thousand people in attendance is not unusual) says to politicians and participants: "We are powerful; our leaders have a real following. The massive interviewing done in preparation for the meeting, the effort to hold public officials accountable, the fact that for one evening those officials have to play by the community organization's rules (with the strict imposition of time limits on their responses, for instance), says: "We are radical democrats." The careful mixing in the speaker corps of women and men, young and old, people from varied religious traditions, Hispanics, African Americans, and European Americans says: "We are inclusive and diverse; we will not be split by the factors that have often divided American have-nots." And of course almost everything about the event cries out: "We are faith-based, we are bringing you the messages you hear on your day of worship but tend to forget the rest of the week."

The use of religious traditions in public meetings is similar to that in MICAH's march. First, these traditions—especially the patterns of worship Christians are used to—provide a structure loosely imitated by public meetings. Furthermore, religious ideas and images serve as sources of inspiration, courage, and perseverance. Keep on knocking, said the passage from Luke, as interpreted by Solis to the people of PACT. And finally, faith serves to legitimate politically progressive sentiments, albeit in a diffuse way, giving preference to the needs of low- and modest-income people over business concerns or the affluent: "bread" over "caviar."

ACTING OUT VALUES IN THE DAILY WORK OF THE ORGANIZATION

In the PACT public meeting just described, the cultural dimension is obvious, with singing, inspirational talks, and so forth. The same is true for the MICAH march. Training programs, similarly, are special kinds of events, removed from everyday life and with a focus on personal transformation and on developing a religio-political perspective. But what about the more ordinary activities that take place within congregation-based community organizing? These are, of course, focused on immediate tasks and goals in a way that training is not, and they lack the color and drama of the PACT public meeting and MICAH march. Yet it turns out that they, too, are in part cultural forms. To see this, we will consider the two most basic daily activities: business meetings and one-on-one's.

Business Meetings

Meetings are ubiquitous in faith-based organizing. In MICAH, for example, the issue task forces have meetings; the board and pastor caucus have meetings; infrastructural committees concerned with matters such as fundraising, personnel, and recruiting new congregations have meetings; *ad hoc* work groups planning particular events have meetings. They are where almost all the organization's work is planned. Most of the tasks participants perform to further the aims of the organization are things they volunteered, agreed, or were assigned to do in a meeting. And most of the entries in the central calendar maintained at a community organization's office are times and places of meetings.

Business meetings vary greatly in their practical tasks. Yet they are quite standardized in *how* they are conducted and constitute yet another cultural form constructed by faith-based organizing. An example that typifies many of the constants in this form is a meeting of MICAH's drugs and crime task force in November 1991. Cheryl Spivey-Perry, MICAH's lead organizer, was present and spoke occasionally, but a lay representative from one of the congregations ran the meeting. The meeting, held in the basement of one of the MICAH churches, started at 7 P.M. with prayer. Then all those present introduced themselves, giving their names and congregations, and the agenda for this meeting and minutes from the last were approved.

The first item of substance was discussion of strategies for dealing with the state legislature and governor about expanding drug treatment programs. Recently the governor had vetoed a bill that would have added more beds for residential treatment programs, and MICAH representatives had left a tombstone at his office to symbolize the death his decision would bring. There had been one meeting with him and another was scheduled. Plans were made for who would attend this meeting and what they would do. The governor, a fairly conservative Republican, was unresponsive and had not been treating MICAH people very well; there was some sharing of anger and frustration over this. A meeting with some other officials had been canceled because task force members had not had time to plan it properly; there was a somewhat indeterminate discussion of what went wrong.

Then, because the task force chair was going to retire in two months, the group considered how and when to elect a new chair. This discussion led to disagreements about precisely how to define eligibility for the position. This was one of the few times Spivey-Perry intervened, pointing out that this experienced and cohesive group—which indeed it was—was hardly likely to elect an inappropriate chair just because such a person might be technically eligible to be elected.

The next item was discussion of the new issue-determination process—for MICAH as a whole—that was about to start. The process was going to involve extensive one-on-one interviews in all the MICAH churches, by which interviewers (members of each congregation, interviewing their co-congregants) would among other things collect information on the concerns about the neighborhood, city, and church that were uppermost in the minds of their fellow members. The "founding convention" (the occasion when MICAH became a formal organization) was coming up in a month, and plans had to be made about who would represent the task force and also about getting turnout from congregations for the event.

The next to last item, labeled "open discussion" on the agenda, was an opportunity for unplanned items to be brought forward by individual task force members. As is typical, there were no such items, and in any case there was almost no time left. Just before the closing prayer, a brief evaluation was made by going around the table and having everyone say in a few words what they thought of the meeting. The meeting ran exactly ninety minutes, as scheduled.

In this meeting, as in all meetings I have attended within faith-based community organizing, there were opening and closing prayers. Some business meetings have another religious component: a biblical or theological reflection, sometimes called a "focus," usually near the start of the meeting. The prayers are sometimes moving, often referring specifically to the people in the room, and sometimes last several minutes. They provide a frame for the meeting. But most of the time in business meetings is spent in secular talk about the specific goals the group wants to pursue and the best means for accomplishing them. What gives business meetings of this kind a cultural dimension is not primarily the explicitly religious content but the fact that such meetings are a highly standardized—one might almost say, scripted—practice, and that this practice serves, like that of large public meetings, as a communicative device. The meeting just described was very similar to dozens I have observed in Milwaukee, Buffalo, and San Jose.

In the first place, it is universal within community organizing that meetings start and end at the announced time and are of moderate length. This pattern is somewhat unusual in religious life. In fact, Pastor Leary of Calvary Baptist in Milwaukee described the impact organizing had on his congregation in this regard. In the old days, he explained, nobody came on time to committee meetings in his church, which were likely to drag on for hours. Once many of the core lay leaders in the congregation became involved in MICAH, however, they experienced a different style of work and rebelled at Calvary's traditional practices, which then seemed to them to manifest disrespect for their time. They eventually forced most church committee meetings into the mold of MICAH meetings. In congregation-based community organizing, that meetings end on time is an almost religious goal. If an agenda item takes longer than expected and the meeting is behind schedule, everyone is exhorted to speed things up. If someone gets long-winded, others complain. But even if the discussion is disciplined and dealing with important issues, going late is simply not tolerated. Not one out of many dozens of meetings I have observed went past its scheduled end by more than ten minutes. There are, of course, practical benefits to this rigor. People who can coordinate their schedules reliably with babysitters, spouses, and children are more likely to come regularly. Attention and energy levels remain high throughout the meetings, in part because participants can assume a sure and early end. But this self-discipline is also expressive. It says that the participants are people of great value whose time is just as important as that of some mayor or corporate executive. It also says that the organization is committed to being practically effective and goal-oriented; it is a place for changing the world, not for fine talk. Ending on time is an outward sign, a symbol, of the efficacy of the organization.

Written agendas, minutes, and a brief evaluation period at the end of the meeting are other elements of the crime and drugs task force meeting described above that are almost universal elements of business meetings in faith-based organizing. These express the systematic character of organizing. They communicate to regular participants and newcomers that, no matter how urgent the task of the day, participants will make sure they know where they have come from and that they are committed to learning from their successes and failures rather than doing things *ad hoc*. Another recurrent feature of business meetings, expressing the organizing concept of "accountability," is that when tasks are agreed upon, notes are taken as to what each person is to do. At a subsequent meeting participants have to report on whether they have in fact accomplished their tasks. Still another common practice is that the chair makes sure that participation is broad, rather than allowing a few people to dominate the meeting. At critical points, the chair may have the discussion go around the table, with each person in turn expressing his or her own views or those of the congregation he or she represents. This procedure is a way of saying that this is a democratic organization, one that believes in open and fair deliberation and that values and seeks to develop each person, not just those who are already articulate.

In addition to the practical and expressive functions meetings fulfill, they are also a source of solidarity. Participants *enjoy* their meetings, and the groups almost always appear cohesive. In fact, the MICAH housing task force insisted on meeting twice a month, while MICAH organizers thought that monthly would be enough.

Purposive Personal Encounters: The "One-on-One"

In chapter 2, while considering the process by which MICAH was built, we saw the important role played by a special kind of personal encounter that organizers call "one-on-one's." In the simplest form, which serves as a model for other varieties, these are interviews lasting about a half hour, initiated by an organizer or active participant in order to learn more about the concerns, capacities, perspectives, life situation, and self-interest of the person being interviewed. Such interviews provide information on constituency (congregational and neighborhood) concerns. A more important function is that they help the initiator assess the likelihood of enrolling the respondent in the organization's work, the kind of contribution the person could make, and the ways in which the person's self-interest (understood broadly) and the organization's could be aligned. These interactions also increase the respondents' attachment to the organization by paying them respectful attention and help them clarify their previously implicit concerns and self-interest. Perhaps most fundamentally they build relationships and community, binding initiator and respondent together.

This is the paradigmatic form such purposive personal encounters take. As a generic form, one-on-one's are conversations undertaken with an intent to clarify self-interests in a way that builds relationships and the organization. In this broader sense, they are as ubiquitous as meetings: most organizing work that does not take place in meetings consists of one-on-one's. Organizing talk manifests fervent commitment to the importance of having large numbers of purposive encounters. Job descriptions for organizers often articulate this as a basic task, and organizers frequently speak of how central this task is to their work. One-on-one's are usually asymmetrical and in a sense unequal: they are initiated by one of the two people, and the initiator may do less of the talking but sets the agenda and asks most of the questions. Asking the questions is an expression (and tool) of power, reinforcing the hierarchical character of these interactions.

But purposive interactions, according to the training and I think in reality, are also strong expressions of respect and regard for the respondents. The process communicates the idea that the respondent is a fascinating, unique, and self-determining person—a child of God whose views deserve to be listened to with care and sympathy and whose self-interest and purposes deserve to be treated seriously. Furthermore, the commitment to doing one-on-one's on such a large scale, and so frequently, bespeaks the importance that faith-based organizing gives to exploring self-interest and building relationships, since the whole purposes of these encounters is to clarify the respondent's self-interest and to start or strengthen the relationship with the interviewer. The pervasiveness of purposive personal encounters also expresses a commitment to working on the basis of empirical information—finding out how the world really is rather than how one imagines or hopes it might be—and the democratic principle of responsiveness. Thus this practice, like the others, has an expressive as well as practical significance, manifesting in action some of the movement's core values.

PRACTICES AS CULTURAL FORMS

I have argued that many of the concrete activities found in community organizing—its "practices"—are quite standardized cultural forms. They have practical, instrumental purposes, to be sure. For example, public meetings like the one staged by PACT can help produce concessions from public officials. Internally, organizing practices and narratives serve to build solidarity and renew the commitment of participants. The practices are means toward ends, and the energy put into them shows how much participants care about the hoped-for result. But in addition, organizing participants engage in their standardized forms of activity as ends in themselves. Their practices serve as a system of communication, as a means of saying certain things to themselves and others. These activities also serve to provide an image or model of how a better world—one that is more democratic and in which each person is more valued—might function. The practices of community organizing, in short, are valued for themselves and for what they express, rather than just for what they accomplish. They are cultural forms, just like religious rituals or victory parades. They combine with the system of ideas described in chapter 3 to provide organizing with a rich cultural life.

Conclusion to Part II

EXPANSIVE AND CONSTRAINED DISCOURSE IN COMMUNITY ORGANIZING

In chapter 1, we saw how an antiwar coalition in Cincinnati refused to allow discussion of anything beyond its immediate goals, which had the effect of leaving the ethical bases for participants' involvement unspoken and invisible. By comparison with that group, and arguably with most progressive movements in the contemporary United States, the discourse of faith-based organizing is expansive. The narratives and practices it has developed only add to this richness in its cultural life. However, the language of community organizing also incorporates various constraints. Since the basic expansiveness of the discourse of community organizing has been amply documented through the last three chapters, we will concentrate here on the constraints and the reasons that are given for adopting them.

In summarizing the ways in which the cultural life of community organizing is expansive and constrained, we will consider three dimensions with respect to which public discourse can vary. These are shown in the table at the end of chapter 1 and are described below.

TEMPERATURE

This dimension has to do with the tone of debate and its relationship to ethical evaluations. At times, political judgments have a hotly passionate and moral tone; they are based on values that are taken to be universal and transcendent. In these cases, a movement's basic principles, whether religious or not, are taken to be "sacred." At other times, evaluations are made on a cooler, more technical, or instrumental basis. Such judgments are about means to achieve ends that are presupposed or thought of as private individual preferences. As with the other two dimensions we will be discussing, a given organization often uses different modes of discourse depending on the context. In Citizens for Community Values (CCV), for instance, people sometimes talked in terms that were strongly infused with moral judgments, while at other times they spoke instrumentally about strategies for achieving the group's ends. The antiwar coalition in Cincinnati, on the other hand, largely suppressed all talk about morality.

We have seen at many points how the language of community organizing makes passionate, transcendent moral claims. On this dimension it is "hotter" or more expansive than what one observes in most American activist movements. The specific demands that community organizations make are not defined as transcendent, but the underlying principles often are, as in the claim that "housing is a divine right," or the assertion one occasionally hears that "this city is holy ground." A skeptic might think that such claims are actually opportunistic, imagining that the "real" motivations underlying them are in fact utilitarian. But in community organizing, the arguments made in private, within business meetings of work groups, are if anything *more* focused on morality and justice than those made to the public.[1]

The choice of means within organizing involves ethical principles in addition to judgments about what will work best. The planning of MICAH's march on the mayor's house is a case in point. Another is the frequently heard idea that opponents are "targets," not "enemies"; they are not to be demonized. Furthermore, the inner life of the organization is constructed following moral and political values, in addition to considerations about what will get things done most effectively. Commitments to widespread participation, respect for each person's views, and civility (the last including a ban on profanity) are manifest in almost every meeting. Some social critics want to argue that religiously based politics inevitably leads to intolerance, absolutism, and even violence—in other words, to people using extreme means because they are pursuing transcendent ends. But there is little sign of such tendencies in faith-based organizing, in part because ethical principles apply to means and the inner life of the organization just as much as to ends.

On the other hand, there are ways in which organizing adopts "cooler" forms of discourse. I have never seen a community organization make its case to local government *primarily* on the basis that "we are a big bloc of voters; do what we want or we'll work against you." But certainly that is an implicit element of the strategy for achieving victories, as one can see from the great emphasis placed on turning out large numbers of people for public events, in part to impress public officials with the size of the organization's constituency. Furthermore, the language of self-interest and power is in part intended as a challenge, telling church people to be more instrumental and less moralistic in planning their political work. This language says something like "Get your hands dirty using means that might actually win concrete victories, rather than just salving your conscience or witnessing to good values." Saul Alinsky was sometimes accused of thinking that any means were acceptable. This is a distortion, but he and organizers since have certainly insisted that before making decisions one should do a cold-blooded analysis of the likely actual outcomes of possible courses of action. To this extent, the mode of action is supposed to be cool and instrumental, rather than passionate and moralistic. In the phrase popularized by Mary Beth Rogers, organizing cultivates "cold anger."[2] Thus organizers advocate certain kinds of discursive self-discipline as a guard against organizing becoming moralistic in a useless and self-indulgent way.

Another form of constraint has to do with how religious claims are made in public settings. As we saw in the mayoral march, they are made in a tentative and modest tone. The reason for this limitation is that in turn-of-the-millennium America one cannot assume a shared religious basis nor in fact any kind of cultural basis more specific than the fundamental democratic principles that commonly undergird American public discourse.[3] Or at least a person of progressive sentiments is not supposed to make such an assumption. That is, the reality or at least the norms of multiculturalism require a constrained use of religious claims.

Sometimes the limitation on using transcendent language goes further, with the language of self-interest leading organizing participants to define the political situation in an almost relativistic way. Consider, for instance, this statement from a trainer with the Pacific Institute for Community Organizing (PICO): "Developers, banks, and chambers of commerce are very clear about their self-interest. I would not begrudge the economic powers their acting on their self-interest. PICO's stance is that mediating institutions are failing to balance these competing interests, and we see ourselves linking families and communities to be more clear about *their* self-interest so that they can sit at the negotiating table as equals."[4] This statement, which is similar to others I have heard in organizing, makes it sound as if the needs of bankers and of inner-city residents were on a moral par. The problem to be rectified is that the interests of bankers are represented while those of residents are not. Organizers and grassroots participants may not be so relativistic in their hearts. But they sometimes frame their views within the kind of assumptions just discussed. These imply that the community organization does not really need to make an ethical case for the *substantive* outcomes that it espouses, such as more resources for inner-city neighborhoods. It needs only to argue for its right to participate in decision making. After that, a "cool" politics of bargaining at the table will do.

ISSUE LINKS

This second dimension concerns the degree to which issues are related to one another and to an overall social vision. Many movements, as a practical matter, deal with only one issue or issue area. However, their discourse—especially internally—may be broad-gauged. What made the discourse of the antiwar coalition in Cincinnati constrained was not so much the group's single-issue practical focus but the fact that it refused even to talk about the wider significance of the Gulf War. Many other peace groups that I have observed *do* talk, especially internally, about the roots of American foreign policy or even about the connections between foreign policy and domestic economic justice issues. Socialist organizations, at the opposite extreme from the Cincinnati group, have an overarching perspective—this being America, it's usually pretty fuzzy—and might in principle take a position or work on any issue. But separation of issues is more typical of American social movements. Economic justice issues, on one side, and questions of individual freedom and cultural diversity, on the other, are particularly likely to be kept apart, although activists sometimes try to surmount this divide.

Community organizers, following Alinsky, believe that the various issues dealt with in American politics are intertwined.[5] And organizing projects describe themselves as "multi-issue." But in practice, faith-based organizing operates under rules that significantly limit the range of political issues that can be discussed and the degree to which different issues can be linked into broader social and political visions.

We have seen that organizing deals with economic justice issues. What issues does it *not* address? The most obvious one is abortion. Even if this issue were not off-limits because the Catholic Church, through the Catholic Campaign for Human Development (CCHD), is the largest source of funds for organizing, it would be excluded by a more basic discursive rule: issues that divide whole congregations against each other are to be ignored. Economic issues bring up serious differences, since participants range from socialists to staunch free-market advocates. But a wide spectrum of views is found *within* each congregation, rather than one congregation being very radical and another very conservative. On abortion, by contrast, the Catholic Church and some traditionalist Protestant denominations are pro-life while most mainline Protestant denominations are pro-choice, to the extent of wanting to keep abortion legal. Accordingly, I have never heard the slightest mention of abortion at a community organizing meeting or event. On the death penalty, denominational stances are less clear and differently aligned than on abortion, but this too is a touchy issue, with the religious traditionalists tending toward conservative positions. Only once, within organizing, have I heard anyone speak to this issue. It was a tense moment, and the remark was ignored.

More generally, organizing does not address the kinds of issues involved in "culture wars," and it does not take up the liberty agenda of progressive politics. Thus faith-based organizations generally do not concern themselves with issues such as civil liberties, gay rights, tolerance for varying sexual mores, or reducing the criminalization of drug use. Political issues about women's rights are not addressed explicitly, although organizing works hard at empowering women in the church. The exclusion of liberty and cultural issues, of course, is driven not just by concerns for unity but also by the fact that they are not as localized as the issues that community organizing commonly deals with. But questions about drugs, such as the debates about the "harm reduction" approach that proposes a degree of decriminalization, relate directly to the local urban concerns characteristic of organizing. MICAH even has a drugs and crime task force. But MICAH spoke only of expanding drug treatment programs, not for or against harm reduction, and the most likely explanation is that this, like sexuality, is an issue strongly correlated with theological positions.

Issues about race are also kept at arm's length, which also could be seen as stemming from the basic rule against doing anything that might set whole congregations against each other. Even in strongly multiracial community organizations very few *congregations* have much racial diversity. In Milwaukee, MICAH sought set-asides for city and county contracts, but in a nonracial way, lobbying for a rule allocating jobs to unemployed inner-city residents. Undoubtedly most of the potential beneficiaries were black, but the proposal could be advocated without having to get into controversies about affirmative action.

An important aim of organizing is to achieve concrete victories, and this is taken to require what is called "cutting an issue": converting general concerns into specific proposals that the organization has a good chance of getting its targets (typically local governments or corporations) to agree to within a couple of years. This is a characteristic self-discipline of organizing discourse, and it has practical advantages. But if discussions about the larger concerns or visions that are behind the "cut" issues do not take place, discourse becomes constrained. Such an exclusion affects the organization internally, as it sets its agenda. It also affects the organization's external discourse, putting the priority on winning specific victories rather than on changing the terms of public debate.

Thus an important discursive dilemma facing organizing is the extent to which political concerns beyond "cut" issues are going to be discussed. Are broader social visions or ways of linking issues to be talked about, even if not agreed upon or articulated in public? Most often the answer in organizing is: only to the extent of expressing extremely general principles of democracy and citizenship with which almost any American would agree. This is true in Alinsky's *Reveille for Radicals,* in statements from network leaders today, in what local organizations say, and in discussions within these organizations. That is, community organizing takes controversial positions on highly specific issues and noncontroversial ones on highly general topics. Intermediate between these two levels on which organizing is heard is what might be called the "middle level" of public discourse. This level is where people debate broader but controversial issues about the direction our society should go, such as what role government should play in economic life, whether we should strive for greater equality, and so forth. It is at this level that general, structured political perspectives, such as populism, socialism, libertarianism, and free market ideology, state their cases. At the middle level, organizing is generally silent. That does not mean that positions on such issues are not present in the minds of organizing participants or intellectuals. Even though Alinsky tended not to articulate any position at the middle level, he became detested by the right: they could tell that he was not their friend. He was in effect something close to a populist, and he even cooperated with communists when he was developing the Back of the Yards Neighborhood Council in the late 1930s.[6]

Today, among organizing intellectuals, there is a debate between people such as Gary Delgado who would like organizing to become more articulate at the middle level, putting forward a clearer political perspective, and those who defend traditional practice, such as Mike Miller.[7] The traditionalists in this debate are afraid of ideological litmus tests that might be divisive. Also, they argue that more discourse at the middle level could inhibit the scope of organizing, undermining one of the strengths of the movement: that it is able to recruit as active participants people who think of themselves as conservative. Traditionalists sometimes also worry that the agenda of organizing might get hijacked. Whatever the outcome of this debate, in the daily life of faith-based community organizations at present one sees relatively little attention to links among issues or to considering questions at the middle level. This is true even in training. In practice, discourse tends to be limited to very general principles or to the highly specific level of "cut" issues, dealt with one issue at a time.

Related to this dilemma is the one of focus on what might be called democratic "process"—gaining an increase in rights of participation for the previously excluded—as contrasted with the "substance" of political proposals. The idea of power is most obviously about process, and it has always been a fundamental goal of community organizing to increase the number of people involved in decision making, to enhance their impact on decisions, and to broaden the range of decisions on which they are heard. On the other hand, organizing discourse often sidesteps questions about what its substantive goals are. As Alinsky put it, "a people's program is whatever the people decide." At the Gamaliel training discussed in chapter 3, after hearing arguments to the effect that congregations and congregation-based organizations should work to develop power, one trainee asked, "Power to do what?" The trainer said this was determined by leaders and members. The trainee, still seeking clarification, asked, "To what end?" The response was: "To whatever end the people decide."[8]

In fact organizers have substantive political purposes. They work to empower people in inner-city Detroit, not Grosse Pointe. Gamaliel advertises for new organizers in the *Nation,* not the *National Review.* And Catholic social teachings put forward substantive principles for economic life—ones that are far more in tune with progressive than conservative politics.[9] Nonetheless, in the discourse of community organizing, a constraint that is clearly operative is a preference for speaking of democratic process rather than egalitarian or social-democratic substance. The basic purposes animating organizing give reason for applying this constraint to some aspects of organizing work. If an organizer, already skilled in thinking about social issues and articulating political ideas, conducts organizing around a set of purposes she defines, the possibilities for indigenous communities to explore their own values and interests and democratically construct their own political agenda are diminished. However, probably broader factors are also at work, given that the reluctance of organizing participants to talk about substantive purposes rather than process is shared with people in many other movements and is found in a broad range of organizing contexts. American social movements frequently prefer the language of process to that of substance. There are gains from this choice. But it also has problems. In particular, it leaves unexamined the bases for establishing, or justifying to others, one's substantive political priorities.

CIVIL-SOCIETAL LINKS

The last dimension concerns the connections between specifically political ideas and the general-purpose cultural traditions to which people are attached in their daily, nonpolitical lives. These general-purpose traditions may or may not have a political dimension, but they do not take their identity from politics and they apply to much besides politics. The most obvious examples are the various religious traditions Americans commit themselves to. But there are others. Every social practice in which people can be deeply engaged, spending many hours with co-practitioners, generates ethical precepts and views of the world. This happens in voluntary or recreational activities such as sports or music, and also in professional settings such as medicine or the professorate. Sometimes, as with the more extreme groups on the religious right, people try to take their civil-societal traditions directly into the political realm. At other times, no connection is made between the two. Avoiding both extremes, activists can ground their political views in the civil-societal traditions they are committed to, forging a connection while also responding to the specific nature of politics.

In faith-based organizing, links to civil-societal traditions—specifically, religious ones—are strong. Religious traditions are not just a motivational force, not even just something participants are aware of in private, but are an explicit and public part of internal discourse and sometimes dialogue with people outside as well.

The language of community organizing is less exclusively linked to a particular religious and ethical perspective than in some combinations of religion and politics. Citizens for Community Values, briefly described in chapter 1, also constructs a rich discourse that brings faith into politics. But it has only been able to appeal to religious traditionalists, and almost entirely Protestant ones at that. By contrast, as part of its public work, community organizations like MICAH take on the task of translating religious claims into various types of discourse such as constitutional or human rights language. By doing this one implicitly forgoes claims to exclusive possession of truth. The rationale for this approach is to develop a broad base of support for one's proposals. Internally, a similar rule applies. The goal of the rule is partly to avoid alienating any religious group or setting groups against each other, given the great diversity of faiths within organizing. But it also stems from what might be called liberal theological principles: an implicit idea that each religious perspective deserves respect and has gleaned part of the truth. David Mann of PICO told me about his desire to strengthen the connections between faith and organizing. But when Jim Shaul, a colleague of Mann's who was present for part of the interview, heard this, he cautioned, "That does not imply disrespect for individual faith traditions. We do not expect a Unitarian to sound like an African American Baptist preacher. But maybe to be able to be as passionately connected to the substance and ground of their faith—whether it's Rilke or Jeremiah."[10]

The norms of American public discourse force the language of governance in the United States to be secular or, at most, religious only in the manner that Robert Bellah has termed "civil religion."[11] Whether officials are personally religious or not, when acting in their official roles they are constrained not to appear to favor one faith over another. All the efforts of Christian right groups over the past few decades has made no real dent in this secularity. When speaking in public, faith-based community organizations often adopt a weaker version of the constraint governing public officials, articulating their proposals in secular, civil languages. To an extent far greater than CCV or religious right groups, they couch their concerns in terms that nonreligious people and public officials can use without embarrassment.

In addition to the constraints just described, there are two important limitations on the capacity of congregation-based community organizing to link politics with civil-societal traditions. Each of these involves what social scientists call a "black box"—that is, something that one simply assumes to be operating without examining how or why it works.[12] In the language of community organizing, there are, it turns out, ways in which faith can become a black box and other ways in which this can also happen to politics.

Faith and Values Examined and Unexamined

While secular progressives tend to assume that the social implications of faith are conservative, socially active Christians and Jews often imagine that scripture and religious ethics automatically lend support to an economic justice agenda like that of congregation-based community organizing. That is, for many people involved in organizing, it seems self-evident that faith mandates a concern for equality and the well-being of the poor. Faith can then be treated as a prepolitical given—a force that is automatically there to help the cause. In the Gamaliel training, there was constant reference to how church people have "good values." The only thing necessary, apparently, was to wed those values with the power required to instantiate them. Only with regard to images of meekness and selflessness and to conceptions of faith as purely concerning private life did the trainers express any need to contest the understandings of faith found in religious communities. In terms of substantive goals for social life, good values were assumed to be already hard at work producing life-affirming political positions, although the particular values in question were not specified. We might tag this set of assumptions the "Christian reform teleology."[13] José Carrasco, taking a similar but more qualified position, allowed that values needed to be "surfaced," "exercised," and "hermeneutically examined," but he was positive that they did *not* need to be reformed.[14]

One difficulty with this approach is that in fact the social implications of religious faith and values are extremely ambiguous. Given the traditions of Christian faith, for example, there are plenty of ways to reach conservative conclusions on economic issues but also plenty to reach progressive conclusions. Faith has backed both slavery and abolitionism, and still today can legitimate the fiercest free-market capitalism or the most utopian communism. Some of the value positions found within widely shared Christian traditions are very supportive of progressive politics, while others, such as St. Paul's teachings on the role of women, are distinctly unhelpful.[15] The social implications of faith vary, and they are largely formed by what happens once people start becoming active on social issues. Well-behaved black boxes serve up consistent outputs, but religious traditions do not oblige.

Many organizing participants, perhaps sensing these problems, want to more carefully examine the connections with faith in the interest of making them stronger. In a meal-time conversation at the PICO training, some participants expressed to each other the view that the faith component of the training was not very well developed, with not enough on "faith, trust in God, [or the] Bible." In another such side conversation, trainees said there was not enough on gospel values and not enough theological reflection. Pearl Cabanilla of PACT said that while she has read the U.S. Catholic Bishops' pastoral on the economy it had never been discussed within her parish's local organizing committee. She observed, "I'm finding out that we need to have time to talk about that, and we haven't had the time. Most of the time what we're doing is working, and not really discussing the values issue and how we might recognize that. I suspect that's true in other parishes as well."[16]

David Mann shared this concern, describing two problems that he wanted to address. The first was that "our leaders are almost illiterate in being able to connect their faith principles up with their organizing principles. In schooling leaders, we've taught power and tactics and strategy and analysis of the social milieu, and we haven't taught what the faith or scriptural connection of that is. So we're catching up now. People [other than African American pastors] are not adept at quickly saying what the faith basis of [their proposals is], for themselves or publicly." Second, "lay people are not *internally* connected to their faith, their spirituality, and their organizing work, so they aren't drawing on the sustenance and encouragement for the long haul that's in them. So our leaders have got to get a lot more faith connected for both of those reasons." He saw this as a tough task, but he was committed to it, hoping that the "common language" of organizing would include not just "power organizing principles" but ones about faith as well. He wanted to "add that to the language. We've learned how important language is."[17] With this spirit of critical self-examination and sensitivity to how cultural processes work, Mann and PICO will probably strengthen the links between faith and politics in the future.

Politics as a Black Box: Civil Society and Empowerment as Heroes

Community organizing projects are incorporated under section 501(c)(3) of the U.S. Code, which defines the criteria for a tax-exempt nonprofit organization, and are therefore legally prohibited from most kinds of involvement in electoral politics. All the same, the most important group of people dealt with outside the organization are public officials. Participants meet with a broad range of staff in local government and become knowledgeable about budgets and agency structure. City administration, for people in organizations like MICAH and PACT, is most decidedly *not* a black box. And community organizing trains participants to value and enjoy the public realm. Yet at times the language of community organizing takes on a cast that diminishes the importance of politics and therefore the urgency of connecting faith traditions to politics.

One way in which this happens in through a heavy emphasis on civil society—the voluntary-associational and familial realm, as opposed to markets and politics—as the source and solution for social problems. In chapter 3, we saw Gamaliel talking about breakdown in community as a central problem in itself and a source of other problems. The document asserting this position also argues that "the ordinary citizen feels more and more powerless in the face of . . . massive political and private forces." It says that both governmental programs and the forces of the market have been ineffectual in solving social problems. Rather, "it is only in community that there can be safe streets, care for the elderly, [and] proper education."[18] Accordingly, Gamaliel argues that organizing can be a means of reconstructing civil society through building richer webs of relationships, strengthening religious congregations, and increasing the capacity of congregations to engage social issues.

It is hard to argue against strengthening civil society.[19] But if this is the central methodology for social change, demands for political change, for change in the economic system, and for using government as a way to improve social life lose their urgency. At times, for this reason, the language of organizing becomes blander and less political, and the links between faith commitments and participants' stance on political issues become weaker.

Focus on empowering individuals can have similarly depoliticizing implications. We have seen over and over again how important the idea of empowerment is to the language of community organizing. In our earlier discussion of statements to the effect that the goals of organizing are whatever people decide they should be, we saw that the discursive rules of community organizing sometimes favor "processual" claims—about rights to political participation—over substantive ones.[20] When this tilt is strong, it puts substantive issues into a black box. All organizing needs to do is to enhance the power of religious people or of those previously excluded from decision making. Movement in the direction of a better society will happen automatically.

The centrality of empowerment also means that organizers often view the development of leaders as their first priority. Pat Speer, an Industrial Areas Foundation (IAF) organizer, went so far as to say that if organizations die but have developed leaders the leaders will find each other again.[21] Thus being empowered becomes a part of people's permanent character.

The implicit assumption in making empowerment one's central strategy for social change must be either that broader participation is the chief political good, with substantive political results relatively unimportant, or else that if a broader range of people become empowered one can count on the results improving. Both of these assumptions are problematic. And they put substantive politics—debates about laws and budgets, about the shape of government policies and programs—into a black box. That is, they assume that improving the quality and capacities of the individuals participating in politics will consistently improve the outputs from politics. If changing and empowering *individuals* is the main way one gets better politics, then it is less important to engage substantive political questions on the basis of religious traditions.

Thus organizing talk is sometimes queasy about addressing substantive concerns beyond specific "cut" issues—the middle level of political discourse we discussed earlier. Sometimes that middle level is tagged, pejoratively, as "ideology." But there are also pushes in the opposite direction by organizing participants who are often quite ready to bring ethical and religious principles to bear on substantive issues, and make links between civil-societal cultural traditions and politics that are much stronger than those usually found in the United States.

While faith-based community organizing adopts a number of constraints, overall it engages in more expansive discourse and has constructed a livelier set of cultural practices than most American social justice movements. Some of the success of the cultural work of organizing is due to the specifically religious roots of this kind of activism. Much of it, however, comes from following more generic principles of cultural action, such as articulating transcendent principles, that are applicable in nonreligious settings. This work deserves to be studied with care by people who hope to enrich the cultural dimension of progressive politics.

Part III: Human Rights and Amnesty International

Chapter 5

THE HUMAN RIGHTS TRADITION AND AMNESTY INTERNATIONAL

Concern for human rights acquired new visibility in the 1990s. The creation of new international tribunals, the 1998 arrest of Augusto Pinochet in England on charges brought by a Spanish magistrate concerning Pinochet's actions in Chile, the international debates around conflicts emerging in the former Yugoslavia—all of these suggest the new currency of proposals to enhance human rights by limiting the power of nation states. That the proposed limits are likely to apply in practice only to weak countries does not negate their importance.

Human rights advocacy is a manifestation of one of the grand projects of progressive politics: enhancing the liberty and dignity of the human individual. Congregation-based community organizing expresses another core progressive agenda: economic justice, community, and equality. We have seen that congregation-based community organizing uses quite expansive modes of discourse—more expansive than are customary in American progressive movements. In this way, it is an example of possibilities other movements might tap. But two questions arise about the generalizability of the cultural approach seen in community organizing—questions that can be clarified by examining human rights discourse.

The first question has to do with the fact that organizing is an explicitly religious movement. Most progressive movements in the United States are not religious. Can they nonetheless construct a cultural life that is comparable to that of community organizing? That is, to what extent do the expansive elements in the cultural life of community organizing depend upon its specifically religious character?

The second question concerns the kind of political issues engaged by community organizing. As we have seen, organizing deals with economic justice issues. It does *not* deal with abortion, women's rights, capital punishment, civil liberties, or gay rights. That is, organizing engages the justice agenda of progressive politics, but not the liberty one. Discourse and activism on behalf of liberty is different from justice politics. Is the kind of expansive cultural work found in community organizing possible in movements that focus on the agenda of individual liberty?

The first question was addressed briefly in chapter 1, where the Greens and a group of ex-communists showed us that expansive discourse is possible without religious underpinnings. Examining the human rights movement allows us to address this question more fully and also to deal with the second one. The human rights movement is secular—probably inherently and necessarily so—since it is international and has to cross deep lines of cultural difference. It is also a movement focused directly and explicitly on protecting individual rights.

Within this movement, Amnesty International (AI, or "Amnesty")—the best known organization in the human rights movement—makes a particularly good case to compare with community organizing. Amnesty is fiercely determined to keep focused on human rights, and the way it does so largely excludes the egalitarian and communitarian thrusts of social justice politics—not from the sympathy of Amnesty activists, but from the political work and talk they conduct within the organization—just as organizing largely excludes liberty concerns. Furthermore, Amnesty, unlike some human rights organizations, has an organizational structure and methodology that engages local members in personal activism and face-to-face interaction. Around the world, one can find local Amnesty groups that have existed for some time and developed their own patterns of activity and discourse. Like organizing, Amnesty provides a context for grassroots public discourse.

The tradition of human rights is much older, as a family of political perspectives, than the language of faith-based community organizing. Organizing in its present incarnation dates only from the 1970s, while human rights work is more than two hundred years old. Furthermore, the human rights tradition is more varied: ambiguities and diverse possibilities for understanding and appropriating it are located deep in its basic ideas. For example, human rights activists have differing views about what "human rights" include and about the moral, philosophical, or religious bases for justifying these rights. Human rights discourse can be quite expansive or quite constrained. The more expansive versions show how progressive politics can be culturally robust even when it is not religious and when the political agenda concerns individual liberty rather than social justice. The less expansive ones allow us to learn more about the forms discursive constraints can take, how and why activists sometimes adopt them, and what consequences flow from them. In this way we can better understand the cultural dilemmas progressive politics confronts.

The human rights tradition is ambiguous, but in the course of action and advocacy individuals and organizations make cultural choices that take the tradition in more specific directions. As a global organization, Amnesty International deals explicitly and seriously with the issue of defining the discursive boundaries within which it will operate. The local groups I observed also confront the ambiguities, making their own choices about how to interpret the human rights tradition.

We will start by reviewing the cultural traditions on which contemporary human rights work relies, with a special focus on three defining documents. Two of these—the French Declaration of the Rights of Man and the Citizen and the U.S. Bill of Rights—date from the age of democratic revolutions. These documents, along with thinkers such as Locke and Voltaire, helped construct the tradition of human rights. The third document is the Universal Declaration of Human Rights (UDHR), adopted by the United Nations shortly after World War II. The UDHR has become the sacred text of the contemporary human rights movement. The discussion of these documents is intended as a sketch of the most important elements of the historical deposit contemporary human rights work draws upon, not an intellectual history of this tradition. In the second half of the chapter, we will take a quick look at the organizational structure and history of Amnesty International and then examine Amnesty's appropriation of the human rights tradition, focusing on the rules it has adopted to govern its work and how it defines its organizational "mandate." The following chapter deals with the interpretation of this tradition within the local Amnesty groups I have observed and the cultural life they have developed. Throughout, we will concentrate on comparisons between the cultural work of human rights activism and organizing; this will be a more limited case study than part 2.

THE HUMAN RIGHTS TRADITION

There are many historical sources for human rights ideas, including religious conceptions of humans as created in the image of God, the philosophical and political ideas of ancient Greece and Rome, and ideas of "natural rights" in European theology and philosophy. From these sources, Enlightenment thinkers created a package of political proposals favoring what were usually called "natural rights." These proposals as a rule had only vague religious groundings, and accepting them required no adherence to any particular religion. They recognizably constituted the political project we now call "human rights."

The Eighteenth Century

One example of the emergence of human rights ideas can be found in the work of Voltaire (1694–1778). Of the many philosophical advocates of human rights, he is particularly striking because of the strong similarities between his methods and those practiced by Amnesty International today. Whenever he discovered a case of arbitrary oppression, he would carefully research the facts of the case and then publicize it, bringing pressure on officials through letters and the media. His skill at rational argument, combined with his scathing wit, brought ridicule to clumsy oppressors. His most famous case was that of a Protestant merchant in Toulouse, Jean Calas. Calas had been accused of murdering his son, supposedly in retaliation for the son's conversion to Catholicism. By the time Voltaire intervened, Calas had already been brutally tortured and summarily executed. But Voltaire, who saw the case as stemming from anti-Protestant hysteria in an intolerant Catholic city, was able to amass such a convincing case for his innocence, and orchestrate such broad condemnation of this atrocity, that Calas's conviction was overturned and the king provided a large grant to his family.

This case manifests recurrent features of Voltaire's work and of the human rights movement. Voltaire frequently took up religious oppression, and human rights advocacy has often meant opposition to dominant religious systems—especially when they are able to use or influence government. Voltaire, living at a time of established churches and repression of minority religions, must have seemed antireligious to many contemporaries. In reality, he was not against all religious faith. He was a Deist, not an atheist, and was able to pursue his work from within religious discourse. For example, in a prayer to God on behalf of toleration he used characteristically Christian parent–child imagery, saying that all humans, whatever their nationality or religion, are "children of one father and creatures of the same God."[1] His rationale for human rights, however, was not primarily rooted in a distinctively Christian theology but appealed to any person with reason and conscience. Thus his was a basically secular understanding of human rights. And he regarded religious fanaticism and prejudice as the most important obstacles to achieving human rights.

The developing tradition of human rights thought was crystallized in a number of late-eighteenth-century documents. The best known of these are the Declaration of the Rights of Man and the Citizen, adopted by the French National Assembly on August 26, 1789, and the Bill of Rights of the United States. While the Bill of Rights was not ratified until December 15, 1791, it was adopted by Congress on March 4, 1789, two months before the Estates-General convened in France. The two documents are reproduced in this book as, respectively, appendices C and D. Both are extremely short documents, and have been given quite varied interpretations. Each lists a number of rights. The French document, in a preamble, also articulates a framework within which to place the rights. Because the Bill of Rights comprises a set of constitutional amendments, its preamble, while describing some of the reasons for adopting these amendments, was not itself included in the Constitution once the amendments were ratified. One might read the preamble to the U.S. Constitution as a whole, and the philosophical part of the Declaration of Independence (beginning, "We hold these truths to be self-evident . . .") as additional frameworks for the Bill of Rights.

Both the French and American statements list a number of rights that could be called "private freedoms." These are rights to be left alone to follow one's own will, unimpeded by government restrictions beyond those required to prevent interference with others. They apply to what we now consider private life—the market, families, and voluntary associations—separating these spheres institutionally from both church and state, and ensuring that one can act within these spheres free of control by outside authorities. Such rights are often called "negative," in that they primarily restrict government and define liberty as freedom *from* forces that might endanger it. In the Bill of Rights, such rights include the protections of privacy, personal property, and due process found in the Third through the Eighth Amendments. The French Declaration contains omnibus statements such as "liberty consists of being able to do all that does not harm another" (Article 4 [my translation]) and a set of more specific protections very similar to the American ones (Articles 7–9 and 17). The most evident difference between the two is that the American rights are stronger and more specific, restricting the powers of government to a greater extent.

Even private freedoms affect political participation, in that they prevent arbitrary actions by officials threatened by a person's political views and associations. In addition, the French and American documents both articulate more "positive" or political rights, including freedom of opinion, expression, and political action. The French Declaration's Articles 10 and 11 provides for these rights, as does the First Amendment to the

U.S. Constitution. In both cases, freedom of religion (which today might be seen more as a private freedom) is subsumed. Beyond this, the only arguably political right in the Bill of Rights is the provision about militias and arms in the Second Amendment. The French Declaration is richer in defining political rights, listing a right to resist oppression (Article 2), to participate in making laws and be eligible for public office (Article 6), and to help determine taxes and know what they are used for (Article 14). This is only one of the ways in which the tone of the French Declaration is more positive about laws, government, and collective concerns than its American cousin. One gets the feeling, reading it, that the authors were suspicious of officials but not of laws. Its provisions for individual liberty, unlike those in the Bill of Rights, are often balanced by clauses about the limits or responsibilities that go with the liberty. For instance, my translation of Article 10 reads: "Nobody should be harassed for his opinions, even religious ones, provided that their manifestation does not disturb the public order established by law." In the same vein, Article 11 asserts: "Free communication of ideas and opinions is one of the most precious human rights; all citizens may therefore speak, write, and print freely, though they may be required to answer for abusing this right in cases specified by law."[2] By contrast, the Bill of Rights, as manifest in phrases such as "Congress shall make no law . . ." (First Amendment) or "No person shall be . . ." (Fifth Amendment), implies that government must be severely restrained and that the rights of citizens are absolute.[3] The preamble to the Bill of Rights makes this impulse explicit: that "in order to prevent misconstruction or abuse of [the Constitution's] powers, further declaratory and restrictive clauses should be added."

These paradigmatic documents show that from the outset the human rights tradition has varied. The American document provides less support for a strong state, but probably more encouragement for the autonomous development of civil society, than does the French one. The American document is more individualistic, while the French one shows that human rights conceptions do not need to be as individualistic as their critics often maintain.

Furthermore, it is apparent in both documents that human rights are of varying kinds. Both the French and American documents contain private rights, on one side, and political rights, on the other. That is, they express aspirations for the autonomy of individuals operating outside the state, and also for the enfranchisement of citizens within the polity. Neither, however, articulates the economic rights found in twentieth-century human rights thinking. The aspect of the French document pertinent to the Marxist concern with modes of production is its rejection of aristocracy: all forms of public office and power, and perhaps some rights in civil society, should be available on the same terms to all, without regard to birth. In America, with no hereditary nobility, there was no need for such provisions. In any case, neither document is concerned with the ways in which rights play out differently depending on a person's class or other social situation. The concern is only with the impact of public policies and authorities, not with the ways in which the liberty and dignity of the individual are affected by what happens in workplaces and families, or by the resources individuals bring to their interactions with public authorities. This limitation is one of the things Marxists have in mind when they talk about "bourgeois rights."

One issue that will be encountered repeatedly in our consideration of human rights documents and activism is that of "grounding" views about human rights. By the term *grounding* I mean whatever accounts people give to explain their own commitments—for example, to human rights—or to recommend similar commitments to others. Sometimes grounding takes a form philosophers might call "foundationalist," where all claims are supposed to lead back to first principles, secular or religious. One has great confidence in those principles and thus they serve, through a chain of deductive reasoning, as a sure foundation for all particular value judgments. But much of the time people account for their views in other ways. They describe a pattern into which a particular view fits; they tell a story about how they came to this view; they refer to their intuition or conscience; or they talk about how the view is connected to their identity, their relationships with others, the way they were brought up, the traditions they have imbibed, or the groups to which they belong. Any of these accounts can ground people's views, although they vary in how effective they are in convincing others to adopt one's perspective.

Religion, which until the Enlightenment served as a major tool for justifying ethical and social perspectives, is notably absent from the French Declaration and the U.S. Bill of Rights. Neither says anything specifically Christian, and both have Deist overtones. The only religious reference in the French document, found in the preamble, is to "the Supreme Being." The Bill of Rights makes no reference to God at all, although the Declaration of Independence speaks of "Nature's God" and more substantively of how humans "are endowed by their Creator with certain unalienable rights." The documents do not have a Christian grounding, and in a sense they do not have much grounding of any kind whatsoever. The preamble to the French Declaration refers to "simple and indisputable principles" and the statement of philosophy in the Declaration of Independence speaks of human rights as "self-evident." Both statements assert, in effect, that there is no need for grounding human rights. That is, saying that a political position is self-evident provides little in the way of explaining how one came to accept that position and, moreover, no reason for another person to adopt it. The implicit assumption in these documents is that every person would come, spontaneously and unaided, to support their claims for rights.

Neither document mentions that there had been a specific historical trajectory, a set of cultural developments and political events (including armed struggles) leading to the emergence of human rights. The documents do not consider the ways in which membership in a particular national community may be a basis for rights. For this reason, the French Declaration makes no clear distinction between "man" and "the citizen."[4] The implicit prospect in both documents is that once superstition, ignorance, and the power of traditional authorities are removed, any person of good will and reason will support the assertion of human rights. We might say that these accounts put the origins and support for human rights in a "black box," parallel to the way cultural processes, as we saw in the conclusion to part 2, become a black box for people of faith who conceive of progressive politics as the natural or automatic outcome of faith. In reality the goal of upholding human rights is a transcendent one, adopted with moral fervor: the French Declaration twice describes the rights as "sacred," the Bill of Rights trumps not only legislation but also the other parts of the Constitution, and the revolutionaries in both France and America risked their lives for their cause. But the basis for the fervor is not evident in either document.

The Twentieth Century

In the twentieth century, the ideas expressed in the French Declaration, the U.S. Bill of Rights, and other documents have been appropriated in new ways. An example of the change is found in the thinking of British social theorist T. H. Marshall. In a famous essay, based on a series of lectures given in 1949, he traced a series of stages in which different components of what he called "citizenship" were established in his country.[5] The components he discussed were all part of what are now considered human rights. In eighteenth-century England, Marshall argued, civil rights were won, establishing freedom from arbitrary government. In the nineteenth century, the spread of suffrage and reforms of the parliamentary system created political rights of citizenship, which had to do with participation in public decision making. Economic rights, manifested in the welfare state, became part of citizenship in the twentieth century. Thus a new category of rights was added to the kinds articulated in the eighteenth and nineteenth centuries. The developments Marshall recounted have a cumulative and (one feels, reading the essay) somewhat inevitable quality, making up an evolutionary account of the growth of "citizenship"—of the rights and dignity that go along with membership in a Western society. His use of a single term, *citizenship*, for all three categories of rights—civil, political, and economic—also represents his conviction that the different rights emerged from the same underlying sources and represented a single trajectory. Not everyone would accept his evolutionary account, but the addition of economic rights to those previously espoused, and the conviction that these new rights represent the same basic principles as the older ones, are characteristic of most twentieth-century human rights thinking.

Another change is manifest in the fact that Marshall spoke of these rights in terms of membership in a specific national community, rather than as natural and universal. This in part reflects a sociological perspective in which the idea of universals existing apart from any cultural and social-structural context makes no sense. Furthermore, as a strong advocate of the welfare state then developing in Britain, soon after World War II, he was probably hoping to legitimate welfare state proposals in terms of national solidarity. Whatever the motivation, the grounding for rights becomes historical.[6] Here again Marshall represents something frequently found in twentieth-century human rights thought. Enlightenment accounts of rights are less persuasive than they used to be. It is hard today for people to deny that ideas arise out of particular groups or communities and are influenced by the experiences, traditions, and needs of their originators. But this change of perspective creates dilemmas for contemporary human rights thinkers and activists. If rights are based on the particular history of specific nations, how does one justify the moral fervor that in fact human rights advocates feel with regard to supporting the rights of oppressed people who live in countries with a very different history and set of cultural traditions? How does one evade relativism? Few human rights advocates are relativistic in their hearts about what they advocate. They believe, for example, that torture is wrong no matter what the cultural context. But in the twentieth century it is not as easy as it was in the eighteenth to know the basis for this belief.

The most authoritative twentieth-century statement of human rights, and the canonical document for Amnesty International, appeared just a few months before Marshall's lectures. This is the Universal Declaration of Human Rights (UDHR), adopted on December 10, 1948, by the General Assembly of the United Nations. It is reprinted in this book as appendix E. The UDHR was written before widespread decolonialization and therefore before the United Nations included many Third World member states. Not surprisingly, therefore, it represents an essentially Western vision (with some concessions to the Soviet Union in return for not torpedoing the proposal). One can recognize in it phrases pulled from the Declaration of the Rights of Man and the Citizen, the American Declaration of Independence, and the Bill of Rights. In many ways it continues the tradition of those statements.

Yet there are also changes. The most obvious shift is that the UDHR expresses concerns for economic justice and well-being. For example, the word *justice* is not used even once in the French Declaration or the U.S. Bill of Rights. By contrast, in the UDHR a whole section (Articles 22–26), comprising about one-fourth of the text, deals with economic rights. This section specifically enumerates rights to social security, "just and favourable" working conditions, "equal pay for equal work," limited working hours, paid holidays, union organizing and membership, "protection against unemployment," education, and "a standard of living adequate for the health and well-being" of the worker's family. In short, a significant part of the agenda of European social democracy is now defined as part of human rights.

One might think that the new attention to economic rights comes out of a correction to the individualism of older ideas of human rights. Not so. The language of the UDHR is *more* individualistic than that of the French Declaration. The economic rights, just like the civil and political ones, are all framed in terms of claims the individual can make on the nation. The rights of all kinds are generally stated without the balancing limitations on behalf of the community or the corresponding responsibilities found in the French Declaration. Only at the end, in Article 29, is there a mention of individual responsibilities and limits on rights. Furthermore, law and the nation, seen positively in the French document, are seldom mentioned as favorable factors in the UDHR. In these ways, the UDHR is more in the spirit of the Bill of Rights than of the French Declaration.

In addition, the UDHR is less concerned with the political component of human rights than is the French Declaration or even the Bill of Rights. That is, the conception of rights is more focused on private life. While the UDHR speaks of rights to political participation (mostly in Articles 19–21), these make up a smaller proportion of the overall text than in the French document, the provisions are vaguer, and some of what the French Declaration included is omitted even though the overall document is much longer. Furthermore, the section on political rights in the UDHR receives less than half as much space as the one on economic rights.

Unlike Marshall's thinking, but like the older documents, the UDHR is not encumbered by attention to culture and history. Membership in a particular community with a distinctive culture and history is almost irrelevant. And the rights are if anything more absolute and universal. According to the preamble, they apply to "all peoples and all nations" and throughout the document they are put forward with few qualifications. Practical or competing considerations are secondary. For instance, no mention is ever made of the fact that for poor nations fulfillment of the economic provisions would be quite impossible. In fairness to the document, one should say that its absolutism may be due in part to the fact that it was designed less for practical implementation than for educational purposes. The UDHR articulates a vision and set of goals rather than a detailed code of conduct. It does not have the status of a treaty, binding on signatories, but is simply a resolution. (However, its principles are implemented in later covenants that *are* treaties and do in principle bind the countries that have signed and ratified them.) It is used primarily as an international moral standard to legitimate criticism of governments.

The UDHR, like the earlier documents, does not much ground its conception of human rights. As an international document, needing to be acceptable to people ranging from libertarians to Leninists and Adventists to Zen Buddhists, it is hard to see how it could have asserted anything very specific. It simply argues that "recognition of the inherent dignity and of the equal and inalienable rights of all members of the human family is the foundation of freedom, justice and peace in the world" (preamble). Thus it does not solve two key problems faced by activists and groups that want to appropriate the principles of the UDHR: how to describe to themselves the bases for their own commitment to human rights, and how to make appeals to others — only some of whom share their religious, ethical, and political perspectives.

Comparisons with Community Organizing

The differences between this cultural tradition and the ones from which faith-based organizing draws are obvious. Human rights concerns liberty and is secular; organizing concerns justice and is partly religious. Yet these traditions are not as different as they look. In fact, they are interconnected. The tradition of radical democracy out of which Saul Alinsky's approach emerged stresses equality of rights to participate in public decision making, and this is only a stronger version of the political rights articulated by the human rights tradition. Furthermore, the claims for justice made in organizing are often couched in a version of human rights language. In the march on the mayor's house by Milwaukee Innercity Congregations Allied for Hope (MICAH) described in chapter 4, housing was described as a human right. This is very much in keeping with the economic rights articulated in the UDHR. And in fact Catholic ideas of human rights have a lot in common with secular ones, although the former are stronger on justice and the latter on liberty. But the core conviction of the sacredness of every human person is shared, as shows up clearly in the passionate opposition to capital punishment on the part of both human rights activists and the Roman Catholic Church. Rights language, in effect, can be and often is used for the pursuit of economic justice and equality, as the civil rights movement in the United States clearly shows. Workers' rights, as we will see, can also be defined as civil rights, and this is another way to bring liberty and justice discourse together. A final similarity is that community organizing pays considerable attention to the agenda of individuation. Self-interest and power are concepts that value the autonomous moral decision making of each person, and this is an essential part of what human rights thinking also upholds, particularly in its emphasis on freedom of religion and political opinion.

Ambiguities in the Human Rights Tradition

Before turning to Amnesty International and its particular understanding of the human rights tradition, let us sum up the possibilities for variation that are inherent in that tradition.

- What priority should be given to the different kinds of things that have been articulated as human rights—private freedoms, rights to political participation, and economic rights? Should one concentrate on private freedoms, extend one's concern to political rights, or work for rights of all three kinds?
- What is the relationship among the different kinds of rights? To what extent and how should they be linked in human rights work?
- How does human rights thinking balance individual and collective claims? To what extent does it take forms that are corrosive of community or collective action, as charged in the many social-critical attacks on "rights language" one hears nowadays?
- How are human rights to be grounded? In what ways (if any) are they connected to civil-societal cultural traditions? What sources of commitment can human rights advocates draw upon? How can they make appeals to people outside the movement? How is the problem of relativism to be dealt with?

AMNESTY INTERNATIONAL: ORGANIZATIONAL BACKGROUND

The story of Amnesty International (AI) begins with Peter Benenson, an English lawyer. In 1961, after many years of *ad hoc* human rights activism, he developed a plan for a permanent organization that would exert pressure on governments to observe human rights and that would support political prisoners, largely through letters sent from other countries. The organization grew quickly, with groups forming in twelve countries within a year. By 1999, it had over a million members in more than 160 countries.[7] In terms of structure, Amnesty has an international secretariat in London with over three hundred full-time staff, national organizations (called "sections") in fifty-six countries, and thousands of local groups. The organization is rather centralized: its *Policy Manual* fairly bristles with regulations requiring the national sections to consult with the international secretariat before taking various kinds of action.[8] Local groups operate under parallel constraints, which are more extensive than those normally accepted by local branches of wider voluntary associations in the United States.[9] However, there is not in Amnesty anywhere near the amount of ongoing interaction between local groups and broader levels of the organization that can be found, for example, in the training process of organizing, or the assistance given to local community organizations by networks.

The section in the United States is one of the largest, with a total of about four hundred thousand members and supporters, contributing over $18 million as of 1993.[10] The U.S. section is in turn organized into five regions, each with its own office and staff, but these are small operations. At the grass roots, there were, in 1993, 359 adult local groups in the United States plus nearly two thousand student groups in high schools and colleges.

The local group we will be most concerned with in chapter 6, Group 425, was one of these adult local groups.[11] It is helpful here to review some basic facts about this group, which will provide a context for examining its discourse and cultural practices. Group 425 was founded in late 1988. Once sufficient members had joined the fledgling group, a staff member from the regional office flew in as a representative of the international organization. He gave the group a charter, which adherents signed, committing themselves to work for human rights. Members remembered the occasion as a moving ceremony. These were heady days. At that time, human rights issues were attracting a great deal of attention—assisted by the worldwide "Human Rights Now" concert tour in which Bruce Springsteen and Sting participated—and the group grew rapidly. Early meetings were attended by forty or more people. When I observed it for eighteen months, in 1995 and 1996, it was smaller but appeared to be holding its own. Throughout its existence there was great continuity in its core membership. The seven most active members in 1995–96—the people to be seen at almost every meeting and who kept the local group running—had all been active since very early in the group's existence. Another group in the same metropolitan area collapsed during this time, but Group 425 persisted, maintaining a very high level of activity for a group of its size, thanks to the energy and commitment of its members.

In 1995–96, the group had about a dozen members who participated regularly. This was typical, according to national statistics compiled annually on local groups. It had a mailing list that ranged during this period from sixty-five to two hundred (depending on how assiduously people who had not recently contributed or appeared were pruned), which was more than average. It usually met twice a month—again, more than the typical frequency. There were no staff and the budget was modest (not much more than one thousand dollars per year). Although small, the group was carefully organized. Responsibilities were clearly divided: one person chaired meetings; one did graphics and posters; one dealt with mail and another with the phone answering machine; one developed plans for educational events (with input from everyone); and another edited the monthly newsletter. The group organized public actions as well as monthly educational events for people outside the core group. Members gave talks to other groups and passed out literature and collected signatures several times a year (for example, at a local peace fair). They placed public service advertisements on local television and occasionally wrote letters to the local newspaper. All this was in addition to the ongoing work of writing letters on behalf of Group 425's adopted prisoners and other prisoners of conscience.

AMNESTY INTERNATIONAL'S UNDERSTANDING OF THE HUMAN RIGHTS TRADITION

Amnesty has developed a number of explicit principles governing its operations. We will briefly review three of them—the primacy of casework, impartiality, and the rule against working in one's own country—and then examine in more depth the organization's understanding of its mission as embodied in what Amnesty calls the "mandate." One of the functions of these principles is to establish a set of boundaries that constrain the activities and discourse of the organization.

The Primacy of Casework

The basic methodology of AI was established almost as soon as the organization was born and is very similar to that pioneered by Voltaire. It focuses on individual prisoners, trying to win their release (if they are "prisoners of conscience") or prevent their torture or execution (in other cases). This approach includes meticulous research into the facts of each case, followed, if the investigation bears out a human rights violation, by a large-scale letter-writing campaign on behalf of the victim. Continuity in these efforts and a planned distribution of effort among the various people the organization has determined to be prisoners of conscience is facilitated by a system in which prisoners are "adopted" by (in practice, at least today, assigned to) particular local groups. The adoption process is far from just receiving a name. Local groups receive extensive files on their prisoners and come to feel a strong personal attachment with them. This is exemplified in the relationship between Group 425 and its first adopted prisoner, Porfirio Suni Quispe. Quispe was a Peruvian village schoolteacher who became an advocate for peasants' land rights and was arrested by the Peruvian government. The group had a photograph of Quispe and faithfully wrote letters on his behalf. When he was released, in 1989, Group 425 held a ceremony of celebration. A letter the group received from him was one of the high points of its life. The next year, when they learned that he had been killed by Shining Path guerillas, they held a memorial service. The group's founder, Michael Cresci, reports that this made group members sad but "galvanize[d them, making them] feel more deeply about the cause and about the issues."[12]

At the international and national level, there is increasing attention to broader campaigns that focus on particular countries or on issues like the death penalty (which Amnesty opposes under all circumstances). But the core subject of Amnesty's work, especially in local groups and in the face Amnesty presents to the world, remains the *individual* prisoner. This is manifest in Amnesty's publications, which are full of the stories and pictures—sometimes the letters or statements—of particular ex-prisoners, showcasing the organization's successes largely in terms of individuals released. The packet of information provided to inquirers in 1995 was largely oriented to casework and individual prisoners.[13] And the organization's international constitution, called the "Statute," embodies this emphasis. (The parts of the Statute relevant to this book are reprinted in appendix F.) The "Methods" section of the Statute defines what the organization will do. It includes eight subsections about working on behalf of individual victims of human rights abuses, compared with only one that is clearly about working for more general changes in laws and policies, plus another that might be taken to have such a focus.[14]

One could make a parallel between the casework focus in Amnesty and the local nature of most community organizing. In casework, each human rights violation is dealt with on its own. Similarly, in organizing the problems of the particular community are addressed primarily as local problems rather than in terms of their broader sources and potential solutions.

Impartiality

"Impartiality" is given various meanings in AI's statements and practices. The Statute states that "Amnesty International shall at all times make clear its impartiality as regards countries adhering to the different world political ideologies and groupings."[15] This provision shows the clear footprint of the Cold War. The organization was in fact very successful at remaining neutral in that war, partly by choice of prisoners, with some from the West and others from communist countries. The *AI Handbook* reprints with pride allegations from government leaders in the West that AI is "an arm of communist propaganda" and from the former Soviet Union that it is "completely maintained by imperialist security services."[16]

What beyond Cold War neutrality is meant by impartiality? A variety of interpretations are possible, of which we will note five, starting with the simplest and moving to ones of greater philosophical import. Each interpretation reflects a way in which Amnesty and its pursuit of human rights differs from other kinds of politics.

(1) The interpretation of impartiality around which there would probably be the strongest and most unanimous agreement within the organization is that Amnesty should not entangle itself with governments or partisan politics. There is a strict rule against accepting public money, and local members spoke of making sure they did not take sides between Democrats and Republicans. (The latter is not a simple issue. Amnesty might, to further its own purposes, want to take a stance that one candidate in an election might also be taking but not the other. For instance, in New York the 1994 gubernatorial election was contested by Mario Cuomo, who pledged to veto any death penalty bill, and George Pataki, who favored capital punishment. In the context of such an election, Amnesty could easily appear partisan when speaking against the death penalty without actually having partisan motivation.)

(2) Another aspect of impartiality is AI's emphasis on careful and objective research: the facts of the case must never be distorted to fit a political agenda.

(3) Amnesty's organizational documents speak of wanting to be, and to appear to be, evenhanded. An example is its approach to revolutionary violence. Violent political dissenters are not adopted as prisoners of conscience, no matter how noble they may be, in part because it would not seem impartial to support their violence but oppose the violence used by governments against them. But on the other hand, Amnesty does not take a position against revolutionary violence so long as it does not involve violations of human rights in territories revolutionaries control.

(4) More broadly, in the language of the Statute, impartiality means carrying out the purpose of defending human rights "irrespective of political purposes." In other words, human rights are taken to be a transcendent purpose and are not to be subordinated to any other social or political goal. This implies, for instance, that a socialist belonging to Amnesty would not support human rights violations in the name of preserving a revolutionary government (as in Cuba), and that a member who was a strong free-market advocate would not think that trying to defeat leftists justified torturing them (as in Chile).

The life of Jacobo Timerman, who died in 1999, modeled this kind of impartiality. Timerman, an Argentine journalist, condemned both sides in the "dirty war" of the 1970s and 1980s, although his political sympathies were left of center in a populist vein. On one side, revolutionaries bombed his house. On the other, the junta arrested and tortured him, confiscated his property, stripped him of citizenship, and deported him to Israel. Although he was an ardent Zionist, shortly he condemned Israeli actions: the Sabra and Shatila massacres during the war with Lebanon and the torture of Palestinians. His commitment to human rights, in short, took precedence over all other political purposes and loyalties.

A corollary of this last understanding of impartiality is that Amnesty activists would not "use" human rights as a tool for advancing other agendas in the way people on both the left and right sometimes do, by highlighting the human rights violations of their opponents and ignoring those of their allies.

(5) A final way of interpreting AI's impartiality involves a separation between "process" and "content." As numerous organizational documents emphasize, "Amnesty International does not support or oppose the view of the prisoners whose rights it seeks to defend."[17] This is close to the aphorism attributed to Voltaire: "Even if I disapprove of what you say, I will defend to the death your right to say it." Or again, it is parallel to the content-free position taken by the American Civil Liberties Union when it defends the right of communists to teach in public schools, but equally the right of American Nazis to march in the heavily Jewish

city of Skokie, Illinois. This kind of impartiality means that one disclaims being connected to the views of a victim of human rights violation: one can defend a communist, or a Nazi, without sympathizing with their political ideas. The goal in saying this is in part to counter criticism—for example, that only a subversive would defend the rights of subversives—but also to be able to claim human rights for *everyone,* no matter how unpopular or even wrongheaded their views may be. It also means saying that human rights claims have priority over normal political claims.

Each of these meanings of impartiality underlies at some point the work of Amnesty, in organizational documents or local discourse. They are not contradictory, although they do represent different emphases. And like the primacy of casework, they have some parallels in community organizing. Organizing also strives to be nonpartisan and to keep what are sometimes called "outside agendas" from taking over. The fifth interpretation of partiality just described has an important parallel in the tendency we saw in organizing to talk more easily about democratic process—empowering individuals and communities to participate in decision making—than about economic justice substance.

Not Working in One's Own Country

A central principle for AI is the rule against doing casework in one's own place of citizenship. Hans Wahl, a national staff person, told me that this norm is really just a procedure rather than a basic principle of the organization.[18] But the precept so strongly colors the practical life of Amnesty groups and activists that whatever its canonical status it functions as a basic principle. Specifically, the rule prohibits local groups from working for the release of individual prisoners or investigating allegations of human rights violations in their own country. They are free to work locally against the death penalty and the groups might be able to work with their national office in lobbying their home government to ratify international human rights agreements. But all casework is directed abroad.[19]

This rule serves various purposes. It protects local activists, since they are not protesting their own government's actions. It also helps preserve the organization's objectivity and credibility; as stated in a national document, it is meant "to ensure impartiality."[20] But perhaps the most strongly desired effect of the rule, according to Wahl, is to promote interdependence and solidarity across national lines.[21] It makes the ideal of internationalism—that we are sisters and brothers around the globe in a way that transcends national boundaries and loyalties—something tangible, something experienced practically by AI members. Since a prisoner of conscience is in one country while activists working on that person's behalf are in another, human interdependence is strikingly made manifest.

One consequence of this rule—probably an unintentional one—is that it conditions members' forms of action and relationship to politics. Except on the death penalty, Amnesty groups and activists address governments in other countries, where they are not citizens and have no political rights. Therefore members do not experience their own rights to political participation through their Amnesty work. Furthermore, since they are addressing officials of countries that are usually culturally quite different from the United States—for instance, that are not predominantly Christian, or where allegiance to democratic ideas is spotty and recent—their appeals on behalf of prisoners tend to be made on the most universal and culturally unspecific basis. In effect, in such appeals Amnesty activists are constrained to speak ethical and social-philosophical Esperanto.

The Mandate and Prisoners of Conscience

Amnesty International is an organization that defines its mission with extraordinary clarity and forthrightness. The limits that this self-definition imposes on the organization's discourse are known and are formed in open debates. The central concepts that perform this function are the "mandate" and "prisoners of conscience" (POCs). In the words of the *AI Handbook,* the organization "believes that all human rights are indispensable, and it recognizes that they are interdependent. In order to get results, however, the movement has chosen to concentrate on specific human rights."[22] The term *mandate* is used to define this focus. In the organizational statement just quoted the decision to limit AI's goals is a strategic one, rather than one of principle. The same view is manifest in the report of the Mandate Review Committee that considered requests for alterations in the mandate during the period from 1988 to 1991. The report argued that the rights Amnesty works on are no more important in any ultimate sense than other human rights. The limitations adopted in the past have served to maintain a manageable organizational focus, rather than to prioritize human rights concerns. The committee therefore concluded that it is reasonable that the mandate should change over time.[23] And indeed, in 1991 the mandate was enlarged, much to the consternation of some national sections and local groups.

Many of the controversies and conflicts within the organization concern the definition of the mandate. Or, on occasion, they concern the definition of prisoners of conscience, since the core of the mandate has always been support for POCs. These controversies flare up nationally, internationally, and among local activists. Group 425 coined an original term to describe what group members oppose: "mandate creep." The Dutch section is similarly skeptical of mandate changes. Related concerns can be found among human rights scholars. For example, Michael Ignatieff, referring to expanded conceptions of rights, complains that "rights inflation reduces the real value of rights language."[24] On the other hand, support for mandate expansions was strong enough to get a number of changes adopted in the 1990s. And this was not easy. National staff person Hans Wahl, hearing that Group 425 was concerned with "mandate creep," remarked acidly that all the mandate did was "creep" since there were so many institutional barriers to change.[25]

The mandate is largely defined by the Statute, Amnesty International's constitution, which can be and sometimes is revised by the organization's biennial convention (called the International Council). The international definition is binding on the national sections and on local groups, both of which are prohibited from working or speaking on issues outside the mandate. (Excerpts from the Statute, including the sections defining the mandate, are found in appendix F.)

The first version of the mandate dates from 1961, a few months after the organization was born. Here the focus of the organization was defined in relation to Articles 18 and 19 of the UDHR, which deal respectively with freedom of religion and of political opinions and communication. The central task of the organization was to work on behalf of anyone imprisoned because of religious or political beliefs. Since then there have been a number of changes in the mandate.

During the 1960s and 1970s, the idea of a prisoner of conscience was formalized as a person imprisoned (or otherwise physically restricted) on account of religious or political belief who "has not used or advocated violence." Those imprisoned on account of race, ethnicity, gender, or language were later added to the category of POCs. The mandate also came to include a category of not necessarily nonviolent "political prisoners," for whom AI demands a fair trial within a reasonable time even though they are not prisoners of conscience. In addition, unconditional opposition to torture and capital punishment were added to the mandate.

After 1977 there were no significant changes in the mandate until 1991, when a series of expansions began. The 1977 version is, indeed, the one that many local activists think of as the mandate and quote from. Some of the changes made starting in 1991 were not controversial.

Extrajudicial executions and "disappearances" were added to the death penalty and torture as things to be unconditionally condemned. Also, there began to be a concern with human rights violations perpetrated not by governments but by other forces, such as guerilla movements that control part of the territory of a country. More controversially, however, the protected statuses defining imprisoned persons as POCs was expanded to include "national or social origin, economic status, birth or other status." Furthermore, Amnesty took on work for women's human rights as a major focus, and the organization decided that it could adopt as POCs people imprisoned because of consensual, adult homosexual behavior.[26]

What trajectories can be seen in this overview of mandate revision? One clear shift over the four decades of Amnesty's life is from an exclusive focus on beliefs—on people who are prisoners on behalf of "conscience"—to a major concern with identity and status as bases for oppression. In one sense, this shift makes the focus of Amnesty's efforts a little *less* political in that most people imprisoned for beliefs are dissidents while those oppressed because of their status or identity are often accidental victims (although victims, to be sure, of political decisions such as the pursuit of ethnic cleansing). But in other ways this shift broadens the range of issues with which Amnesty deals, raising questions about racism, patriarchy, and homophobia.

Another shift—probably the least popular one—is toward dealing with issues of gender and sexuality. This is evident in the adoption of gays as POCs, in the increased focus on the ways in which human rights issues affect women, and in discussions over the past few years about whether to take up the issue of female genital mutilation. Making this shift means incorporating some of the concerns that were brought to prominence by the new social movements of the 1960s and 1970s, a change that rubs some people the wrong way.

A third trajectory is toward an ever more comprehensive sense of the kinds of physical oppressions that can be visited upon people and the circumstances in which this can happen. Signs of this trajectory are the addition of capital punishment, "disappearances," and nongovernmental human rights violations to the mandate.

Let us conclude our discussion of the mandate by thinking about it in relation to the ambiguities in the human rights tradition identified earlier in this chapter.

The first two ambiguities are about the kind of rights one will work for and the relationships among the varied kinds of rights. The economic rights delineated in the UDHR have never been part of Amnesty's mandate. This restriction remains largely in force, although the first two of the trajectories just mentioned push the organization's concerns ever so slightly in that direction. "Economic status" is now an explicit aspect of the definition of POCs, and work on women's issues tends to bridge or make ambiguous the formerly strict and clear boundary between private or political human rights and ones with economic content. It may be that in the future the mandate will evolve to include greater attention to economic rights. But such a change would encounter opposition not only out of concern for keeping the organization's tasks manageable but also on principle: some activists reject demands for economic "rights," saying that these are only expressions of wants rather than the kind of indisputable claims on the community represented by civil liberties. The expansions in the mandate that have taken place, even the controversial ones, are actually more in the area of private rights, although certainly the political right of free speech remains the center of Amnesty's work. Even political rights are addressed only partially by the mandate. The focus on *individual* victims of human rights violations means that Amnesty is more articulate about free speech than about more structural political rights, such as the right, stated in the UDHR and the French Declaration, to have public policy be determined by elected representatives. For example, a monarchy that retained legislative power in royal hands but allowed free speech and a free press might not generate prisoners of conscience and therefore not be seen as violating the human rights Amnesty includes within the mandate. In short, Amnesty deals with some kinds of political rights but not others. The restrictions it adopts with regard to linking issues are to some degree parallel with those that arise in organizing because of the insistence on "cutting" issues (that is, converting all broader concerns into discrete issues).

With regard to the question of individualism (the third ambiguity), Amnesty's selection among the different ideas available within the human rights tradition does have an individualistic cast. Amnesty takes much more from the U.S. Bill of Rights and the UDHR than from the French Declaration, and it does not use the economic sections of the UDHR, which are the most communitarian. At the same time, however, Amnesty clearly stands for building *international* community, enhancing solidarity across national lines. Furthermore, the center of Amnesty's work concerns free speech, which is more than anything else a tool for public involvement. Thus it is hard to see how Amnesty's conception of rights could be corrosive of community. On the other hand, it does not have the same kind of positive agenda of community building that one finds in organizing.

The fourth ambiguity is about grounding human rights. Amnesty has always been a strongly international organization, and by the 1990s the majority of delegates at International Council meetings were from non-Western nations. Faced with this diversity and with the limited persuasiveness, even in the West, of Enlightenment ideas about natural rights, Amnesty is not in a position to adopt any clear organizational position on what grounds human rights. This leaves individuals and groups within the organization to grapple with the issues about relativism mentioned earlier. In essence, individuals can make links between human rights concerns and civil-societal cultural traditions, but the organization cannot. We will see later how local activists deal with this situation.

Amnesty International's understanding of the human rights tradition draws upon both eighteenth- and twentieth-century ideas. Its use of this tradition is selective, as any organization's would be: it largely ignores the philosophical ideas grounding eighteenth-century human rights ideas, the valuation of collective life found in the French Declaration, and the economic rights found in the UDHR. The selectivity installs some constraints within the potentially enormous field of human rights discourse, but it also leaves large areas open. In the next chapter we will see how local activists employ this tradition when operating within the context for human rights work provided by Amnesty International.

Chapter 6

CULTURAL WORK

IN AMNESTY INTERNATIONAL

Within the context provided by the human rights tradition and the structure of Amnesty International, local human rights activists in the United States and other countries pursue the cause of individual liberty and dignity. In the course of this work, activists develop narratives, practices, and their own appropriations of the human rights tradition. They deal with the ambiguities in that tradition described in chapter 5. They make decisions about what nature of constraints to impose on their discourse. They think about the balance of concern for private, political, and economic rights, which leads to the question of the extent to which various issues should be linked. They grapple with issues about relativism and how to ground human rights, which means that they link or decouple their human rights activism to civil-societal traditions.

We will begin our account of this local cultural work with the story of one activist, a story that manifests recurring patterns in the personal narratives of Amnesty members. Then we will examine, as cultural practices, the activities Amnesty members engage in and the events they organize. Finally, we will consider the various kinds of discourse engaged in by local activists and the explanations they give for the constraints they adopt.

A NARRATIVE OF SOLIDARITY: CATHERINE DUNCAN

Catherine Duncan is one of the seven core members who helped sustain the ongoing work of Amnesty International (AI) Group 425, described briefly in chapter 5. At the time that I interviewed her, in 1996, she was thirty-five years old, married to a construction project manager, and had three children, one of them adopted from Guatemala. She grew up in a heavily Catholic and Democratic environment, and hungered from early on for a role in the world. Her political formation happened in the shadow of the social movements of the 1960s and early 1970s, and she spoke of coming of age after those movements. Amnesty work, she said, is "a social activism. I grew up in the seventies, and there was a part of me that needed to carry a banner somewhere, and that didn't exist in the seventies for us kids in high school and college. Thank goodness, I'm not complaining, [but] the Vietnam War was a settled issue by the time I was a teenager. And this is a way for me to feel like I'm doing something to help those who might need a little help."[1] Thus, while the need to be politically involved was clear to Duncan, how to do so was not. Amnesty solved the problem, becoming one of her principal loci of activism.

"Those who might need a little help" turned out to be people in other lands, especially poor ones. Duncan has traveled in Latin America. "There are certain things that are very important to me," she reported. "My kids are extremely important, I'm important, my husband is extremely important, that nucleus in my life. But I see the world as my family. I find it so exciting to travel; I travel with tears in my eyes, because I meet with kids and people. . . . We're all in this together, and [people who are] doing a little bit better [should] help" those who need it. This perspective, Duncan said, was encouraged by Amnesty, her faith, and missionaries speaking at her church. The result is a passionate attachment to the well-being of people abroad. For Duncan, this is *not* an abstract or processual universalism, as it might be for someone who simply rejects national chauvinism and racism. She thinks concretely about the practical well-being of people she has met or heard of, and by extension of others like them. The result is international solidarity: a strong sense of kinship with and concern about people elsewhere in the world, especially in poorer countries or countries where torture and imprisonment of dissenters occur more frequently than in the United States.

Similar stories were told by many of the Amnesty activists I interviewed. Four of the seven most active members of Group 425 had lived or traveled extensively abroad (three of them in Third World countries) and reported having had personally transformative experiences during these sojourns. Another two had had parallel experiences in this country. One, for instance, had grown up in the South before 1960 and reported having seen close up what happened to people whose basic human rights were denied. The seventh was influenced toward human rights concerns by experiencing minority status as a Jew and witnessing the repression of writers at a point in his life when his professional aspirations were to write. By one or more of these routes, all came to feel a concrete and passionate attachment to the oppressed in other countries. The stories they told about their lives and the basis for their passion for human rights could be called "narratives of solidarity."

These narratives are parallel to the narratives of empowerment told in organizing. Both function as interpretations of life events within a framework that relates them to political values. In Amnesty, however, they were not to the same degree parts of the organization's collective life. For instance, no narratives of solidarity were told in meetings or public events during the eighteen months of my observation. Instead, the stories that *were* told in such settings generally concerned particular victims of human rights violations.

The content of the personal narratives told in Amnesty present a paradoxical contrast to organizing. In organizing, a movement dedicated to justice and community, the most frequent narratives are of becoming more individuated. In Amnesty, devoted to individual rights, the stories tell of learning altruism and solidarity. The character of both kinds of story hints at the connections between justice and liberty talk and suggests that communitarian critiques of rights language may often be wide of the mark. In part 4 we will return to these issues.

After high school, Duncan attended a well-known professional art and design school, where she received an associate degree. Although this was the end of her formal education, she continued to hunger for new information and understanding. As she put it, "I crave knowledge. I loved school. As a thirty-five-year-old adult, I like the nuts and bolts of making organizations run but I'm also intrigued by constantly learning about the death penalty, Jordan, places I've never been. And the knowledge I gain makes me feel better." Here, as with internationalism, Duncan expressed something heard repeatedly from Group 425 members. They all loved to find out more about the political and social life of the whole world. The educational programs organized by the group provided a concrete reward, giving them direct personal compensation for the time and effort they devoted to Amnesty and thus supplementing other motivations.

Group 425 had a major impact on Duncan's life and thinking. "I am a very strong-minded, -willed person," she reported, "but I vacillated on the death penalty and this group has helped me to form my opinions and stand strongly behind them. [Now] I can talk about the death penalty" in a wide variety of settings, even social ones. "It's a wonderfully diverse group," she said, "and I think it's great. It's added depth to my life. The knowledge I've gained from interacting with all of us—everyone's changed my life in this group, and I hope that I've changed other people's lives because of the knowledge I've gained."

The rewards of educational activities that Duncan described are parallel to those experienced by people involved in organizing—Phil Reifenberg, whose story is recounted in chapter 3, is the most obvious instance. Even more important, we see here how Amnesty nurtured Duncan's political sensibilities and skills, forming her views and giving her increased capacity to articulate them to herself and people outside the movement, thus operating as an actor in the public sphere. As we have seen, community organizing does the same thing systematically, as did the Cincinnati antipornography group, Citizens for Community Values, described briefly in chapter 1.

At the time I interviewed Duncan, she had multiple involvements and affiliations. Occupationally, she was running a graphics design business out of her home. Using her professional skills, she published and marketed a calendar to raise money for Amnesty each year, designed striking T-shirts sold at Amnesty tables, and laid out the monthly newsletter. Beyond her extensive work in Amnesty, she was president of her local arts society and did volunteer work in Habitat for Humanity and the parent-teachers organization where her oldest child went to school. She was actively involved in political work through the local peace center and an organization working on Latin American issues. She was also a member of Greenpeace and several other advocacy organizations.

While Duncan was exceptionally energetic and socially engaged, almost every member of Group 425 had multiple affiliations. The organizations they were engaged with included charitable or service enterprises with no particular political valence. But most of the members were also involved in groups such as the peace center that are part of progressive politics, and none was a member of any conservative organization. Thus Amnesty was in most cases part of a "package" of progressive causes, pursued to some extent independently of each other but all manifesting the activist's underlying values.

The relationship among various causes and issues, however, was not a simple one. The mandate and the principle of impartiality govern this relationship, but we have seen that the mandate is a subject of controversy within AI and that impartiality can mean various things. When I queried Duncan about the idea of human rights and what it included, the responses were complex. She affirmed that there was not a clear separation between civil rights and economic ones: "You can't have one without the other." On the other hand, she said that she wanted Amnesty as an organization to pursue a narrowly defined agenda that did not include the economic breed of human rights, and she did not talk about the links between different kinds of rights during meetings. She reported in an interview that she suspected that the group was regarded by conservatives as "a bunch of bleeding heart liberals." But she said that she didn't join with any "political-mindedness, just human rights-mindedness." In these statements she articulated recurrent themes among the activists in Group 425. That is, members *as individuals* had multiple concerns and many of them at least implicitly made connections among issues. This became apparent when they were interviewed. Catherine knew, as her statement about Amnesty's being regarded as liberal shows, that within American public discourse the agenda she was furthering as an Amnesty activist tended to be linked to wider currents of progressive politics. But she still wanted to maintain the independence of "human rights-mindedness." This is a statement in the spirit of the impartiality principle: human rights are not to be subordinated to any other political agenda but remain a transcendent goal. Furthermore, the group governed its collective life by a strong discursive rule against making connections between the particular human rights addressed by Amnesty's mandate and other causes, or even other matters widely regarded as human rights.

However, this rule was sometimes relaxed. In a short talk that Duncan gave at a candlelight vigil in 1995, she began by framing the event as a commemoration of the Universal Declaration of Human Rights (UDHR). After paraphrasing several articles from the UDHR, she moved to a discussion of women both as victims of human rights abuses and as activists opposing such abuses. (This kind of victim/activist pairing is found frequently in Amnesty's discourse.) As Duncan discussed the ways in which women are victims and in which they work to uphold human rights, she mixed issues that fit the traditional definition of Amnesty's mandate with ones that did not. On the traditional side, she spoke of women as victims of gender-specific infanticide and of "disappearances" and torture. This fit within the definition of a prisoner of conscience in the mandate and had to do with private and political rights. Not so traditionally, however, she talked of struggles for "equal treatment at work . . . [and] land rights." Here she moved into the area of economic rights, which Amnesty does not include in the mandate. This was particularly striking given that Group 425 members, Duncan included, felt that the mandate had expanded too much already. In speaking of human rights violations against women, she said "most of the casualties of war are women and children; most of the world's refugees and displaced persons are women and children; most of the world's poor are women and children." In the last clause, and to some extent the previous one, we can see a trajectory toward concern with economic rights.[2]

In one of the vignettes she used to make her talk more concrete, Duncan linked traditional and nontraditional aspects of human rights, talking of an East Javanese woman who was tortured and "disappeared" because of her work as a labor activist fighting for women's workplace rights. Duncan's support for this victim encompassed not only the victim's right to political freedom but also the economic rights she was working for. These economic rights were within the scope of the UDHR, but not within Amnesty's mandate. Thus her talk expanded Amnesty's (and especially Group 425's) traditional areas of concern. Furthermore, it was not constrained by Amnesty's traditional understanding of "impartiality"—that one does not support or oppose the views of the victims whose rights one advocates. Certainly Duncan believed strongly in the free speech rights even of people she disagreed with, but here she *was* supporting the victim's views. She had been formed by travel, missionaries, and involvement with activist groups, and she sympathized with struggles for social justice. To be sure, one can have such sympathies as an individual but discipline oneself to remain silent about them in one's role as an Amnesty speaker at a public event. But in her talk Catherine did not do so. Her talk was *not* in the Voltairian mode of defending to the death a person's right to say something even if one disapproves of it.

In sum, her talk illustrates how work on women's human rights—which has become an increased emphasis within Amnesty over the past decade—has made it harder to maintain some of Amnesty's previously clear discursive lines. This applies to the line between the human rights defined in the eighteenth century and the newer, economic rights articulated in the UDHR, and also to the line between process and content discussed in chapter 5 with regard to "impartiality." Duncan's talk, in effect, linked the concerns of contemporary feminism to those of traditional human rights work, adding new dimensions to the group's understanding of the human rights tradition.

How do these ambiguities surrounding the relationships among issues, which in Amnesty often concern the relationship among different kinds of rights, compare to the discursive patterns of faith-based community organizing? At times organizing, parallel to Amnesty, seeks to disengage itself from more general struggles for social justice. Pat Speer, for instance, described himself as a "recovering social justice Catholic."[3]

But Phil Reifenberg was a social justice Catholic who showed no signs of recovering or of wanting to. In short, in both organizing and human rights work, the degree to which there should be connections among issues is a matter on which there are debates or at least diverse proclivities.

Catherine Duncan was a practicing Catholic. She personified, simultaneously, why American Catholicism is so vibrant and why Pope John Paul II is so suspicious of it. Not only did she attend Eucharist regularly, but she also paid close attention to the social teachings of the Church and reported that she was "raising a family Roman Catholic." She felt, on a religious basis, a strong sense of mission, saying that she had "been placed on this planet for a reason." But she was no passive receptacle for church doctrines. "I believe in birth control; I'm probably not a real good Catholic," she said. After a brief pause, she continued, "I *am* a good Catholic, I *am,* I believe in the majority of the doctrines, but I also will not be spoon-fed." To her more orthodox relatives, however, she was "a heathen," to which characterization she replied, "So be it, I'm a heathen, but at least I'm a heathen that goes to church. I answer to God, not to Aunt Ruth. And that's what I believe."

Here we have a strong affirmation of theological and ethical autonomy. But Duncan did not take a position hostile to institutions. She did not leave the church, despite her disagreements with some of its teachings. Thus she formed her autonomous conscience in constant interaction with the liturgy and teachings of the Roman Catholic Church. This is different from the kind of individualism criticized in *Habits of the Heart,* where one of the most memorable characters is a nurse named Sheila Larson who describes her religion as "Sheilaism."[4]

Duncan said that she felt "a connection" between her human rights work and "my religion." The simplest instance of this connection was the strong influence that talks given by missionaries at her church evidently had on her. A more subtle connection was that the religious autonomy she asserted for herself paralleled the freedom of conscience her work in Amnesty was upholding for others. In the church and the wider world, for herself and for others, she advocated liberty of opinion. A third way in which her faith was connected to her work in Amnesty was that her sense of mission was personalistic. As she put it, "I believe in the power of one person, times a few other people—the ripple to me is a very exciting thing; it happens. My religion has helped me believe in that." Thus faith encouraged her to take personal responsibility and action on behalf of the world. Simultaneously it encouraged her to do so in a person-by-person mode that was a good fit with the primacy of casework in Amnesty. She, like several other activists, strongly affirmed the importance and efficacy of writing individual letters on behalf of individual prisoners: "It's a system that works. If it didn't, these prisoners would never be let out."

Summarizing in an interview the religious and moral bases for her Amnesty work, Duncan said, "So I see a direct tie with what I believe is my religion, and what Christ says. It ties in with my religious beliefs quite a lot. I don't really talk about that much, but that was kind of nice to talk about." As with links among issues, this comment described a difference between two contexts. In the interview, she felt free, and in fact enjoyed, linking her activism to the primary civil-societal tradition—her faith as a Roman Catholic—that nourished it. But in the life of Group 425, her faith remained a private, almost secret source of passion and concern, something one would not want to discuss. The opportunity to do so provided by the interview was welcome but not something to which she was accustomed.

With regard to connecting civil-societal traditions to politics, as with regard to linking issues, Duncan expressed a pattern that was frequent among Amnesty activists. Religion was not necessarily the source of their commitment to Amnesty. Another member of Group 425 specifically disavowed such a connection: "I'm a practicing Roman Catholic, and this [her work in Amnesty and views on human rights] has nothing to do with my religion at all. I don't see the two as meshing at all." And most members of Group 425 did not attend church or synagogue. (Two were Jews, three Catholics, one a Protestant, and one a Buddhist; but only Duncan and the Catholic just quoted were regular worshippers.) The bases in civil-societal cultural traditions or in ethical or philosophical commitments that grounded their involvement in Amnesty remained unspoken within the group. This decoupling is perhaps the most important difference between the cultural life of Amnesty and that found in community organizing.

PRACTICES AND SYMBOLISM IN AMNESTY

Local work in Amnesty International, as in organizing, includes a rich array of practices that have expressive as well as practical significance. These practices, in addition to having an effect on the world, communicate values and identity to members and outsiders. They express and build the solidarity of members with each other and with prisoners overseas. We can describe these activities as "rituals" if it is clear that the often negative connotation of that term—activities that are useless, irrational, or obsessive—is not intended.

The Candlelight Vigil

Each year Group 425 held a candlelight vigil on or near Human Rights Day, which is December 10, the anniversary of the adoption of Universal Declaration of Human Rights. In this ceremony, candles held by participants in the midst of winter darkness (in a gray, snowy, northern city) symbolized continued hope for human rights in the face of oppressive governments and other discouragements. The flame was passed around from candle to candle, short but carefully crafted talks were given, color was provided for the media (who covered the event on television every year), and food was shared. It was at the 1995 vigil that Catherine Duncan gave the talk described above.

This ceremony, whether intentionally or not, drew on the cultural traditions found in Hanukkah and Christmas, linking them to the continued pursuit of human rights, which in Amnesty sometimes takes on, often self-consciously, an obdurate, stubborn quality in which participants maintain hope and action despite many reverses and the daunting power of human rights violators. The ceremony also served as a birthday party for the group (with candles again fitting in), since the group was chartered in 1988 only a few days from Human Rights Day.

Writing Letters

Writing letters, or at least addressing and mailing them, is the most pervasive and characteristic practice of local Amnesty members. For members of Group 425, letter writing took place at home, during meetings, and in public places where they set up tables. Sometimes the letters were individually composed, but in recent years they were more often preprinted, in which case participants signed, addressed, and mailed them. Each monthly issue of the newsletter came with at least three letters attached. These were ready to sign and send, and the group's expectation was that most recipients would do so. The first half hour of one of the two monthly meetings was usually devoted to signing and addressing other preprinted letters.[5] The same thing happened in the Amnesty local group in Brooklyn, New York.

The letters expressed the group more than the individual. Whether preprinted or not, they were often on Group 425 letterhead, and group members were very conscious of the boundary between writing in their identity as AI members and letters they might write on their own or in connection with their participation in other groups. The content of the letters was quite standardized. Shown below is the text of one used in 1996 by Group 425 on behalf of its adopted prisoner. Group members, using Group 425 letterhead, wrote many letters during that period.

September 1996

Director of Drapchi Prison
Jianyuzhang
Xizang Zizhiqu Diyi
Lasashi 850000
Xizang Zizhiqu
People's Republic of China

Dear Director of Drapchi Prison,

I am writing to you on behalf of Ngawang Choezom, a 24 year old Tibetan Buddhist nun, who is serving a prison sentence for having participated in a peaceful pro-independence rally in March, 1992. For this act, she was sentenced to five years.

During this imprisonment, Ngawang Choezom and other nuns held in Drapchi Prison wrote songs and poems expressing their feelings on imprisonment and independence. None of the songs or poems advocated the use of violence. Because she joined other nuns in composing a poem or song, Ngawang Choezom's sentence was increased by another six years.

China is a member of the United Nations. As a member of Amnesty International, I consider Ngawang Choezom to be a prisoner of conscience who has been imprisoned, and has had her sentence increased, in violation of the United Nations Universal Declaration of Human Rights guarantee of freedom of expression.

Due to this violation of her human rights, I urge you to grant an immediate and unconditional release to Ngawang Choezom. However, while she is in Drapchi prison, I urge you to make sure that Ngawang Choezom's health and well being are protected.

Sincerely yours,

____

Letters were almost always addressed to an official abroad—in China, Iraq, Nigeria, or wherever human rights were being violated. Less often, they were addressed to a U.S. official, usually requesting inquiry with regard to human rights cases in other lands. The official was addressed respectfully, using customary titles such as "Your Excellency." The letters usually identified a particular person, normally a prisoner (but occasionally a person who had "disappeared"), and in flat, matter-of-fact terms recounted the story of what had happened to that person. The letters said, in equally unemotional terms, why AI considered the person to be a prisoner of conscience or a person whose human rights had been violated. Normally they referred, as a basis for authority, to international standards or agreements such as the UDHR. Finally, letters requested immediate corrective action, but only for the specific individual named in the letter and only the minimum required to end the violation of that person's human rights. No threat was ever made—even of negative publicity.

This blueprint was not the idiosyncratic creation of one local group. Many of the letters were downloaded from Amnesty web sites. Even when new letters were created, they were written within an explicit and detailed structure of norms. An AI–USA information packet for people who call or write to inquire about the organization describes the letter and the telegram as "Amnesty International's primary tools." It goes on to articulate conventions implicit in the letters used by Group 425: that the letters be respectful and "assume a government is reasonable." A more detailed guide to letter writing spells out similar rules: "Do not express anger or hostility. . . . Assume that the official is either not aware of the facts or is willing to cooperate in improving the prisoner's situation." It urges that specific facts about the case be clearly stated and that the appropriate articles in the UDHR or other international agreements be cited. The coordinator of Group 425, Daniel Levine, told me that in earlier days "many people, especially inexperienced members, had trouble learning how to write letters in the style Amnesty strongly recommends (almost demands). We tried letter writing seminars [but] many had trouble adapting their personal feelings and writing styles to 'Amnesty-speak.'" In his view, this was why the letters used in more recent years were preprinted. However, other group members, when interviewed, explained the use of preprinted letters as an effort to maximize speed and volume of letter production. Whatever the reasons, preprinted letters were used in both groups I observed.[6]

The letters mailed by Group 425 could serve as models for civics classes. While the missives expressed a strongly held moral concern, they were unemotional, respectful, and unthreatening. They spoke in an impersonal or altruistic voice, in that the personal interests and situation of the author and recipient were implicitly taken to be irrelevant. They were written as if human rights principles were universally accepted, one could expect the recipient to be convinced by rational argument based on these principles, and the recipient cared more about moral rectitude than power. They were also educative in spirit, providing information about the facts of a case and about international human rights agreements and principles.

Amnesty members are not fools. They know that rational argument is not all-powerful and that not everyone values human rights as much as they do or defines them in the same way. They expect success from a high volume of letters, manifesting widespread disapproval. Recipient officials, they hope, will find this attention embarrassing or politically harmful.

Yet the surface assumptions of such letters are also important. They manifest a model of democratic discourse and of the kind of person appropriate to that model.[7] Such a model is one in which political decisions are made after broad, open, unconstrained, and careful deliberation. It assumes that officials operate conscientiously within the guidelines established by laws and constitutions, and that citizens are rational, free, active participants in the political process. The letters act out this model. They represent AI members' belief in the superiority—compared with the present order of things—of a hoped-for world in which reason, discussion, and toleration rule. That is, they show commitment to a transcendent, nonempirical reality. They manifest hope that the imagined world will come into actual existence some day, or at least that movement in this direction will happen in practical human affairs. The letters appeal to some kind of innate goodness or universal values that are assumed to exist in the heart of even the most hardened violator of human rights. The transcendence of this vision is an expansive element in Amnesty's cultural life. The vision is not intended as a realistic description of how life works today but as a beacon to reduce human-rights shipwrecks in the future. The shared vision builds solidarity among Amnesty members and assists in making appeals to others.

That letter writing was central to the life of Group 425 was obvious from the work of the group but was also explicitly articulated. For example, the postcard announcing the October 1996 planning meeting was headlined "Back to Basics," and described letter writing as the key "basic." On the address side of the card, there was a picture of a broken handcuff along with "Amnesty Works" in large type. "Works" appeared to have two meanings: the character of Amnesty's work, and something that successfully "worked" to accomplish goals. In short, the postcard asserted both the importance of letter writing to the group and its practical value.[8]

As we have seen, casework is primary to Amnesty, and letters are the core of casework. As a national and international organization, Amnesty is increasingly emphasizing work beyond casework, such as country or issue campaigns. And national staff would like even work on behalf of individual prisoners to be pursued in a broader way than just writing letters. But Group 425 members felt that they did not have a surplus of energy by which to add country campaigns to traditional AI work, and the core activists preferred to concentrate on letter writing. In fact, they were passionately attached to writing letters. We have already seen Catherine Duncan testifying to her belief in the efficacy of letters. Daniel Levine spoke in similar terms in a public talk, giving the example of a Tibetan monk who had been a prisoner adopted by Group 425 until his release. "Amnesty International methods work. Not always. Not every time. But they work. Prisoners get released because of letters sent to governments by ordinary people like me, like each of you. . . . Even though we may be half way around the world from someone in prison, and even though we can never know what it is to be in their place, we are their lifelines without which they might sink, never to be heard from again." Another member of Group 425 spoke of how earlier in her life "I thought one letter never made a difference, [but] now I realize, of course, that every letter, every phone call is important." I have heard similar testimony from Amnesty members in other groups.[9]

Letter writing, as a cultural practice, celebrates the importance of the individual activist and the individual victim. It tells the letter writer that he or she, no matter how isolated or seemingly powerless and no matter how hard it may seem to influence world events, can be an agent for social change. One's letter can help rescue a suffering fellow human being. Furthermore, letter writing can contribute to the establishment of human rights, since the assumption behind casework is that social change can be brought about through an accumulation of victories in individual cases.

Letter writing can be carried out in isolation or in groups. In the Cincinnati antipornography group, Citizens for Community Values (CCV), writing letters to the owner of an adult video store entailed a large amount of discussion and became an almost collective activity. In Amnesty, some letter writing is done in solitude and some in group settings, and the amount of interaction varies. In the AI local group in Brooklyn there was a higher level of group interaction than occurred in Group 425. As at many Group 425 meetings, the first half hour was devoted to signing and mailing letters. In both groups, the letters were preprinted. But whereas the accompanying conversation in Group 425 consisted mostly of catching up on each other's lives, in Brooklyn members spent most of the time talking about the cases their letters concerned.

Petitions and Tabling

Some causes are addressed not by letters but by petitions. In Group 425, these were passed around at meetings and more signatures were gathered at public events. Sometimes the petitions then went to an AI group in another city, where yet more signatures would be added. Or petitions came to Group 425 that had originated in another group. Here the process of signing petitions manifested tangibly the interconnectedness and common purpose of local groups. Signing petitions is not intrinsically entertaining, but it is much more so when one sees signatures from people in other cities. Also, the petitions seem more likely to have an impact, and one's signature therefore seems more useful, when large numbers of people from several different communities are involved.

Tabling at concerts given by sympathetic rock artists, at peace fairs, and other occasions where people inclined to sign letters or petitions were likely to be present was another recurrent activity, happening several times a year. This was done in a quite standardized way. The same inventory of pins, T-shirts (designed by Catherine Duncan), literature, and so on accompanied the table on every occasion, and the table was an excellent setting for conversing with fellow group members. Tabling was enjoyable and built solidarity.

Thus tabling was another standardized activity. It lent richness to the internal life of Group 425. In a way that was not immediately evident, it also reinforced international solidarity. Many religions provide solidarity through beliefs or rituals shared by adherents around the world. For example, Catholicism has a more or less fixed liturgy worldwide, which allows a believer to visit a Catholic church in any city in the world and feel oriented and comfortable. I had a parallel experience in 1995, when I was in Italy and attended a celebration commemorating that nation's liberation late in World War II. Mixed in among other elements of the event, I found an Amnesty International table that looked almost identical to Group 425's. At this table there were petitions and letters of exactly the same kind I was used to thousands of miles away, and even though I knew almost no Italian it was easy to figure out what to do: sign them, purchase a pin—more graphically sophisticated than pins found in the United States, which is only what one would expect of the Italians—and chat a little with the Amnesty activists staffing the table. It was apparent visually and through practical, physical actions that one was encountering the same movement. And even though my trip was short and anything but lonely, and my role in AI primarily that of a researcher, I found the encounter heartwarming, making me feel more at home in a foreign country.

The Amnesty Logo and Understandings of Good and Evil

Many of the practices of AI manifest a definition of the particular kinds of good and evil the organization is concerned with. These are compactly symbolized in the Amnesty logo (see below), a candle encircled by barbed wire, which is AI's most widely used visual symbol. On the evil side are the oppressive structures that destroy human rights: police, prisons, torturers, and soldiers. These are symbolized by barbed wire in the logo. On the good side, represented by the candle, are the courage and patience of the prisoner or victim, in solidarity with the concern, energy, and perseverance of the Amnesty activist. While oppression degrades the human spirit, the activist and even more the prisoner use oppression as an opportunity to demonstrate reserves of nobility in the human person and possibilities for human solidarity that are not apparent in everyday, nonoppressed life. The barbed wire encircles the candle, but in the image the candle pokes out from the top and its flame is not hidden, thus manifesting the organization's faith in the eventual triumph of good. Some people viewing this image might also respond (perhaps unconsciously) to the spatial contrast between outside and inside. The barbed wire is represented as on the outside—something outward and material, keeping the prisoner's body within the walls. The candle, on the other hand, because it is on the inside, can be understood to represent something inward, spiritual, and personal: the indomitable spirit of the prisoner of conscience. Since symbolism in which the spiritual domain is morally superior to the physical one are endemic in Western culture, the inner/outer contrast reinforces the conception of good and evil conveyed by the logo.

The same assumptions symbolically expressed in this logo are also found in Amnesty-generated texts and the talk of Amnesty activists. These discourses repeatedly refer to the terrible things that happen to innocent persons, but almost always with a tone of awe at the heroism of the prisoner, her or his capacity to endure unspeakable suffering and remain a caring, dignified human being. Recruitment mailings from the national office frequently speak of or even describe torture. A headline may say, quoting the torturers, "We are gods in here." Certainly the dramatically evil quality of torture and the blatant effrontery of those who commit it while describing themselves as godlike are used in such mailings to attract the reader's attention. Such mailings may evoke the rec-

An Amnesty Logo (candle with barbed wire)

ognition of parallel experiences of pain in the lives of those who receive them, making tangible the evil deeds of oppressive governments. But at the end of all Amnesty narratives is the endurance of the victim and the solidarity of AI activists who do not forget prisoners. This results only sometimes in the material victory of release for a particular prisoner, but always in a moral victory. Thus in the end the oppressor, contrary to his or her will, contributes to exalting the human spirit.

Group 425 possessed a three-dimensional version of the logo: a very large candle with barbed wire around it. This was placed on a table for important events. At one time, I was told, it was brought to every meeting and kept lighted while the group was meeting, paralleling the practice of many religious denominations in which a candle is lit at the start of worship services and extinguished at the end. This ritual, however, had lapsed by the time I observed the group.[10]

The recurrent activities we have been examining—the candlelight vigil, letter writing, tabling, and so on—were integral parts of the cultural life of Group 425. It would be wrong to view them simply as instruments for achieving the group's values and purposes. The activities are valued for their own sake as well. They are cultural forms created by drawing on longstanding cultural traditions, religious, ethical, and civic. They dramatize understandings about who we are and should be as individual persons and as a society. They are expressive and communicative tools, not mute ones. That is, Amnesty members mean these practices to be useful, but also to serve as outward signs manifesting their values and image of the world.

While the cultural practices of Amnesty are different from those found in organizing, they are similar in the respects just described.

Moreover, practices in both movements express strong commitment to models of democracy that depend upon rational and unconstrained exchange of ideas. In both settings, activities often serve to symbolize the value and agency of individual activists. The things people do in both contexts symbolize hope in the possibility of social change, and even that some day most Americans might be enlisted as supporters of the cause.

LOCAL DISCOURSE IN AMNESTY INTERNATIONAL

Now we will turn from practices to the ideas expressed by local Amnesty activists. In this section, we will look at four kinds of talk these activists engaged in and discuss the ways in which talk varied depending upon context. In the next, we will look at the accounts activists gave for the nature of their talk.

Sharing Information about Human Rights Issues around the World

Group 425 generally met twice a month during the period of my observation. One of the two monthly meetings was called a "program meeting." Normally this was an educational event, usually with a speaker from outside the group presenting information and a perspective on the human rights situation in a particular corner of the world, or occasionally a film or video. The range of topics was wide. For instance, during the eighteen months I observed the group, in 1995 and 1996, the events included a presentation on the human rights situation in Bosnia and the international war crimes tribunal; a film about Bosnia; a report by a participant in the 1995 international women's conference in Beijing; a presentation on political change and human rights in Jordan; a speaker on Nigeria; a report from the director of the National Interreligious Committee for Peace in the Middle East about the peace process in Israel; a dialogue with staff from the local peace center; a talk by a Tibetan Buddhist monk who was on a national AI tour; and a film about the Chinese student democracy movement of 1989. This last was a large fundraising event held at a local university campus; it was widely publicized and drew several hundred people. The rest of the events had anywhere from fifteen to sixty people in attendance, and drew peripheral members and nonmembers as well as core activists.

We saw earlier how letter writing focused on individual victims rather than social patterns or political structures, and manifested faith in the power of individual action. The individualism implicit in this practice was balanced, in Group 425, by what happened at program meetings. The effort put into staging these events demonstrated enormous interest in the affairs of the entire world. As we have seen, members greatly enjoyed the educational opportunities that Amnesty gave them. The quality of the information and sociopolitical analysis in the programs was high. The presentations were sophisticated, providing far greater insight into various world events than could be gleaned from diligent reading of the *New York Times,* let alone from television news. The analysis given in these programs was far from individualistic. On the contrary, the presenters usually examined whole constellations of social causes, most of them beyond the control of individuals, that lead to human rights problems or progress. The programs considered ethnic relations and histories, political systems, and economic factors. The message implicit in the education programs was that human rights were interdependent with other social and political issues and that the causal forces affecting human rights were complex and often collective. In the educational programs, the duality of good and evil mentioned before was fleshed out with care and in detail, and the sources of human rights violations turned out to be largely impersonal. The villains and oppressors lost their human face, and so did the heroes: instead of individual victims and activists, they were often international tribunals and social movements.

At the program meetings, the focus was informational. Although there were questions and answers after presentations, there was little debate or discussion. The questions were generally informational. Although these events were very stimulating, they were not occasions at which members shared or debated views on the ethical or religious basis for human rights, differing conceptions of rights, the links among different kinds of rights, or the relationship between human rights and other social goals.

Detailed Planning of Local Activities

Talk of this nature mostly occurred at the other kind of meeting held monthly, a "planning" or business meeting. This was usually attended only by core members of the group (although advertised in the group newsletter and occasionally bringing in other people). Attendance was usually seven to twelve people. Aside from the half-hour often spent writing letters on behalf of particular prisoners, most of the time at these meetings was devoted to dealing with the nuts and bolts of organizing public actions, fundraising, and other local activities.[11]

The following account of a business meeting I attended early in my period of observation will convey a sense of the kind of talk that takes place in this setting. First everyone wrote postcards (an occasional substitute for letters), and then there was a report on the group's participation in a recent peace fair: how many signatures had been gathered on a petition that was now going to another group, and so on. The city's newspaper had printed a letter to the editor supporting the death penalty, and the group talked about how best to respond. There was clearly some difference of opinion about how much priority to give this. Later I learned that two of the seven most involved members were in favor of the death penalty, but this was not clear at the meeting. Rather, members talked only about who should write what kind of letter to whom. A large block of time was then spent going over plans for program meetings for the next few months: what the topics would be, what speakers could be brought in, and so on. The remainder of the meeting (which ran two hours total, including the postcard-writing time at the beginning) was spent preparing for a human rights film festival to be held in a couple of months. The only item that went beyond nuts and bolts at any point in the meeting was the discussion about the death penalty, but even this was discussed only in terms of specific activities.

Discussing Amnesty's Mandate

A third recurring kind of discussion was about the mandate and related questions. Most of this talk concerned Amnesty as a national and international organization. Discussions of this kind occurred at business meetings, but took up only a small proportion of the total meeting time. Often, members complained about the expansion of AI's purposes beyond those defined at the founding of the organization, explicitly referring to "the mandate." It was clear from the very first meeting I observed that this was an important concept for the group. However, there was little or no disagreement on mandate questions—the group was united in a traditionalist position—and people seldom spoke about the *reasons* for their stance on the mandate. Furthermore, during my period of observation the group did not discuss the national and international issues—many having implications for the mandate—that were to be debated at the national Amnesty General Meeting held each June.

At one meeting, there was a lengthy discussion, precipitated by a critical article in the *New York Times,* of the group's dissatisfaction with the national office. Out of this discussion came a letter, drafted by Daniel Levine, that expressed the group's opinion. Group 425, the letter said, "would prefer to see Amnesty International resist the temptation to expand its mandates." The missive mentioned some issues—female circumcision, land mines, and slavery—that the group would *not* want to see included within AI's agenda. In the group's view, "[t]here is a whole world full of problems. For instance, many people would state that adequate nutrition and access to adequate health care are human rights. Should Amnesty International adopt these issues as part of the mandate? We think it is unwise for Amnesty to try to take on so many of the world's problems."[12]

At another meeting, the group dealt with an invitation to cosponsor an event with a local group concerned with Latin American issues—an organization to which Catherine Duncan and one other Group 425 member belonged. According to one member, the potential partner organization had "a definite political stance" and was clearly a "left-wing group." It was, she said, against the School of the Americas (a U.S. government project training Latin American military and police forces that has often been accused of contributing to torture and supporting dictators). "Of course everyone should be against that," she continued, but then she said that AI couldn't take a position, although members as individuals could be involved. She concluded, "I don't think that we should be connected" organizationally with the Latin America group. Nobody contested this, and Group 425 did not cosponsor the event.

The group was united in wanting Amnesty to use a fairly constrained version of the mandate. Members' opposition to "mandate creep" meant that they emphasized the human rights articulated in the eighteenth century. (However, they did not adopt the natural rights philosophy dominant at that time; rather, their grounding of human rights was largely narrative.) The reasons for their stance on the mandate were not uniform. All the group members agreed with the practical arguments for mandate limitation: to keep a manageable focus so the organization could do a good job of what it took on. One core member of the group, whom I will call Sarah Browning, was a socialist. Socialists normally have a highly structured political perspective that weaves varied issues into a more or less unified social vision. Nonetheless, she had "great problems with the expansion of Amnesty's mandate." She didn't "disagree with expansion in principle." But in her view expansion reduced "effectiveness" and resulted in the organization being "spread too thin."[13]

Other members did disagree in principle with some of the expansions of the mandate. Two of the seven most active members of Group 425 dissented from Amnesty's unconditional opposition to capital punishment (a relatively early mandate expansion). Levine, articulating a broader dissent, described his view of human rights as "fundamentalist." "I wish Amnesty would stop this mandate creep," he said. "For me, human rights are fundamental things that people need to exist in . . . a civil society." He referred to the U.S. Bill of Rights as defining these basic rights. "Other things people want out of government," he argued, "might be nice but are not fundamental."[14]

While I was looking for a second group to observe—which turned out to be the one in Brooklyn, New York—I had a phone discussion with Bob Antonucci, the coordinator of a group in Queens, New York. When I began asking about his group's responses to the mandate changes of the 1990s, he immediately jumped in, "They destroyed my group." When these mandate expansions were adopted, the group "seemed too liberal" to people who might otherwise have become involved. The death penalty was an especially touchy issue, with emotions running particularly high after innocent people were killed in his neighborhood. He himself was ambivalent about Amnesty's stance on capital punishment. Furthermore, the national office had recently issued a report on police brutality, singling out the New York police department. "They're right," Antonucci said, "the cops are bad." He thought they were out of control and racist. But now, as a result of this report, every time he went tabling he was frightened of the police. "I love the organization," he reported, but he felt "very frustrated," wishing it could be "more successful." Thus he, and apparently the former members of his group, shared Group 425's repugnance for expanding Amnesty's organizational purposes.[15]

The Brooklyn group, too, was concerned with the mandate, although it seemed to apply the strictures a little more loosely. It engaged in discourse and practices that were somewhat more expansive, although still observing the same basic constraints. As mentioned earlier, letter writing included more discussion of the issues raised by the cases. This group did a considerable amount of work on the death penalty and also on campaigns beyond casework. One member I interviewed was in charge of the group's work on Turkey. "In the case of Turkey," she told me, "Amnesty International has actually made the very controversial statement that our military assistance to Turkey is being used to decimate civilians. Amnesty has made the very rare stand against a political decision of our congress. Because normally Amnesty does not get involved with politics. It's only a human rights organization, ok? [But] in this particular case the politics *is* a human rights issue. . . . Certainly our campaign about Turkey is not about a particular individual. It's much broader."[16] Here, as in Group 425, there is an awareness of the line drawn by the mandate separating Amnesty from politics; but at the same time there appears to be more willingness than in Group 425 to take the risk of occasionally blurring that line, as in the case of Amnesty's "country" campaign regarding Turkey. The Brooklyn group also made regular visits to their elected representatives to discuss human rights concerns.

In Group 425, during the period of my observation, there was a little involvement in Amnesty's China campaign but nothing that led to "political" stances in the way that the work on Turkey did for the Brooklyn activists. The closest parallel to this blurring, in Group 425, was the ambiguity about espousing economic rights that occurred in Catherine Duncan's talk about women's rights at the candlelight vigil.

Grounding Human Rights

As we saw in chapter 5, the UDHR as an international document and Amnesty International as a multicultural organization do not attempt to ground human rights in any religious tradition or in the Enlightenment account of natural rights. In Group 425, correspondingly, nobody consistently grounded their advocacy of human rights either in religious principles or (as in natural rights theory) in a secular political philosophy. Rather, they tended to explain their allegiance to human rights by telling stories about their lives and how they had come to feel so strongly about human rights. These are what we have termed "narratives of solidarity." The stories were often powerful, and a plausible argument can be made that narratives are a good mode of ethical thinking. Underlying the particular stories, or as part of them, what one heard over and over again from group members was an intense and concrete concern for vulnerable people throughout the world. The implicit vision of human brotherhood and sisterhood expressed in this concern was a shared underpinning for their commitment to human rights.

The basic subjectivity of the narratives—that each was an account of someone's personal trajectory toward concern for human rights—raises the question of why and how one could make transcendent, universal claims for those rights. After all, other people's life experiences might have led them, for instance, to decide that the preservation of threatened communities is so important that sometimes individual rights need to be suppressed. The frequently expressed feelings of concern for people in other lands had a similarly subjective quality, raising the same kind of question.[17]

The fact is, however, that Group 425 members showed little sign of relativism. The organization's practices reflected an unquestioned faith in the existence of *something* universal that allows human rights appeals to be made. Members had no real doubt about the universality or objective value of human rights. In one of the group interviews, when I asked what the members present thought of the criticism sometimes made that human rights advocacy is a kind of cultural imperialism on behalf of Western ideas, they rejected the argument totally. One person explained that she believed a person being tortured within a political system where that is an accepted practice suffers no less than where torture is disapproved. On the controversial issue of female genital mutilation (also termed "female circumcision"), although members did not believe that the issue should become a priority for Amnesty, they rejected arguments that communities for which this is a traditional cultural practice should have the right to continue it.

The ways of grounding human rights commitment just described were expressed mostly *outside* of meetings in the course of interviews conducted with AI members, either individually or in small groups. In meetings, whether educational or business, one heard little discussion about the basis for human rights activism. One result was that the group, at least during the period of my observation, conveyed to newcomers little about the grounds for human rights politics. In a sense, the group had little to say to them beyond what was encoded in organizational documents. In fact, newcomers were not even given written materials, let alone any oral orientation as to what the group stood for and did. The perspective of these potential members on human rights, their decision to come, and the decision they would ultimately make about whether to return—all these were implicitly taken to be random and private, rather than something to be influenced by the group through cultural work. Perhaps partly for this reason, newcomers seldom returned.

The Contextual Character of Modes of Discourse

The fact that grounding happened entirely outside of meetings points to the fact that the discursive constraints manifested by Group 425 were contextual. Group members were perfectly capable of more expansive modes of discourse, as they showed when they were interviewed. Most of the members were interviewed in groups of two or three, and the interview sessions consisted largely of interactions among group members. In these conversations members talked freely about the meaning of human rights, disputed issues about the mandate, and so forth. But in the context of Amnesty meetings and actions, they observed a set of norms that narrowly limited the range of discussion. The difference between these two contexts, and the rules applying to them, was manifest in Catherine Duncan's remark that talking about her faith was unusual but "kind of nice." Another group member, departing after an interview, commented to a comrade as they went down the stairs, "It isn't often that you get a sanctioned evening of talking." That this person would use the term *sanctioned* points to the rule-based character of modes of discourse. In group meetings, a set of rules applied that were far more restrictive than those applying in the interview. Daniel Levine, the group coordinator, explained to me in a letter that the absence of discussions about grounds for human rights, connections among different kinds of human rights, or other controversial questions in the meetings I had observed was the result of "what the group sees as a 'normal' meeting."[18] Thus Levine made it clear that a set of rules, not just accidents or lack of time, determined the group's discursive patterns.

ACCOUNTS FOR CONSTRAINED DISCOURSE IN AMNESTY INTERNATIONAL

There are a number of constraints manifest in the grassroots discourse we have been describing. Political issues remained fairly disconnected, since economic rights were not linked to other human rights. Connections between human rights and civil-societal cultural traditions were not articulated.

One of the impressive things about Amnesty is that it continuously and systematically addresses issues about its purpose and identity, by discussing its mandate. That is, Amnesty's structure and self-understanding encourage members to carry on explicit internal debates about the modes of discourse the organization should adopt. One result is that discursive constraints are more clearly formed in Amnesty than in most organizations. In addition to observing a set of constraints, local activists constructed *accounts* for why the discourse in their groups was constrained. Such accounts described what activists saw as obstacles to more expansive discourse. Sometimes the accounts were critical, but more often they justified the constraints their groups enact. That does not mean that the accounts were celebratory in tone. On the contrary, they often included statements to the effect that "More expansive discourse would be beneficial in many ways, and I'd prefer it personally, but it just isn't possible, for the following reason: . . ." Accounts like this can be more or less plausible. Whether plausible or not, they are believed and mold behavior. In this way *the accounts themselves* often serve as obstacles to more expansive discourse.

The accounts provided by Amnesty activists took quite varied forms. They can be roughly grouped as accounts based on not having anything to discuss, on organizational processes and necessity, and on principles of individual autonomy.

Not Having Anything to Discuss

One of the most frequently encountered explanations for constraint, which we will term the "unanimity" account, is that serious exchanges about matters of principle do not happen because everyone is in agreement. Two members of Group 425 told me that everyone in the group thought pretty much alike. Sarah Browning said, "I think we have a basic level of mutual understanding of certain issues and things [that] does make life very bland." But she also thought nondiscussion of divisive issues might have gone too far. "I worry about the fact that there's . . . some of us who have been working together for a number of years now, to the extent that we don't talk about things that sometimes we should" discuss. The basic principles, she said, are not very controversial, and so "it's quite easy to opt in" and therefore sometimes "the underpinnings are very loose, they're not as concrete or developed" as in other organizations. That is, a least-common-denominator kind of agreement with the group's purposes was all that was expected of members. Specifics were not inquired about and people joined without a serious enough self-examination of their values and purposes.[19]

A member of the Brooklyn group articulated this account even more strongly when I asked her whether people in her group ever talked about why they are opposed to the death penalty. "No," she said, "we don't talk about it. We don't have intellectually interesting discussions in the group. Maybe we did a long time ago. When everybody's in big agreement there's less to discuss. Great discussion tends to come up when there are people who are disagreeing. So there's no discussion. The people in this group are in incredible agreement. Most of the stuff that's up for discussion is just extremely obvious. The stuff that we're fighting is obviously wrong. I almost wish that we did have a devil's advocate in there to stir the pot a little." This woman also belonged to an animal rights organization that had meetings filled with very intense discussions. She told me that she wished her Amnesty group could move a little in that direction, and thought that this might be possible. Thus she not only regretted but criticized the degree of constraint that was found in her group.[20]

Organizational Processes and Necessity

The unanimity narrative just described is sometimes linked to a conception of how organizations evolve. Honoring Max Weber's classical conceptualization of the trajectory of originally innovative movements, we might call this the "routinization" narrative. In Group 425 and also in Brooklyn, activists reported that discourse had become more constrained as time had passed. Basically, both groups told me that I had arrived too late to see expansive discourse. The gist of this account is that exciting ideas and energy for cultural struggle are found at the inception of an organization but tend to die out later. This is evident in the

Brooklyn activist's words that more stimulating discussions may have happened "a long time ago." A member of Group 425 said that she saw "an evolution of our group": at one time meetings were more "passionate" and "informal," but not now. Sarah Browning explained that I had arrived at a time when the group had "been together so long" that people "know what each other is thinking," resulting in the blandness I had observed.[21]

A more utilitarian argument is that any discussion of matters beyond nuts and bolts would be divisive. Some Group 425 members said that the more expansive discussions of the past had been dangerous. In Levine's words: "I can remember times when we actually have had disagreements or personality clashes or whatever [that] were threatening the existence of the group. And . . . that tended to fall off, because we . . . all thought that human rights were important, and that it was more important that the group stay together than we sit and have a debating society that might rip the group to pieces. . . . Discussions like [one about the death penalty], I think, threatened the existence of the group." Levine explicitly disagreed with the members who had told me that everyone thought pretty much alike. According to this "conflict-avoidance" narrative, wider topics were embargoed as a peace-keeping and organization-saving move. Only by focusing on a narrow agenda could one find the area of agreement enabling members to work together.[22]

A different but even more utilitarian explanation for minimal discussion of issues of principle came out in a group interview with three core members of Group 425. These people did not remember the kind of serious conflict just described, even when I told them, at the end of the interview, that other members had reported such conflict. Their story, instead, was that as Group 425 grew smaller and had to work harder to carry out its tasks the time for such discussions vanished. Every minute was needed for business. As the member quoted above about the evolution of group life away from passionate and informal meetings put it, at this point "it's gotten to the point of survival of the group. We're efficient at the business meetings because we have to be. [But] I know our passion still exists." This "efficiency" account was not universally accepted. Catherine Duncan, who was in this group of three being interviewed, answered the person just quoted, arguing that the move toward only discussing nuts and bolts had gone too far and that time should be taken for broader discussions.[23]

The need for efficiency was also used as an argument against "mandate creep." In the view of one Group 425 member, "We can't get behind. We're taking on too much, we're getting too far afield, with all these country campaigns, and fundraising, and our prisoners, and this, and this—there aren't enough volunteers." This was at once a cry from the heart of an overworked activist and a statement in favor of a traditionalist conception of Amnesty's priorities. She was suggesting that the constraints implicit in the mandate had been relaxed to an unfortunate extent in the wider organization, but that Group 425 had retained some of those constraints, partly in order to be efficient.[24]

Principles of Individual Autonomy

Respect for ethical autonomy is a core progressive value. Closely allied to it today is the idea of tolerating, in fact respecting and valuing, cultural diversity. While nobody in Amnesty argued outright that these values should exclude more expansive forms of discourse, one could see hints of such a view. Sarah Browning said that "the local group has a very disparate group of people comprising its membership, and I think a lot of people believe in what they're doing for very different reasons." She went on to say that one reason for the constraints in the group's discourse "might be because people don't want to express a specific reason for why they believe." Then she talked about the mutual respect that exists between her and Levine despite their differences on the death penalty: "I don't think less of him for it—I think he's wrong, actually, but that's all right." Thus she articulated a basic principle of liberty: respectful toleration of differing opinions. And she seemed to be saying that respecting the variety of grounds for involvement had led to constrained discourse. She expressed a norm of privacy and self-determination. Each person, in this view, was entitled to have his or her own reasons for doing human rights work, without being held accountable for those reasons by others. More expansive discussions would put people under pressure to articulate their grounds, and that would invade their privacy and reduce their freedom. We should note that Browning also believed that nondiscussion had gone too far and that more expansive discourse, despite the problem just mentioned, would be better. It was not clear whether she thought group members would accept a move in that direction.[25]

This "privacy" account is connected to the emphasis on subjectivity evident in the use of personal solidarity narratives as the primary approach to grounding human rights. That is, if individual life histories and ethical instincts are the basis for human rights concern, it is easy for that concern to remain inarticulate. In other words, the concern for human rights can be conceived of as a private set of motives that individuals come to the group already possessing, and about which they are not to be asked. Group 425 manifested this possibility: the basis for members' passion about human rights was seldom expressed, and to some extent *was not supposed to be* expressed or asked about. This constraint applied not only to the external discourse of the group—what group representatives said in public on behalf of the group—but also to the conversations within it. One difficulty this presents is evident in Group 425's ineffectual approach to newcomers mentioned earlier.[26]

The Nature and Implications of Accounts for Constraint

There are several features of these narratives that deserve note. The first is the contrast between the multiplicity and disparate character of the narratives and their essential agreement in what mode of discourse they supported. The reasons varied, but the outcome did not. The conflict-avoidance and unanimity accounts partly contradicted each other. The people who told me the efficiency story explicitly took issue with those who told me about avoiding conflict. Yet the stories largely grounded the same set of discursive rules: ones banning discussion of connections among issues or between issues and civil-societal traditions used to ground them.

This indicates that the rules had an authority in themselves, independent of the principles mentioned in the accounts. The similarity of rules in spite of differing accounts also suggests that the rules stemmed in part, not from the particular history and needs of these Amnesty groups, but from blueprints for activism—from broadly (if implicitly) shared ideas about voluntary political activity. I have observed constraints similar to the ones evident in Amnesty in many activist groups, and have read scholarly accounts of similar phenomena in many others. Furthermore, some of the accounts of constraint we have reviewed represent metapolitical principles—for example, the idea that people should not be asked to talk about the grounds for their opinions—to which many Americans are deeply committed. In short, we are looking at ways of thinking that exist far beyond Amnesty.

Another fact cutting across the narratives is that at times members offered criticisms of constraint and advocated or at least wished for more expansive discourse. Sometimes they did not accept an account of constraint given by another member, and at other times they accepted it as a correct description of how certain constraints had come into existence but not as a justification for them. Quite a few Amnesty activists, in sum, hungered for more expansive discourse. Some thought it was possible, but even those who were pessimistic on this score, such as Levine, acknowledged that it would have advantages.[27]

A third observation, of a more evaluative nature, is that many of the accounts did not make a good case for the necessity of the constraints they purportedly explained. This lack of plausibility suggests that the constraints partly stemmed not from the practical considerations described by many of the accounts, but from norms to which activists were committed. The Brooklyn activist who spoke of unanimity contrasted her Amnesty group with an animal rights one. But the latter group sounded like it had if anything a higher level of internal agreement than Amnesty, indicating that unanimity is not an entirely plausible explanation for constrained discourse. In Group 425, the unanimity account overstated the actual level of agreement in the group. Two members supported the death penalty, while the other five most active members opposed it, many quite strongly. Browning was a socialist, while three held fairly conservative views on domestic economic issues.

The conflict-avoidance account also has problems. Group 425 activists had a long history with each other and had formed strong bonds transcending such differences. Quite likely, differences could have been dealt with in a nondivisive mode of mutual respect—like the spirit in which Browning expressed her disagreement with Levine on the death penalty—especially since the group would not have been taking official positions on the broader questions that were not discussed. In fact, the problems with the unanimity and conflict-avoidance accounts suggest, as sociologist Nina Eliasoph remarks, that the ability of activist groups to discuss matters of principle and controversial topics is largely independent of the actual level of agreement found within the groups.[28]

The efficiency narrative was presented as if this were a purely practical issue. But other groups, such as the community organizations described in part 2 of this book and the Cincinnati antipornography organization thumbnailed in chapter 1, manage to combine a great deal of practical work with taking some time to deal with questions of principle. Furthermore, Group 425 itself devoted time to the monthly program meetings, not just to make its case to the public outside the group, but because of the opportunities for political education and development these provided to the core members. All these facts suggest that "efficiency" has as much to do with a group's identity and preferred mode of interaction as with what is technically required to achieve its ends.

Finally, some of the accounts point to important discursive dilemmas for human rights work. The Brooklyn activist talked about how "obvious" Amnesty proposals are, and Browning said that the basic principles are not very controversial. And in a sense they are right. Amnesty's premises so nearly resemble the democratic principles that are central to American national identity—the ideas in the Bill of Rights, for instance—that activists easily occupy the discursive high ground. Nobody in the United States is going to say that torture is a good thing or that imprisoning people for nonviolent political advocacy is just. But this assent happens in such a generalized and vague way that it gives little leverage on the policy debates within the United States that relate to human rights and *are* strongly disputed: the death penalty, military assistance to Turkey, and so forth. Furthermore, the assumption that the things Amnesty opposes are "obviously wrong" puts culture in a black box, reducing one's motivation to figure out why people disagree and to engage in cultural work aimed at persuading those who are not yet convinced that the group's claims are correct.

If one's political purposes are "obvious," then adherence to those purposes happens naturally or automatically once one provides information on what is happening. In this spirit, Group 425's program meetings, including both the presentations and the discussions that followed, were predominantly informational: members almost never expressed their own evaluations of the political and economic phenomena under discussion at these events. Similarly, the letters its members wrote on behalf of prisoners of conscience were largely recitations of facts. But if information isn't enough—if, for example, it is *not* obvious to one's representative in Congress that military aid to Turkey needs to stop, once one has presented the facts—then the conversation simply stops. In short, the Amnesty activists I observed and interviewed, while not adopting natural rights philosophy, were mostly committed to something like the optimism of the Enlightenment about what the natural reason and conscience of human individuals can accomplish—morally, not just technically—once ignorance, prejudice, and oppression are removed. This kind of optimism is found far beyond Amnesty. In chapter 8 we will discuss the ways in which it obstructs effective cultural work by progressives.

Conclusion to Part III

DILEMMAS IN HUMAN RIGHTS DISCOURSE

The human rights movement gives us an opportunity to see different aspects of the cultural dimension of progressive politics than are seen in congregation-based community organizing. Like organizing, human rights activism has robust cultural practices. The modes of discourse it adopts are in some respects expansive and in other ways constrained. When they are expansive, human rights work shows how such discourse can be constructed in a different context from that provided by organizing—a secular context, and one focusing on liberty—manifesting potentials that are present even when not active or visible. Similarly, the richly expressive character of Amnesty's practices shows that a movement does not need to be religious in order to construct modes of action that convey meaning as well as contribute to goal achievement.

When human rights discourse is relatively constrained, on the other hand, the limits it manifests are instructive in two ways. First, examining these constraints challenges us to clarify the implications of adopting a secular stance in one's political work and of pursuing the agenda of individual liberty. In what ways do those choices entail discursive constraints, and with what degree of necessity? Second, some of the constraints exemplify ones found in many forms of progressive politics. In turn-of-millennium America it is hard to construct expansive discourse. In periods when there have been high levels of social activism, such as the 1930s and 1960s, one could observe a considerable amount of extremely expansive discourse. This was sometimes even the expected model for people seeking social change. In less activist periods, however, the norms of American public discourse, along with other factors, tend to constrain what happens in social movements. The factors that lead to discursive constraints in human rights work point toward obstacles to effective cultural work, arising out of these norms, that affect many progressive movements, not just human rights activism. Amnesty International (AI) is especially instructive in this regard because it is so explicit about its discursive rules and so systematic in developing and discussing them.

We will begin by summarizing the expansive and constrained elements of local Amnesty discourse, and how that discourse compares to the language of faith-based community organizing, using the three dimensions described in the conclusion to part 2 and schematized in the table at the end of chapter 1. Then we will mention some dilemmas of progressive politics that have come to the surface in our consideration of human rights—dilemmas that will be addressed in part 4.

TEMPERATURE

The members of Group 425 were committed and passionate activists, and the ethically charged character of their human rights work was evident. They maintained a robust sense of their personal and group purposes. Furthermore, they clearly regarded human rights as a transcendent goal. Their investment in their work was very different from that one would probably find, say, among lobbyists for tobacco companies seeking legislation to limit product liability. The discourse of the Amnesty activists I observed was moralistic, not in the sense of trying to make people feel guilty, but of expressing values that members believed to be in essential respects universally applicable, and therefore a basis for making ethical evaluations of the conduct even of people who are not part of their own community or cultural traditions.

Although Group 425 members tended to use narrative and subjective modes of grounding their commitment to human rights, they were not relativists. At least with regard to the issues that fall within Amnesty's original mandate, human rights were, for these people, universal and objective standards. They were principles that transcended cultural differences and the say-so of any human community. Furthermore, the way in which activists wrote letters and went about their work clearly manifested their faith that there was *something* universal to which one could appeal across all lines of political and cultural difference. This faith functioned, among other things, to sustain hope in the possibility of progress toward a fuller attainment of human rights.

In some ways, the political stance of Amnesty activists was more ethically intense than that found in faith-based organizing. In organizing, issues are not the central concern, and are chosen and addressed in a fairly cool manner. They are particular manifestations of the congregations' sense of their mission and of the community organization's basic agenda of empowerment, justice, and community. In human rights work, by contrast, the issues constitute a cause—something of transcendent importance. Furthermore, Amnesty activists took even more care than those in community organizing to make sure that their *means* corresponded to their values. Letter writing, Amnesty's major local methodology, expressed in microcosm members' implicit image of a good society. In organizing, while ethical considerations often govern decisions about means, ideas about power and self-interest are often used to ground a cool, instrumental choice of means.

Despite the efficiency account described in chapter 6, saying that time excluded expansive discourse, nearly half of Group 425's meetings consisted of educational programs. These gatherings were not task-oriented and provided opportunities for learning about the social and political structures that result in human rights violations. As social analysis, they were more sophisticated than what one commonly finds in community organizing. However, Amnesty's local activists did not have a context like that provided for participants in community organizing by training events. Such events, in organizing, are loci in which participants can explore, as part of the group's collective life, the grounds for personal commitments. No such loci existed in the life of the Amnesty groups I observed. The bases for the passion felt by Amnesty activists—the life experiences, religious faith, ethical commitments, political involvements, and other factors that lay behind commitment to human rights work—rarely surfaced at either the program or business meetings held by Group 425. These bases remained private rather than becoming part of the group's collective life. The grounds for commitment to human rights were hardly ever used to help the group think through its mission and communicate its perspective to others. Catherine Duncan's report that the group helped her become articulate on the issue of the death penalty suggests that at an earlier time such discussions may have taken place. But they did not occur during my period of observation. In this respect, organizing adopts a more expansive mode of discourse.

ISSUE LINKS

The question of the range of issues Amnesty will deal with and how different issues should be linked is at the heart of the mandate controversies within the organization. Since a great many social and political issues can be understood as human rights concerns, the question about issue links, in Amnesty, largely takes the form of debates about what range of things should be considered human rights, what subset of this range Amnesty as an organization should address, whether other rights should be discussed within the organization, and what the connections among different kinds of rights are.

Bob Antonucci of the Queens group, Daniel Levine, and the other members of Group 425 all took a traditionalist view of the mandate. While some agreed and some disagreed in principle with recent mandate expansions, all believed them to be a bad move organizationally. The result, whatever the motivation, was to keep human rights activism fairly narrow. Economic rights were largely excluded. In addition, impartiality as interpreted by some activists meant that one was to exert constant self-discipline in order to adhere to the rule of defending people's rights to free speech without supporting what they said. In sum, the perspective of these local activists largely separated different issues from each other. As we have seen, many of them were active in a variety of causes. But this might almost not have been true from what one could see within Group 425. The practical work taken on by any local group, under the AI statute, has to stay within the bounds of the mandate, observe the injunction against working on behalf of prisoners in one's own country, and manifest "impartiality." But these norms impose no gag rule on discussions within local groups. Such rules were self-imposed. Their implicit result was to define human rights fairly narrowly, in an individualistic, largely eighteenth-century mode.

Furthermore, the norm of impartiality and rule against work in one's own country put politics in a black box to some extent. Only with respect to the issue of the death penalty were Amnesty activists in the United States encouraged to act as citizens, taking on their own government. While this would not necessarily have blocked discussion of other issues, in practice such topics were not much discussed, even internally. This is especially striking given the links often argued to exist between U.S. foreign and military policy and human rights abuses by U.S.-allied dictators overseas. Impartiality, interpreted in a Voltairian sense, meant keeping one's distance from the actual substantive issues that the victims of human rights violations were dealing with. This discursive situation had some parallels with how in organizing (and many other American social movements) it is easier to talk about democratic substance or empowerment than about substantive visions of social justice.

Nonetheless, at times Amnesty discourse did connect a variety of political or social issues. In her talk at the candlelight vigil, Duncan linked feminist and human rights stances and articulated concerns that in effect constituted some of the economic rights normally excluded by the mandate. Sarah Browning saw her Amnesty work as part of being a socialist—as a way to pursue justice. The educational events conducted by Group 425 frequently related human rights to other concerns, such as lack of economic development, inequality, or superpower interference.

On this dimension the discourse found in AI was no more constrained than that of congregation-based community organizing. Community organizing, also, has trouble linking issues. Local concerns are largely separate from national ones because of the predominantly local character of organizing projects. Organizing is "multi-issue," but the multiple issues are largely addressed in isolation from each other. The methodology of "cutting" issues largely separates different political issues from each other: local groups pursue particular, immediately winnable victories rather than any broader agenda of social and political change. (To be sure, participants in organizing have a broader agenda of enhancing citizenship and strengthening civil society, but this is so general as to give little guidance on contemporary political struggles and debates. What we have called the "middle level" of political discourse, intermediate between "cut" issues and very general but noncontroversial principles, is mostly absent.) The difficulties both Amnesty and organizing have with connections among issues reflect broader dilemmas facing American social movements. Finding ways to engage larger issues without losing focus or encountering major internal dissension is a grave difficulty for many kinds of activists in the United States. Partly for this reason, single-issue groups have often fared better in this country than movements linking issues.

CIVIL-SOCIETAL LINKS

The grounds for political commitments are largely to be found in civil-societal traditions, which Americans imbibe more thoroughly and earlier in their lives than they do political ideas. Therefore the private quality of such grounds, in Amnesty, constituted a decoupling of politics from civil-societal life. When I talked to local activists in a context outside of Amnesty activities, some of them made strong connections to such traditions, some made vague ones, and some made none at all. Even when they did not make such connections explicitly, they did seem to be drawing on an implicit but nonetheless powerful substratum of values grounding human rights, acquired from various traditions such as American democratic thinking, Catholic conceptions of human rights, Protestant emphases on individual conscience, and the traditional American Jewish commitment to protecting ethnic and racial minorities. But whatever connections were made, they remained entirely private—a source of personal motivation, but not something to talk about within the group, even in meetings consisting solely of core activists who had known each other for years.

It is here that perhaps the greatest difference between Amnesty International and organizing can be seen. In organizing, the participants' religious membership is publicly stated and serves as a practical basis for involvement, rather than only as a private source of motivation. Furthermore, religious ideas—that is, a civil-societal tradition to which participants are typically far more attached than to their political views—are explicitly linked to the political world.

CULTURAL PRACTICES

Beyond the three dimensions of discourse just discussed, the cultural life of a social movement includes practices. In this area, the activists of Group 425 did almost as robust cultural work as their counterparts in community organizing. Drawing on the human rights tradition and the resources provided by Amnesty as a wider organization, they constructed a rich set of cultural practices that gave powerful support to their values and beliefs and to the solidarity they experienced as a group. For example, the act of letter writing expressed faith in the efficacy of individual action more powerfully than could any verbal affirmation. Group 425 had a ritual life that nurtured the members and brought distinctive contributions to public discourse. The symbolization of hope and steadfastness in the candlelight vigil, for instance, was transmitted by the cameras of local television stations into the homes of people living in the metropolitan area. In sum, Amnesty activists attended carefully to the symbolic, noninstrumental side of the life of their group.

THE SECULARITY OF AMNESTY INTERNATIONAL

Human rights activists construct cultural forms that do many of the same things accomplished by congregation-based community organizing. Transcendent ideas provided Amnesty activists with passion and mission. But there are differences: in some respects Amnesty discourse was more constrained than the language of organizing. Was this a result of Amnesty's secularity?

Secularity for Amnesty is not negotiable. As a far-flung, multicultural, international organization, it could not possibly ground human rights in any particular religious perspective. It could not even adopt, organizationally, a particular philosophical position, such as the one advocated by Locke. But does this situation necessarily imply as stringent constraints as those found in the Amnesty local discourse described in this book?

In constructing a transcendent stance on behalf of human rights—a stance that was absolutist in the sense of not yielding to utilitarian or situational arguments for violating human rights—Amnesty activists articulated secular principles in a way that performed the role that faith plays in the cultural life of community organizing. In this respect the secularity of Amnesty was no barrier to expansive discourse.

However, in Amnesty links between politics and civil-societal traditions—general-purpose, not-directly-political value commitments—were weak. Obviously the cultural task here was harder for Amnesty than for community organizing. One could argue that organizing does its cultural work without assuming that everyone shares any particular religious faith: faith-based organizations are not Christian. But in practice few participants in community organizing are alienated by hearing Christian talk, which would not be true in Amnesty. Catherine Duncan would have been ill-advised to explain to a newcomer that her human rights commitment was based in her faith as a Roman Catholic, whereas a parallel explanation given to members of a congregation considering joining a faith-based organizing project would be unlikely to give offense, even to non-Christians. (An exception is the complaints I have heard from Unitarians about Christocentric language in organizing.)

Yet Amnesty's secularity would not bar members of a group from expressing to each other their grounds—ethical, political, or religious—for human rights commitment. In fact, such sharing, if done carefully, might strengthen a local Amnesty group. Also, the connections of secular ethics to human rights politics could be developed. The experiences Americans have in their schools, workplaces, families, and any sports, cultural activities, or volunteer work with which they become involved, teach a variety of ethical perspectives. For example, such settings frequently induct Americans into commitment to equal opportunity. They communicate ideas about the dignity, value, and rights of human individuals who are quite different from oneself, and they act out or at least affirm the precept that everyone gains when people of varied races, religions, and nationalities work and play together. All of this constitutes a civil-societal basis for human rights discourse. Thus the passionate and concrete sense of international solidarity felt by Amnesty activists could be linked to secular ethics, rooted in civil-society, in something like the way community organizing is linked to faith. The Seaview Greens observed by Paul Lichterman—his analysis is summarized in chapter 1—did this kind of cultural work. The secularity of human rights work, in short, is a hurdle but not an impassable obstacle on the road to expansive discourse.

DILEMMAS IN HUMAN RIGHTS AND PROGRESSIVE DISCOURSE

It is not easy, nor always advisable, to engage in expansive discourse. In part 2 we saw a number of discursive constraints that are characteristic of faith-based organizing. These were adopted because participants believe them to be important rules to follow in order to achieve the basic purposes of organizing. Similarly, the constraints found among Amnesty activists reflected their considered judgment about what would best advance human rights.

There are, however, other ways of interpreting the human rights tradition. We have seen that this tradition has varied potentials. One example of a more expansive interpretation of human rights is found in a local organization in Portland, Oregon—the Workers' Organizing Committee (WOC). In WOC, the boundaries between liberty and justice talk break down. Rights language concerns social justice and building community, thus partly losing the somewhat individualistic quality it has in Amnesty.

Starting in the mid-1990s, WOC has engaged in an unconventional form of labor organizing. It has concentrated on unorganized, low-income workers in the service industry, beginning with hotel workers. Much of its work is concerned, not with wages or the usual kind of working conditions, but with raids by the Immigration and Naturalization Service or the use of toxic chemicals by hotels and restaurants. WOC is a multicultural organization comprising blacks, new Asian immigrants, and Latino/as. From the outset it used the language of rights to articulate its proposals. It has managed to get the Metropolitan Human Rights Commission in the Portland area to adopt a "Workers' Bill of Rights." Thus it has positioned itself in the mainstream, as an organization working not just for workers' particular interests but for what an established public body is willing to consider human rights. Furthermore, WOC contextualizes its work as related to the Universal Declaration of Human Rights (UDHR). The Workers' Bill of Rights begins with an explicit reference to the UDHR as "outlining the basic economic rights of all peoples."[1] The body of the document mostly articulates more specific or elaborated versions of the economic rights found in the UDHR. Thus this organization takes seriously the economic rights articulated by twentieth-century human rights thinking. Furthermore, it links various kinds of rights. It is deeply concerned with free speech questions, in part because the suppression of free speech that happens when employers fire or use violence against people who speak out against their working conditions is a basic impediment to organizing.

In Amnesty, the discourse was more constrained. In chapter 6, we examined five explanations or justifications given by local Amnesty activists for this constraint: the unanimity, routinization, conflict-avoidance, efficiency, and privacy accounts. These accounts are far from unique to Amnesty. Many progressive groups use them. Thus the accounts manifest a cultural structure that is widely adopted. This structure consists of a set of discursive rules and the rationales for them, and it is independent of the actual public discourse carried on by activists. It includes reasons *not* to link issues with each other, *not* to connect politics with religion and other civil-societal traditions, and *not* to engage in transcendent, ethically charged modes of discourse. Thus our examination of human rights discourse leads to an encounter with ideas that influence the conduct of many kinds of progressive politics, not just human rights work.

These ideas are not uncontested: there were Amnesty activists who questioned each of the accounts for constraint, and the same is true more generally for progressive politics. For example, the member of the Cincinnati antiwar coalition who wanted to discuss the broader purposes of the coalition's work was a dissenter from the discursive rules operative in his group. And the WOC as a collective enterprise implicitly contests Amnesty's way of understanding human rights. Thus we can see an implicit debate being carried on among progressive activists concerning the right way to engage in public discourse.

The issues at stake in this debate become quite explicit in Amnesty because of its ongoing attention to defining its "mandate." But the issues are broader than AI, manifesting dilemmas faced by progressive politics. Each of the accounts makes an argument that has some weight even if one does not find it fully persuasive. Each identifies potential dangers of more expansive discourse, dangers that would have to be considered and minimized if one wanted to engage in more expansive discourse but also be practically effective and remain true to basic principles of liberty. (The fourth row of the table at the end of chapter 1 lists some of the dangers of extremely expansive discourse.) What kind of constraints to retain, and what risks from relaxing others to accept, are basic questions for contemporary progressive politics. In part 4 we will address these questions.

Part IV: How Should We Talk about Politics?

Chapter 7

INDIVIDUALISM AND ITS DISCONTENTS

How do the case studies and the way of thinking about public discourse presented in this book speak to contemporary debates about the American cultural scene — our ideologies, religions, and views of the world — and about the impact of these cultural forms on the potentials for progressive politics? In this concluding part of the book, I will address this topic by considering the views of various social critics (along with scholars and journalists) and comparing them to what one sees when one observes activist groups. I will evaluate the diagnoses and prescriptions proposed and suggest my own. This chapter discusses the problems and possibilities of individualism and civil society in America; the next examines the perils and opportunities that arise when politics is richly cultural.

When it comes to explaining the weakness of social democratic and socialist politics in the United States, individualism is often taken to be the chief culprit. Substantively, individualism is assumed to foster conservative politics. Processually, it is seen as a cause of disengagement from public life and concern, and also as a force eroding civil society and its ability to support democracy. Probably the most sophisticated and best-known expression of this argument is presented by Robert Bellah and four coauthors in *Habits of the Heart*. A partly overlapping perspective is the one best known from Robert Putnam's work on "bowling alone": that weakness in civil society is the source of our ills. Many scholars have criticized Bellah or Putnam, and I will use these debates to address two basic issues about individualism.[1]

The first is the extent and manner in which individualism and deficits in civil society dominate American political culture. Are we really so individualistic? Is our associational sector falling apart? How does all this affect American politics? I will argue, drawing on the case studies in this book and other evidence, that individualism and deficits in civil society are not in themselves the main obstacles to progressive politics. Rather, the problems arise from decoupling of civil society from politics. When this happens, the nonindividualistic resources that are plentifully present in what is still a robust civil-societal sphere fail to influence the tenor of public discourse.

The second issue concerns the ambiguities of individualism itself. What different forms does it take? Which forms should progressives affirm or criticize? I will argue that progressives actually need individualism, but of a particular kind: an individualism that seeks justice and liberty equally, that neither rejects rights language nor accepts it uncritically, and that does not assume that liberty or the individual are "natural" phenomena, based on the intrinsic nature of human beings and requiring from cultural traditions only that they not interfere or oppress. I will also show how elements of such an individualism can be found in contemporary activism.

AMERICAN INDIVIDUALISM

In their influential and widely read book *Habits of the Heart: Individualism and Commitment in American Life,* Robert Bellah, Richard Madsen, William Sullivan, Ann Swidler, and Steven Tipton assess the moral state of American culture, primarily on the basis of in-depth interviews. One of their central conclusions is that while biblical and what they call "republican" traditions exist in America and are appropriated at times, the "first language" of most Americans is either utilitarian or expressive individualism. Utilitarian individualism is a perspective that assumes that people should and do focus on advancing their self-interest—typically, their wealth, power, or security. Expressive individualism, a reaction to the utilitarian form, gives room for developing and expressing one's feelings, spirituality, ethical identity, and relationships, but still within the framework of serving no will or purpose other than one's own. Both kinds of individualism take individuals to be more real than social institutions or culture. That is, Americans tend to articulate grounds for decisions in terms of what will get them ahead or express themselves, even though their actions and feelings often inchoately manifest richer possibilities.[2]

The argument Bellah and his colleagues made has been frequently misunderstood as saying that Americans are individualistic as a trait of personality or behavior. Some of their respondents fit this model, having little involvement with voluntary associations or public life, or regarding their personal self-interest or emotional fulfillment as the purpose of their lives. Others, however, have broader aspirations and are engaged in civic improvement efforts, political activism, churches, or volunteer work. But even the more engaged respondents, as the book describes them, are largely unable to make their public-spirited or altruistic practical activities accountable. They are unable to use less individualistic cultural traditions fluently as ways to explain the bases for their involvements. Thus the argument is about cultural patterns rather than moral character (although certainly the book has an element of exhortation). *Habits* argues that American moral language tends to take individualistic forms. Our culture and public discourse, the authors believe, have been seriously impoverished, diminishing our capacity to articulate visions of the common good or reasons to be involved in public life.

Not everyone is convinced by this argument. The book is sometimes dismissed as mere preaching or wistfulness. More to the point, other scholars argue that Bellah and his colleagues have not correctly analyzed the American cultural situation. One important critique comes from ethical philosopher Jeffrey Stout. In Stout's view, nonindividualistic ethical languages are much more alive and well in America than a reading of *Habits* would lead one to believe. To find them, however, one needs to look at social practices. The real "first languages," in the sense of ethical perspectives Americans actually use routinely, are *not* general social theories or philosophies, whether individualistic or communal. Rather, our native tongues are the varied sphere-specific languages generated within particular social practices. Such languages include occupational ethics, the values and norms of cultural and recreational activities in which Americans become involved, and so on. As a recreational/cultural example, we might think of amateur choruses and choirs—the most widespread form of performing arts participation in America. Choristers subordinate personal self-expression to the necessity that everyone do as the conductor says, practicing and valuing teamwork. They pursue excellence (as we know, not always successfully) for its own sake rather than as a means to other ends, spending countless hours in rehearsal and putting up with criticism ("Sopranos, you're flat!") in order to do justice to music they love. The implicit ethic learned and acted out in a chorus is neither individualistic nor utilitarian. An example of occupational ethics is the code governing research practices espoused by social scientists, which includes the principle of keeping the promises of confidentiality customarily made to respondents. This principle has no legal standing and is therefore harder to observe than the confidentiality norms of doctors, lawyers, or clergy. Nonetheless, social scientists have been known to go to jail or to destroy documents that have been subpoenaed, thereby risking imprisonment, rather than violate it.[3]

The languages learned within such social practices often contain strong nonindividualistic and nonutilitarian frameworks but do not constitute overarching ethical or social theories. Stout thinks that these sphere-specific languages are understudied and undervalued in *Habits*. Furthermore, he believes that the authors of *Habits*, through their interviewing techniques, often pressured their respondents into talking as if they had a philosophical commitment to the position that all values are arbitrary individual choices. "We may parrot individualistic sayings, on occasion," in Stout's view, but we engage in "varied and supple" moral languages that are anything but individualistic.[4]

It is hard to disagree with Stout's argument for the potentials found in social practices. Associational contexts—including ones like choruses where political goals are not primary—link people to nonindividualistic cultural traditions. The links are reinforced by ongoing interaction and take place in ordinary life rather than just when a person becomes politically active. When these traditions are connected to public issues, in activist groups with expansive discourse or in nonpolitical voluntary associations that occasionally relate their distinctive values to political and social questions, one starts seeing the very real capacity Americans have to frame issues in terms that go beyond individualism and utilitarianism. Thus there are grounds for a more optimistic assessment of American ethical culture and its political implications than the tone of *Habits* suggests.

But Stout says little about how sphere-specific languages connect with public discourse. If they operate in isolation, the argument of *Habits* could be true in practice. That is, the central public spheres of economy and politics might still evoke predominantly individualistic discourse from most Americans. In that case, the sphere-specific languages Stout describes would make daily life in America better, but would not improve American politics. A great many associations compartmentalize their concerns from broader issues and many activist groups, as we have seen in previous chapters, adopt discursive rules limiting connections to civil-societal traditions. Thus there are grounds for a less optimistic view of our cultural situation than Stout appears to adopt.

Furthermore, public issues have a kind of generality transcending the limits of the particular spheres Stout discusses. Such questions cannot be dealt with adequately through sphere-specific ethical frameworks by themselves, although these frameworks *can* potentially inform or help ground one's political conclusions. To put it simply, it may be very nice that choristers transcend individualism and utilitarianism when they sing, but this will not do much to improve politics unless what they learn in their choirs somehow informs their thinking in their role as citizens, voters, and (on occasion) activists. For a robust political culture we need cultural tools, available to ordinary citizens, by which the issues that come up in political debate can be addressed in their ethical dimension rather than just as technical questions or as issues to be negotiated based on the balance of power of contending forces. Sphere-specific languages, by themselves, cannot provide these tools.[5]

So the key is not the ethical languages of civil society but rather the cultural *connections* between civil society and political life. We cannot say how individualistic American culture is, as a basis for the creation of public discourse, without knowing to what extent and with what implications the ethical languages generated in social practices encourage or discourage public involvement. Do these languages help Americans think and talk about what should be considered just and unjust, preserved and changed, in American society? The debate between Stout and the authors of *Habits* cannot be resolved without evidence on the sources, nature, and implications of compartmentalization and integration between the cultural resources generated in civil society and those used in politics—evidence that Stout does not give us and *Habits* provides only in part.

The evidence from our case studies suggests that the question of compartmentalization and integration is an ambiguous and contested area in the discourse carried on by local activists. Congregation-based community organizing constructs significant links between religious faith and public issues.[6] However, sometimes faith is treated as a "black box" in this process, with an assumed rather than examined relationship to politics. That is unfortunate, given the power of individualistic languages. For religious languages to bring their alternative resources into public discourse, participants in community organizing need to learn to articulate links rather than assume them. Otherwise, faith might serve at a psychological level as a source of public-spirited motivations but would not contest the power of individualistic themes within American political culture. As we have seen, organizing intellectuals are thinking about this issue, and already the links are much stronger than in most American activism. Many organizers would agree with the statement quoted earlier from Pat Speer, that "what church-based organizing is doing around America is a relentless frontal, total assault on the philosophical and epistemological individualism" in our country.[7]

The purpose of Amnesty International, of course, is to advance individual liberty and dignity, and so one cannot expect it to contest individualism in the same way as organizing does. And the links between human rights discourse and civil-societal traditions are weaker than in organizing. Nonetheless, Amnesty does favor a very different kind of individualism than the kind criticized by *Habits of the Heart*. And the kind of international solidarity that it manifests is a definite challenge to American individualism.

Weakness in Civil Society?

Another major argument about the problems in American politics comes from those following in the tradition of Alexis de Tocqueville, a nineteenth-century French historian and observer of America. One of de Tocqueville's central arguments was that the pursuit of equality was compatible with the preservation of liberty in America because of a vibrant voluntary sector linking individuals to wider societal concerns. Since the mid-1990s, the leading proponent of a neo-Tocquevillian perspective has been political scientist Robert Putnam. His widely cited 1995 article, "Bowling Alone: America's Declining Social Capital," takes its title from what bowling operators and the bowling industry told him: bowling is up, but *league* bowling is down. (In other words, it isn't really that people are bowling alone but that increasingly they are bowling in small groups of friends or family. The bowling industry is unhappy with this trend because league bowlers are more profitable—they buy more beer.) Putnam compiles a mass of statistics to support his view that associational involvement is significantly declining. This trend, he argues, weakens civic trust, political participation, and democracy.[8]

Putnam's work has occasioned serious disagreements among scholars about the actual degree of decline in associational involvement. There are also theoretical and comparative issues that can be raised about the argument. For instance, whatever decline there has been, American involvement is high compared with other Western countries, and yet when it comes to voting these other countries have higher mass political participation than the United States. Perhaps most important, Putnam's argument pays insufficient attention to the role of different kinds of associations and to the question of how civil-societal involvement and public concern interact. Involvement in a local neighborhood improvement association is quite likely to make a citizen more interested in social and political issues, while joining a religious sect that shuns the world may decrease interest and the effect of participating in a bowling league is debatable. Some private involvements compete with public ones—some former activists now spend their spare time on Little League activities—while other associational commitments contribute to public engagement. Thus the *kind* of involvement may be more important than the *amount* of it.[9]

Furthermore, parallel to what we argued with regard to the disagreements between Stout and the authors of *Habits of the Heart*, a central question is the degree to which civil society and public life are linked or decoupled. In the voluntary sector, Americans are often concerned with the well-being of others and with social issues beyond their immediate lives. But as with the "varied and supple" ethical languages Stout describes, the question is what difference this involvement makes. The unsatisfying answer is: sometimes a lot and sometimes very little.

Sociologist Theda Skocpol, in an analysis far more nuanced than Putnam's, puts her finger on some of the factors that determine the result. She shows that there was a shift over the second half of the twentieth century in the *kind* of associational involvements Americans have that relate to public life. In particular, large membership federations, such as the National Congress of Parents and Teachers (PTA), have greatly declined. These organizations typically existed at a local, statewide, and national level. In their local branches, they provided a context for personal involvement, interaction, learning, and fellowship. But they also provided opportunities for those participants who had or developed the requisite skills and interests to become involved in wider levels of the federation. These levels interacted with state and federal governments. Since the 1960s, Skocpol shows, such federations have become much weaker. They have largely been replaced by professionalized advocacy organizations, such as the Children's Defense Fund, often operating out of national offices in Washington.[10]

The key point is that compared with the federations, such advocacy groups provide only weak connections between public concerns and civil society. Supporters are called upon mostly to make contributions that will pay national staff to work on behalf of the supporters' values by lobbying government officials, developing policy proposals, researching issues, and so forth. The organizations have no roots in local communities and provide their supporters (who are often not even defined as members) with no significant opportunity for personal participation in public life, and certainly no interaction with other members. That is, they are only in a weak sense part of the associational sphere. They can do only a small part of the things de Tocqueville and Putnam have in mind. The contexts in which ongoing interaction and personal participation *do* still happen in American civil society are generally organizations, such as amateur sports teams and choruses, that take little or no interest in public life. If they are democratic, their internal affairs may nurture love for the kind of activity and participation that the public realm allows. But unlike the traditional federations, they make no connection between their organizational concerns and public life.

The key exception to the bleak situation just described, of course, is the bevy of local groups found in every American community that engage public concerns on the basis of grassroots participation. Whether such groups consider themselves political or not, whether they are left or right of center, whether they use expansive or constrained discourse, and whether they work for social change or just to solve particular social problems, these groups involve their members in personal activity relating to domains beyond their private lives. They still play the role de Tocqueville scripted for the voluntary sector. While good data on such groups is hard to come by—they are often almost invisible to outsiders—it is possible that they have held their own while the federations have declined.

Nonetheless, the decline of the traditional federations is a loss, leaving a bifurcated situation in which there are national advocacy groups, with the disadvantages just mentioned, on one side and highly localized activist or service groups on the other. It is hard for the latter to address public policy issues that could only be solved by levels of government beyond the local community, and they do not link their members to statewide and national debate or provide opportunities for them to move into public activity in wider arenas. In faith-based organizing, for example, many participants know that statewide or other initiatives beyond the local organization are necessary to change the dire conditions found in inner-city neighborhoods, but not very much energy actually gets funneled into such broader projects. And organizing has the benefit of the networks, whereas many grassroots activist groups have hardly any contact with the world beyond their communities.

The up side is that the localism of activist groups gives them the freedom to be more unconventional than federations and to find a more specific cultural consensus grounding their work than a broad federation could possibly construct. In addition, they are as capable as federations of empowering their members. Community organizing of all kinds, including the faith-based version we have studied in this book, comes out of the tradition of radical democracy in America, a tradition that stresses the role of the individual activist as an independent agent in public life. Radical democratic values encourage forms of politics that often transform and energize participants.

Amnesty International is in principle closer to the traditional federations, with a true organization, not just networks, beyond the local level. But as we have seen, the interactions between different levels of Amnesty are weak. Therefore, local chapters such as Group 425 operate to a large extent in the same way as localized activist groups, while the national organization operates somewhat like professionalized advocacy organizations. When fundraisers call from the national offices, they never mention that a local group exists in one's city.

To the extent that Americans are involved in local groups concerned with social issues, of whatever kind, civil society is organizationally linked to public life. However, when involvements are confined to apolitical associations and national advocacy organizations, these sectors are decoupled. The organizational problem is roughly parallel to the cultural one described in relation to individualism: civil society is not so much the problem as is compartmentalization between spheres.[11]

In short, neither individualism nor weakness in civil society is in itself a plausible explanation for the political woes of progressives. Rather, the key factor is what kind of linkage or lack of linkage one finds: whether the nonindividualistic values nurtured in many sectors of American life have an opportunity to influence our political and social life, and whether civil-societal institutions are able to do so. This is why the kind of choices activist groups make about their discourse are so important. If no connections are made between civil-societal cultural traditions and public issues, the chances of bringing energy and public support into progressive politics are greatly weakened. The groups making up the religious right construct such connections, gaining strength far beyond what their actual base of support merits. But progressive activists, for the reasons found in the accounts for constraint described in our case studies, are often reluctant to do so. A change in this situation would significantly improve the chances of success for progressive politics.

WHAT KIND OF INDIVIDUALISM SHOULD PROGRESSIVES ADOPT?

Whatever the problems with individualism, it is hard to imagine a progressive politics without a major agenda of individual freedom—defense of civil liberties and so forth. Furthermore, a politics that tried to be systematically anti-individualistic would have scant chance of success in the United States. So far, communitarianism as a movement has acquired quite a number of leaders and spokespersons, but not too many followers. So the interesting question is not whether to espouse individualism, but what kind of individualism to endorse—how to appropriate and interpret America's powerful cultural traditions about liberty. There are many individualisms, and they are not all created equal. In the remainder of this chapter we will look at some initiatives toward articulating forms of individualism that are in keeping with progressive politics.

New (Actually Old) Cultural Strategies for Labor

In the conclusion to part 3 of this book, we briefly described the Workers' Organizing Committee (WOC) in Portland, Oregon, as an example of an understanding of human rights that incorporates economic rights and becomes a search for justice as well as liberty. Some progressive intellectuals have been trying to articulate this strategy more broadly. Let us consider one example.

In 1998, Nelson Lichtenstein, a labor historian who has been actively involved in progressive movements, addressed the cultural predicament of American labor in an article published in *WorkingUSA,* a magazine for labor activists. The article was titled "Workers' Rights Are Civil Rights: How to Put the Labor Movement Back at the Center of American Political Culture." In this essay, Lichtenstein argues that labor needs to reclaim the links between its basic principles and ones that are central to American ideology: assertions of rights. During the New Deal period, new forms of unionism "represented a doorway that opened onto the democratic promise of American life," but too often in later decades labor has been isolated from the core of American political culture.[12]

In Lichtenstein's view, "the most startling disjuncture faced by American progressives arises from the sharp dichotomy that puts the 'civil rights' of workers in one conceptual box and the collective workplace rights of those same employees in quite another." Thus, for instance, any American worker is entitled to freedom from discrimination at work on the basis of race, sex, religion, or national origin. These rights are enforceable by law and strongly supported by public opinion. State and local "human rights" agencies will defend them. But that same worker has very limited rights to organize or even to talk with coworkers about workplace issues. The agencies charged with protecting these rights, such as the National Labor Relations Board, often work in practice to destroy them. There is little public outcry when they are violated. This disjuncture is essentially the one found in Amnesty between civil and political rights, on one hand, and economic ones on the other. Like the Workers' Organizing Committee, Lichtenstein wants to bring together economic and civil rights.[13]

In the past, key labor struggles acquired "transcendent meaning," and this needs to happen in the future, Lichtenstein argues, by constructing "social and ideological linkages between civil rights and workers' rights." In essence, he is proposing a cultural struggle within American public discourse to increase the proportion of Americans who understand human rights in an expansive way. And in doing so he is proposing a return to something quite traditional in America. The major thrust of the work of civil libertarians in the early years of the American Civil Liberties Union, after World War I, was to defend radical trade unionists from repression of their basic civil liberties. Correspondingly, labor unions have sometimes understood civil liberties and civil rights, not as a separate agenda, but as an intrinsic part of their struggles.[14]

Lichtenstein is not just proposing that we add economic rights, as a separate package, to civil and political rights, but that we understand all rights in a more integrated way. Rights, he acknowledges, belong first of all to individuals, but he wants a kind of rights language that supports our capacity to act collectively. He does not go very far, however, in developing this.

Individualism as a Source of Public Involvement

Sociologist Paul Lichterman, who has studied environmental activism, argues that there are forms of individualism that enhance public life. His argument does not necessarily contradict *Habits of the Heart,* but it certainly contradicts the usual interpretations of this book and the critiques of individualism frequently encountered in American social criticism. The stereotype that Lichterman wants to counter sees individualism and public concern as being on opposite ends of a seesaw: if one goes up, the other goes down. In his view, this is not necessarily true.[15]

In the past, many popular movements could be based in shared communal culture and solidarity. These counterbalanced the individualism that was also part of American culture. Militant labor struggles, for instance, were often conducted by communities that were ethnically and religiously homogeneous. In turn-of-millennium America, progressive movements of any scope cannot and should not rely on such homogeneities. Yet Americans continue to get involved in activist groups and are frequently public-spirited. What is the basis for this? One could refer to our shared democratic traditions, but they are extremely indeterminate.[16] Lichterman suggests that there is a form of individualism, which he calls "personalism," that "might *enable* public commitment" rather than undermine it.[17]

The possibility of such an individualism is at the center of what

Lichterman calls "radical democracy," as found in such otherwise dissimilar perspectives as those of Jürgen Habermas and Chantal Mouffe. In these radical democratic theories, individualism has to do with autonomous, activist individuals working together in the public realm. Critique of existing communal structures (patriarchal ones, for example) goes along with public commitment. Such an individualism presupposes and reinforces public concern and altruism, rather than undermining them. The only problem is that radical democrats do not give empirical or cultural substance to their conception of individualism: it comes off as hypothetical (and in the case of Habermas, rationalistic and deracinated).

Lichterman gives an instance where an individualism of this kind *does* exist in describing the discourse of the Seaview Greens, discussed briefly in chapter 1. He shows activists who preserve a long-term commitment to active engagement in the public sphere, who articulate a kind of altruism, and who are willing to spend time and effort on unpleasant tasks (such as dealing with difficult individuals)—all within the matrix of a mode of political action that is intensely individualistic. The Seaview Greens take the freedom of speech and conscience of individual participants within the movement, and each person's political development and empowerment, as central ends, not to be subordinated to external practical objectives. This does not mean that the group becomes a therapy or support group, for the goal is long-term social change and the engagement of individuals in public life. But the process of political work becomes as important as short-term visible outcomes. Furthermore, for the Seaview Greens, emphasis on the individual becomes a source of solidarity.[18]

It would be easy to think of faith-based community organizing as the polar opposite of this kind of politics: organizing seems businesslike, rooted in traditional religious solidarity, and more in tune with communitarianism. But in fact organizing originated in an American version of radical democracy. Like the Green groups Lichterman describes, it shows enormous interest in developing and empowering individual participants, helping them become active participants in public life. The philosophy of "Green values" and the basic commitments of organizing converge on the goals of building community and enhancing economic justice. Thus both in organizing and among the Greens, individualistic and communal purposes are linked within a single perspective. Individuation becomes a resource for public life.

There are some limitations to the capacity of the kind of individualism Lichterman describes to contribute to public life. Although he does not draw this conclusion, from the accounts Lichterman gives of the Seaview Greens and another Green group it appears that the members had a strong and enduring personal commitment to being involved in social change work but had great difficulty sustaining their *organizations* over time. The same people revolved through a rapidly changing array of Green organizations, none of which lasted very long. Furthermore, they sometimes tended to think of social change as a process of change in the attitudes and values of individuals, to be achieved through dialogue and education. If building institutions and enduring organizations is an important part of seeking social justice and building community, and if institutions need to be addressed up front rather than as a follow-up concern once consciousness has changed, then the kind of individualism Lichterman describes may be to some extent an obstacle.[19]

Nonetheless, Lichterman's analysis helpfully presses us to look at how in actual practice people negotiate the relationship between public commitment and individualistic ideas, rather than deciding *a priori* that they are inimical to each other. Doing so shows that the version of individualism found among the Greens can be a source of solidarity and facilitate public engagement. Thus Lichterman's analysis offers hope that the individualistic strands that are so strong in American culture can help rather than hinder progressive politics.

Individualism as a Transcendent Moral and Political Vision

The two initiatives just described are promising, but they do not delve deeply enough into how to understand individualism. For that, let us turn to some ideas developed by sociologist Emile Durkheim in the 1890s. Durkheim's perspective, updated to some extent, provides a promising framework for a progressive interpretation of individualism.

In response to attacks by the conservative social critics of his day on the liberalism of the Third Republic, Durkheim explicitly took on the task of articulating the nature of individualism. He did this in various writings, but most pointedly in an 1898 essay entitled "Individualism and the Intellectuals."[20]

The political stance that Durkheim puts forward in this essay and other works is similar to that of many contemporary progressives. He endorses the human rights framework found in the French Declaration of the Rights of Man and the Citizen and expresses views very close to those articulated fifty years later in the Universal Declaration of Human Rights (UDHR). His analysis of the *bases for support* of rights, however, is different from the views of most liberals and human rights advocates.

It is a fully cultural analysis, emphasizing the collective, historical, and suprarational character of the culture of human rights—as opposed to seeing rights as self-evident, natural, or otherwise independent of culture and history. Durkheim calls the worldview he favors "individualism," but he gives a specific meaning to that term, thereby differentiating his views from others.

Durkheim talks, first, about the kind of individualism he would *not* wish to defend: that of the utilitarians. This, as he describes it, is a perspective in which each person should pursue individual self-interest, with the common good enhanced by some kind of invisible hand. This worldview is essentially the utilitarian individualism described in *Habits*. If this were what French civil libertarians were supporting, Durkheim says, conservative social critics would be right.

The kind of individualism that Durkheim defends is entirely different. This individualism is a defense of the dignity and liberty of the individual in general, of "*la personne humaine*," to use Durkheim's term. Such an individualism, which we might call "communal individualism," does not counsel us to put our self-interest first. On the contrary, a person acting in congruence with this framework might die in a war against Hitler, go to jail (as a reporter or editor) for publishing what the government wishes to suppress, or be fired and blacklisted rather than "name names." Here we have a secular cultural tradition that has much in common with religions. In this tradition, *la personne humaine* is the object of worship, the sacred object. This kind of individualism is a collective and constraining cultural structure, demanding discipline and sacrifice.[21]

In Durkheim's view, this is actually the only cultural tradition capable of uniting an entire modern society. Christianity and other traditional religions, he says, are too particular, with too limited allegiance. In our increasingly differentiated, complex society, no inherited system of beliefs and practices is universal, and the circumstances of people's lives are too varied to provide much in the way of shared experience or destiny. (It is remarkable that Durkheim would conceptualize modern France in this way, describing what in contemporary terminology would be called "multiculturalism," as early as 1898.) But the sacredness of *la personne humaine* can be accepted by people of all religious faiths, all ethnic groups, all nationalities, and all social classes. Furthermore, its focus is the one thing we *do* still have in common: our shared humanity. Thus it is not just a tool for individual liberation (although Durkheim was passionately attached to civil liberties) but also for social unity, and for ethical meaning and purpose in the face of the diversity of modern societies. Durkheim, while a steadfast liberal, *accepts* the argument put forth by conservative critics of modernity that there have to be moral bases for action in any society worth living in, and even the argument such critics make that a certain degree of moral or cultural unity is necessary.[22]

Durkheim's conception of individualism is intimately related to social justice. In this respect, he is closer to the Universal Declaration than to the French one. In fact, he says that the principles of 1789 need to be broadened. Some political stances imply that there is a tension between individual liberty and the usual progressive economic agenda—equality, social welfare, and a degree of public decision making in economic life. Free-market conservatives on the right and Leninists on the left take this view. Durkheim, however, saw no such tension. Politically, Durkheim positioned himself as what we would now think of as a social democrat or moderate socialist. In his book *The Division of Labor in Society,* he says that our interdependence in a complex modern society can be a source of solidarity, but only if, among other things, market forces are constrained so that those weak in bargaining power can still have their needs respected.[23] He also argues that modern societies are far from operating on a purely contractual basis and show no sign of moving in that direction. In his view, the political freedoms achieved by the process started in the French Revolution and completed (in Durkheim's view) in the Third Republic, while essential, were not the ultimate ends but rather a means toward enhancing the dignity of *la personne humaine*—a goal that now requires amelioration of social conditions. Respecting the dignity and freedom of every person requires a variety of collective supports and constraints, and also that economic issues as well as civil liberties and political participation be addressed. In other words, a degree of social justice is required for the fullness of human rights. In adding economic concerns, Durkheim is taking a position like that of the UDHR or T. H. Marshall. Thus, like Lichtenstein and the Workers' Organizing Committee in Portland, but unlike the more traditionalist members of Amnesty, Durkheim's vision integrates the goals of liberty and justice.[24]

Durkheim is closer to the French declaration than to the UDHR, however, in the attention and positive value he gives to collective life. (We saw in chapter 5 that the UDHR, despite its concern with economic rights, is very individualistic—more so than the French declaration.) As a sociologist, Durkheim criticizes the attempt of Enlightenment thinkers to "deduce their individualist ethics not from society but from the notion of the isolated individual." That is, such thinkers wanted to base human rights in a conception of the state of nature—taken by the more optimistic, such as Locke and Rousseau, to be one of freedom. In such a view, the rights of the individual would be rooted in the basic character of the world, and specifically in human nature. Durkheim takes the contrary view. Individualism, he says, "is a social product just like all moralities and all religions." Liberty is not the natural and original state of humans, destroyed by society and needing to be recovered. Rather, it is an idea and set of institutional arrangements we have come up with as our culture has matured. That is, individual freedom emerges not from the absence of society or constraints, nor from the separation or liberation of individuals from society, but from the development of kinds of collective life that contain cultural and organizational forms supporting liberty. It is by collective and partly suprarational influences that the rights of individuals to participate freely in rational-critical discourse are preserved.[25]

Durkheim's argument articulates a narrative about Western history, one that describes how our society has become increasingly diverse and honors individual freedom, yet can and often does retain a moral center and even unity. Obviously, this is a more optimistic narrative than the one found in *Habits of the Heart* or contemporary communitarianism. In this narrative an individualistic society is more rather than less interdependent, and no less "social," moral, or coherent than its predecessors. The discourse of human rights is therefore about freedom and diversity but also about social integration. To be sure, the greater complexity requires changes in order to maintain a moral center, which is why Durkheim argues for broadening conceptions of human rights to include economic considerations. Thus Durkheim evinces a nonstandard liberalism. In broadening the concept of human rights to include economic issues, he lends support to the more or less social-democratic and civil-libertarian agenda of twentieth-century progressives. But the *basis* for his support is a set of collective and cultural considerations.

Durkheim's vision is in accord with core progressive values in a way that much individualistic thinking, even on the left, is not. His perspective would argue for a discriminating attitude towards rights languages, rather than the blanket condemnations one sometimes hears—especially from people in the communitarian camp—or the uncritical acceptance sometimes manifested in progressive rhetoric. Some rights languages can be affirmed as they stand. The civil rights language of Martin Luther King, Jr., for example, or the assertion of the political rights of dissidents by civil libertarians can be accepted happily as manifestations of our collective worship of *la personne humaine*. Other kinds of rights talk, however, require reinterpretation and a more qualified acceptance.

For example, progressive health care advocates sometimes talk about access to high-quality medical care as a human right. Surely in most cases they do not mean this in the usual, literal sense: they do not mean that this is an absolute demand one should make of government—with no exceptions or limits and no concern for competing claims on the public purse. This demand is not like that for freedom of religious belief. Possibly the intention in using rights language is to connect the policy proposals such progressives make—for universal health insurance and so on—to values dear to Americans. In a sense, this is similar to the course Nelson Lichtenstein advocates for labor or the strategy of the WOC.

This does not really work very well as a discursive strategy. At a forum where I heard an intelligent, articulate activist present this position, her conservative opponent got the upper hand, interpreting her rights language literally and thereby making it look silly. Free-market advocates are not deceived; they realize that behind rights language on health are proposals for what they most oppose: increased government intervention in economic life. Communitarians have as much disdain for rights language in this area as in any other. And human rights traditionalists, such as Daniel Levine, the coordinator of Group 425, see this use of rights language as diluting the struggle for the eighteenth-century rights they take to be fundamental.

But in my view the more important problem in trying to tie progressive health policy proposals to rights language is in what tends to get left unsaid when one takes this approach. The activist just mentioned is a social democrat. For her, like most health activists, equality of access to medical care, regardless of wealth, is a primary concern, and she values other public purposes. Yet these points were hardly mentioned in her talk. The communitarian critique of rights language makes some sense here. Health care politics has to do in part with distributing resources and should be about our mutual responsibilities as well as our individual rights. Health care policies can be validly formed partly by the criterion of trying to maximize reduction of suffering across the whole population—a criterion in tension with assertions of rights. In short, a rights language that speaks just about individual claims and not about collective ethical decision making is seriously incomplete. It also downplays progressive principles. Progressives should not be ashamed to say that social justice and equality are core values driving their health policy proposals. Rights language of a simple and unexamined kind can play into the hands of conservatives, who argue that market-based approaches maximize people's right to choose their health care. This is an example of how standard versions of individualism can work in ways that undermine the value bases for progressive concerns for economic justice.

Despite these criticisms, one can affirm many of the purposes that are behind the expansion of rights talk to the health care field. Rights language about health points to the sacredness of human beings and our collective commitment to the dignity of every person. Those principles imply that persons should not have to endure physical suffering unnecessarily and that their physical integrity is a higher purpose than the bottom line of insurance companies or pharmaceutical firms. A Durkheimian individualism would endorse using rights language to talk in this vein about health, thus integrating justice concerns with commitment to the value of the individual.

Durkheim's vision is realistic in a basic sense: of taking into account the cultural and collective character of people's allegiances. The Enlightenment narrative of the origin of rights was never true to the reality of human life—of how rights really emerge—and is losing support. To continue to espouse rights by thinking that they are natural and will emerge automatically once inhibiting institutions and cultural frameworks are removed is a recipe for constructing discourse that will be, and deserves to be, unpersuasive.

Yet, however valid Durkheim's point of view, the question remains: is it a plausible option within the range of forms of public discourse of which contemporary Americans are capable? Varying answers to this question are possible. For instance, Durkheim's assertion of the unifying potentials in human rights discourse could be supported or opposed by examples drawn from American political discourse. Patriotism and nationalism in America have always been mostly justified not by referring to a shared history, experience, land, or culture, but by asserting that we have a special role as the chief bearer of values of liberty. Jimmy Carter tried to articulate human rights as the central basis for American foreign policy—a basis that he hoped would unify the country after the Vietnam experience. However, response to Carter's initiative was tepid and American foreign policy, even in its rhetoric, has only sporadically been focused on human rights. Many Americans, furthermore, understand freedom primarily in terms of not having anybody interfering with our decisions about how we live our lives—that is, in a negative and apolitical sense that lacks the collective meanings found in Durkheim's vision or even the French declaration.

The fact that it has been so easy for politicians to demonize the American Civil Liberties Union (ACLU) could be interpreted, pessimistically, as showing a low commitment to freedoms that concern the public rather than the private realm, or more optimistically, as evidence that Americans have a communitarian streak that leads them to doubt the unqualified rights language used by the ACLU. Durkheim saw the individualistic and collective elements of honoring *la personne humaine* as equally essential. If only the individualistic ones are present when Americans think about liberty and human rights, it is hard to see how to enrich rights thinking in the way Lichtenstein proposes, or to have individualism serve to promote public concern and provide a basis for unity in a diverse society, as Durkheim hoped it might. That is, it is an empirical question to what extent Americans can or do appropriate a Durkheimian form of individualism instead of (or perhaps alongside) the forms of individualism described in *Habits of the Heart.*

In this regard, the evidence from activist groups is mixed. The members of Amnesty Group 425 *did* adopt more than a utilitarian individualist view of human rights. Their political commitment was rooted in the solidarity they felt with people in other countries. They were deeply attached to respecting the dignity of every human person. They partook, in short, of the kind of transcendent commitment Durkheim describes. However, some of the time they disavowed the kind of integration of liberty and justice concerns that Durkheim's conceptualization implies. Yet such an integration does seem to be a possibility within American culture. The WOC manifests this possibility explicitly, using human rights language. In addition, the Seaview Greens are individualistic in the sense Lichterman describes, while strongly public-spirited and concerned for economic justice. And in faith-based organizing, concerns for individual empowerment and building community come together in a way that expresses the same spirit.

Participants in community organizing, however, could benefit from greater examination and appreciation of the kind of individualism Durkheim espouses. Faith-based community organizations do not deal much with liberty issues, and it is hard to see how they could do otherwise, at a practical and organizational level, in view of the cultural diversity they contain within them. (Paradoxically, they are far more diverse than human rights groups in the United States—which are largely composed of middle-class whites—even though rights groups work on behalf of cultural minorities while organizing projects generally ignore cultural differences.) Organizing work does adopt a degree of rights language, as we saw in the mayoral march staged by the Milwaukee Innercity Congregations Allied for Hope (MICAH). But I have observed no discussion of the nature and limits of rights, or their relationships, within organizing. To have such discussions as part of training events, yet with no expectation that the organizing projects would do practical work on liberty issues, could be beneficial for organizing and for the tenor of public discourse. The savvy demonstrated by organizers every day could easily be applied to making sure that such discussions did not become divisive. In short, organizing as well as human rights activism needs to, and in my view could, pay more attention to the integration of different kinds of rights and different political agendas.

DOES CONCERN FOR LIBERTY IMPLY CONSTRAINED DISCOURSE?

An argument could be made that principles of liberty inherently lead toward a fairly constrained mode of discourse. Progressives tend, for good reason, to be committed to tolerance and equal rights for all religious and nonreligious traditions. The value of individual ethical autonomy is central to progressive politics. So is the ideal of democracy, which implies that procedural principles, such as the right of every citizen to work on behalf of his or her political agenda, should be observed even when that is detrimental to the success of the substantive political purposes we prefer. All of these core ideas about liberty can be interpreted in ways that require strong discursive constraints. Some social critics—Richard Rorty, for example, as we will see in the next chapter—even believe that the maintenance of liberty requires stronger constraints, such as embargoes on religious language, moralism, and transcendent talk. One can go so far as to see any highly structured philosophical or political perspective as a danger. In such a view, issue links are potentially a danger to liberty, as are links to civil-societal traditions and passionate, transcendent discourse. The fact that the right engages in more expansive discourse than the left, according to this view, is connected to the intolerant and antiliberty strands in its thinking. It may be unfortunate that conservatives thereby get the discursive high ground, but that is the price liberals pay for their principles. We saw a hint of this kind of analysis in the privacy account sometimes given for constrained discourse in Amnesty: that no one should be put in the position of having to make accountable the nature and grounds for their commitment to human rights.

The case studies in this book and observations of other grassroots activists in the United States do not support this argument. The experience of faith-based organizing indicates that talking about religion need not lead to intolerance or divisiveness. This may be even more the case when secular cultural traditions are linked to politics. Amnesty, for instance, manages to be moralistic and transcendent without yielding any ground whatsoever in its support of liberty. And within Amnesty, the privacy account was not entirely believable. Did respect for the freedom of conscience of one's coworkers for human rights really demand that grounds for individual commitments never be discussed? There were clearly mixed feelings about that claim within Amnesty; and to me as an observer, looking at the actual persons in Group 425—their style and predilections—it seemed implausible that conversations about the grounds for human rights commitment would have become attacks on freedom of conscience. Organizing is a counterexample in a different sense: while it does not pursue a liberty agenda it manages to remain culturally diverse and tolerant. Organizing projects may not support reproductive rights, but they are neutral on this issue, strongly promote understanding across lines of religious difference, and operate under a discursive rule prohibiting claims for the superiority of any particular faith.[26] In short, the work of many local activist groups of quite varied politics often has expansive consequences, such as bringing the links between politics and civil-societal culture out into the open, without manifesting totalitarian proclivities.

Local groups are, in fact, the best place for this to happen, since strong nonideological factors—personal relationships, a collective history, and shared practical goals and activities—are at work in this setting. Groups like Amnesty might, for example, experiment with creating occasional contexts for discussions that are more expansive. Such discussions inherently could not result in the adoption of organizational positions. Differences would arise, and the discussions would have to be carried on under a strong discursive self-discipline of respect for the diverse civil-societal bases for commitment to human rights. Disagreements would have to be expressed in something like the way, as we saw in chapter 6, that was manifested by Sarah Browning—one that respects and tolerates differences. But gains from such discussions would accrue not only to the groups holding them but to any others in which the group's participants became involved.

In light of Durkheim's perspective, fear that expansive discourse would undermine liberty seems misguided. Attachment to the freedom and dignity of the individual is a social product. It comes from the history of our culture and specifically the development of *la personne humaine* as a shared object of worship. This attachment is passionate and transcendent, rooted in our experiences and civil-societal lives, and in order to make any sense in contemporary society must link concerns for justice with continued allegiance to the human rights articulated in the eighteenth century.

In journalistic parlance, "liberals" are people who take something like the ACLU's position on civil liberties and lifestyle issues but also favor government activism in economic life, while conservatives are the reverse. Many Americans, of course, combine their views in patterns that do not fit easily on this continuum. But in addition, recently there have been a number of political writings suggesting that the left/right distinctions of old are now obsolete—that, for instance, a political stance combining free-market economics with pro-choice and pro-gay rights stances is the most logical. To be sure, there is historical warrant for such a stance, particularly in the libertarian tradition. But most progressives are not persuaded that they should abandon their traditional economic views, and Durkheim's argument provides cogent reasons why: that individual freedom and dignity are incomplete, precarious, and partly dependent on wealth if economic justice issues are not addressed.

Durkheim's vision is extremely plausible descriptively or sociologically. There is no doubt that individualism is a cultural and collective phenomenon, a product of history, and that individual freedom comes not from the absence of society and culture but from the kind of society one lives in and the resources for freedom it provides. These resources are both cultural and social-structural. An organizational situation in which authority is not overly centralized, and in which the associational sphere can prosper and act independently, is conducive to freedom. The same is true of a cultural situation in which the traditions providing bases for making ethical and political evaluations cannot be controlled by any person or organization.

With regard to the acceptability of Durkheim's kind of individualism in the United States, the evidence, as we have seen, is mixed. There are bases for both optimism and pessimism about the capacity of Americans to adopt such an individualism, but it seems plausible to say that there is at least a possibility that it could influence public discourse. In my view the effort to communicate this vision needs to be made—in fact, is an indispensable task for progressives—even if success is not certain. The other forms of individualism that circulate in America, and the other bases on which Americans commonly support liberty, are downright harmful. They involve putting forward stances that actually undermine concerns for economic justice and community. On the other hand, to take a stance like the communitarians and make the critique of individualism the center of one's politics does not seem likely to succeed in America—or, more important, to accord with progressive goals—since progressives usually back individualistic causes ranging from civil liberties to reforming gender roles. That is, progressives in the United States are usually radical democrats, with a strong commitment to expanding the scope of liberty and self-government. Thus neither acceptance of the usual kinds of individualism, nor anti-individualism, seems a possible or appropriate approach for progressive politics. Instead, an individualism like Durkheim's that brings liberty and justice together is required. To develop greater understanding of this kind of individualism; to apply that individualism to how progressives think and talk, among themselves and in public, about the issues of the day; and to build public support for this version of individualism—these are urgent cultural tasks for progressive politics in contemporary America.

Chapter 8

INTEGRATING CULTURE AND POLITICS

What kind of relationships between culture and progressive politics are possible and desirable? I will first clarify this question by examining its context—the increased salience of cultural themes within late-twentieth-century American politics—and distinguishing between two different senses in which politics can be cultural. Then I will present some suggestions for how the cultural dimension of progressive politics could be enriched.

THE QUESTION OF POLITICS AND CULTURE

Cultural Factors in Recent U.S. Politics

Since the 1960s, there has been a flowering of social movements with what is sometimes tagged a "cultural" or "noneconomic" focus—for example, gay and lesbian rights initiatives, feminism when it challenges traditional family patterns and gender roles, and movements concerned with ethnic and racial identity. The new movements have generally pushed for what their opponents describe as relativism, in that they challenge received certainties about the right way to live, promoting new choices in private as well as public life. Some of the new movements are also distinguished by their concern with "identity," that is, with asserting the particularity of their group and the value and distinctiveness of its culture and way of life.

During this same period, in academic venues, the rise of postmodernist thinking represents a parallel trajectory. Traditional modernist ideas focus on striving for maximum universality in how one expresses values, whereas postmodernist perspectives point out the value of cultural specificity. Postmodernists argue that attempts to achieve universality can lead to emptying out everything that makes culture powerful and reducing discourse to some ghastly moral Esperanto. Even worse, from the point of view of postmodernists, attempts at universalizing discourse are dangerous and potentially oppressive, since they obfuscate the one-sidedness and partiality of the hegemonic perspective that claims universality.[1]

The same ideas have had a strong influence in other intellectual movements as well. Contemporary developments in pragmatist social philosophy, most visibly in the work of Richard Rorty and Michael Walzer, draw on these ideas, as does the postliberal theology of Stanley Hauerwas and the ethical and social philosophy of Alasdair MacIntyre. Both Hauerwas and MacIntyre are deeply critical of liberalism and of modernist universalism. The former they blame for the deficits in public discourse found by the authors of *Habits of the Heart,* and the latter they take to be a surrender to the Enlightenment agenda.

These new movements have not gone unchallenged. Although the left pioneered the idea that the personal is political, the religious right also took up questions of personal life, leading to the conflicts commonly dubbed "culture wars."[2] Traditionalists in academe have staged a parallel struggle against postmodernist and relativist currents. And many social critics worry that our public discourse—on the left as well as the right—may be too floridly values-based, with cultural factors encouraging forms of political engagement that destroy civility and democracy and undermine the chances of progressive politics. As over against "identity politics," some leftists are reasserting the traditional universalism and economic focus of the left. Thus there are ongoing debates about whether it is a good or bad thing when culture plays a larger role in American politics.

What Does It Mean for Politics to Be Cultural?

Such debates, however, often take place without much clarity about the kind of link between culture and politics under discussion. Consider, first, two political perspectives as articulated in the late 1990s.

Ellen Willis, a radical journalist, has described three main paradigms or tendencies on the left. (She cautions that any particular person or group may represent a mixture of these.) The first comprises progressives single-mindedly concerned to improve the distribution of income and wealth. In Willis's view, people operating within this paradigm put aside too many cultural questions and have a constricted idea of human liberation. She is no more pleased with a second tendency, which includes communitarians and the "politics of meaning" advocated by the progressive Jewish magazine *Tikkun*. *Habits of the Heart* would presumably be an example of this tendency, which she labels "moral utopianism." This approach, she thinks, is excessively focused on moral reform and is often quite conservative with regard to gender and sexuality. Also, like the first, it is often elitist, failing to question the power of the highly educated, mostly white male leaders who design our public policies and social arrangements. The heroine of Willis's story is the third paradigm, cultural radicalism. This approach makes freedom, including sexual freedom, central to politics, and looks toward cooperative self-government and creativity. This tradition has been expressed in anarchism and radical feminism. It seeks equality, not as the main goal, but as a means for freedom. Willis is certainly committed to seeking economic justice, but she is first of all a cultural radical and radical democrat.[3]

A very different view is found in the thinking of Todd Gitlin, a sociologist who was a leader in Students for a Democratic Society during the 1960s. He represents a reaction against the focus on particularity found in some recent social movements and in postmodernism, and wants to reassert the modernist universalism that until a generation ago was characteristic of progressive politics. While his critique is similar to those often made of incivility and intolerance in conservative cultural politics, Gitlin is concerned with the sins of the left—above all, the bane of identity politics. His basic criticism is that this kind of politics hurts the chances of creating and sustaining the alliances that are crucial to the success of left-of-center politics. In addition, identity politics has too strong a focus on culture, on goals of pride, distracting us from the economic justice questions that Gitlin takes to be the real issues. Even worse, identity politics is divisive, creating a disassembled jigsaw puzzle of different groups unable to unite or find common ground, each concerned only with its own agenda.[4]

Gitlin makes this argument in *The Twilight of Common Dreams*. The case study that occupies the book's introductory chapter and serves as a paradigm is a conflict over multiculturalism in the Oakland, California, public schools in 1992. His villains, the proponents of extreme multiculturalism, are easy to hate. As Gitlin tells the story, they got their facts wrong and viciously vilified those who disagreed with them. They were not interested in "compromise" but "wanted all or nothing. The debate was . . . about symbols, overloaded with emotional meanings, totems of moral conviction." The concern with symbols introduced irrationalism, substituted for struggling against actual inequalities, and produced "acrimony among potential allies." Such struggles "demoralize the proponents of commonality, choke off the forbearance, the reciprocity and yes, the deal-making that are the prerequisites of a successful democratic politics in a complicated society. . . . Identity politics is a very bad turn, a detour into quicksand."[5]

This argument contains a number of themes. Not only is there supposed to be tolerance, but also a "cool" tone: one should simply negotiate with people one disagrees with politically, refraining from making morally charged arguments. Symbols and emotions are better left out of public discourse, and struggling toward a symbolically defined goal is taken to be at odds with trying for real social change. Since pursuing cultural goals divides progressive forces, it would be better to concentrate on the economic ones that presumably unite them.

The contrast between Willis's and Gitlin's views represents a frequently found polarity in progressive perspectives. On one side progressives are counseled, by Gitlin and others, to focus on economic issues and to engage in constrained discourse. On the other, as in Willis's thinking, the issues are chiefly cultural and they are to be engaged with passion. What makes the argument confusing is that the question of *what kind of issues* progressive politics should address is conflated with that of *how* progressives should carry on public discourse. Both questions raise issues about how to deal with culture, but in a quite different way. The first question has to do with variations in our choice of substantive issues to address. The second concerns variations in modes of discourse. The diagram below puts these two dimensions together.

From the polarity as defined by Gitlin, one might think that the only choice was between Willis's position (possibility A) and his own (possibility D). But this is not so. Identity politics in fact varies tremendously in the modes of discourse it adopts. For example, some gay and lesbian activism is expansive, aiming for fundamentally different ways of think-

Different Ways in Which Politics Can Be Cultural

	Preferred Mode of Political Engagement	
Issues Addressed	Expansive, Richly Cultural	Constrained, Excluding Ethics and Symbolism
"Cultural" (sexuality, gender, etc.)	A: Cultural radicalism, some identity politics (Willis)	B: Negotiation for group interests by culturally defined groups
Economic (equality, welfare, etc.)	C: Morally based politics on economic issues	D: Deal-making on economic issues (Gitlin)

ing about sexuality. This fits in possibility A. On the other hand, gay and lesbian rights can be pursued in a "cool" vein, where advocates make no attempt to say that gay sexuality is equally legitimate ethically, but instead position themselves as representing a bloc of voters that is of significant size, has gotten organized, and wants some of its needs met in return for political support. Within the schema, this fits possibility B. There is little in the mode of discourse of such politics that is different from that of any other group pursuing its interests. Thus we see that cultural issues can be addressed in varying modes. The same is true on the economic side. A progressive economic agenda can be pursued in a narrowly interest-based mode (possibility D), as Gitlin advocates. But one can also seek economic justice in a morally charged and culturally rich way. This is what happens much of the time in faith-based community organizing, which fits in possibility C.

The data in this book indicate that progressives can choose their issues and modes of discourse independently. A focus on economic issues need not imply a culturally anemic way of doing politics. In fact, the importance of expansive discourse and lively cultural practices is arguably *greater* in the economic realm. The forces arrayed against progressive economic proposals, after all, are usually wealthy, powerful, united, and well organized—more so than on "cultural" issues. On economic issues, after all, not just political forces but also the economic power of many corporations work in support of conservative goals, whereas corporations generally remain neutral on cultural questions. Occupying the discursive high ground, calling upon all the life-affirming resources in American culture, is essential to having any chance of success. Unless progressives engage the cultural traditions and debates that bear on how Americans think about economic life and form judgments on economic issues, explicitly addressing ethical issues concerning what kind of economic order our nation should work toward, they are unlikely to garner the public support they need.

HOW CAN PROGRESSIVE POLITICS BE CULTURALLY ROBUST?

Progressives need to attend just as carefully to the cultural dimension of politics when pursuing economic justice as they do in other issue domains. In the remainder of this chapter I will offer some suggestions for doing so. The first point is negative: to discard ways of thinking that lead to ignoring cultural factors. Then I will address issues about the use of expansive versus constrained discourse, and discuss the need for adopting a realistic and critically affirmative stance toward American culture and engaging in wide-ranging dialogue across lines of cultural difference.

Rescuing Cultural Factors from Black Boxes

As was indicated earlier (see the conclusion to part 2), activists and social critics often put political or cultural processes into a "black box." That is, they assume that certain ideas and motivations emerge predictably, automatically, or even naturally from a process that one does not examine or seek to affect. Thus the cultural bases for political discourse and action are treated as if they were something random, or something found privately in each individual. Examples mentioned in earlier chapters include the Christian reform teleology, with its assumption that Christian values are faithful friends of progressive movements; the idea that if one can only ensure fair and equal popular participation in decision making, one does not need to worry about the substantive policies that emerge; the assertion that the agenda of organizing is "whatever the people decide," leaving the nature and basis of the deciding unaccountable; and conceptions of human rights as "obvious" or "self-evident."[6]

Consider, as one more example, how Amnesty International (AI) deals with capital punishment on its web site. Although the site devotes considerable space to this issue, almost all the material is informational: details of impending or recent executions and legislative updates. Surprisingly enough, it is hard to find a document that actually makes the case against capital punishment. "Human Rights v. the Death Penalty," by AI staff member Eric Prokosch, is the one philosophical statement on the site. Even this is written largely in the mode of argument one would use in a legal brief addressed to a court for which the Universal Declaration of Human Rights (UDHR) was the kind of supreme authority the Constitution is for U.S. courts. The statement does not include the kind of moral or political argument that might influence legislative debates. Instead, it supplements legal points with social-scientific arguments against the idea of deterrence and for seeing the death penalty as a form of discrimination. These arguments are sound, but they do not seize the moral high ground. Although it is clear that Prokosch feels ethical passion about capital punishment, the statement is weak on making an ethical (as opposed to legal) case.[7]

Prokosch himself seems aware of this problem: "For Amnesty International, the human rights argument is paramount. But in practice, it is only one of several powerful arguments against the death penalty which need to be part of the national debate. While Amnesty International is making the human rights argument, others need to make the other arguments. Statements from religious leaders, other respected public figures, influential organizations and the news media can create a moral climate in which the legislators will be more willing to vote in a way which they know will be unpopular with many of their constituents." This part of Prokosch's essay reveals his awareness that Amnesty's position is *not* self-evident, not something one can count on being accepted by any person who uses reason and is not blinded by prejudice. Prokosch is evidently not confident that the kind of argument he is making will be widely persuasive. He apparently feels that Amnesty, which is secular, has to piggyback on the moral persuasiveness of religious (and other) leaders and the cultural traditions they can tap into. One might say that Amnesty, being able only to treat culture as a black box, counts on allying itself with cultural practitioners who know how to get inside the box: that is, to appropriate, interpret, communicate, and transform the cultural traditions to which people are most committed.

Why do people put cultural processes in a black box? The most important reason is arguably the influence of what might be termed the "Enlightenment teleology." This is a secular story, but many religious Americans adopt it as well. The story line is that humans have an inbred tendency to come down on the side of progressive values through the exercise of their natural capacities. "Good" values are assumed to be in some way built into our nature: a predictable result of something hardwired into human beings. As a sign of such faith, Saul Alinsky argued for a focus on learning as a core purpose of organizing by quoting Jefferson: "Enlighten the people generally, and tyranny and oppression of body and mind will vanish like spirits at the dawn of day."[8] In Amnesty, the focus on giving and receiving information and the oft-repeated conviction that Amnesty's stances are "obviously" correct manifest a similar confidence that political views can be counted on to take a good turn if people have the right information. This outlook reflects the basic Enlightenment optimism that good social values will emerge naturally once obstacles such as ignorance, prejudice, and superstition are removed. If one holds this belief, one does not need cultural traditions at all, although one may have to fight retrograde ones that sustain bigotry. (This perspective, we should remember, emerged in the historical context of the early modern era, in which religious authorities were often enemies of liberty and justice, and a struggle against received cultural traditions therefore seemed liberative.)

A less radical way of ignoring cultural factors is to assume that one can count on the cultural traditions to which one is attached to help support favored political causes, as for example when participants in organizing, adopting what I have called the "Christian reform teleology," assume that church and synagogue people will have good values. In a secular context, a parallel assumption is evident when activists believe that other Americans will surely reach the same conclusions they do from the democratic principles to which almost all Americans are committed. (Many people combine this belief with the Enlightenment teleology.) Yet another example is the frequently found assumption that family values will help one's cause—that, for example, people who care about children will surely support one's proposal. (Progressives and conservatives are equally likely to make this assumption.) In all these cases, culture becomes a force that one does not systematically examine or try to influence. One merely draws upon the helpful consequences—the outputs of the black box.

There are countercurrents. One of the virtues of postmodernist thought is that it has carried on a systematic campaign against this kind of thinking. In his seminal book, *The Postmodern Condition,* Jean-François Lyotard argues that today "meta-narratives," which means above all the Enlightenment story about human nature and progress, but also includes the Christian reform teleology, are no longer convincing.[9] All legitimation now is local—that is, persuasive only within particular groups of people with common cultural commitments. Lyotard may underestimate the continuing power of meta-narratives, at least in the United States. But it seems clear that arguments for natural rights based in the universals of the human condition are made more hesitantly than they were two centuries ago. And the incredulity Lyotard describes (and favors) is a good thing, helping to temper the frequent American assumption that everyone should do things the way we do, as long as incredulity does not mean loss of faith in the possibility and value of pursuing social and ethical visions.

Postmodernism is not the only intellectual current that can help overcome Enlightenment ideas of natural values. Alasdair MacIntyre argues that there is no way to do rational ethical thinking except by being grounded in a particular tradition.[10] The pragmatist tradition rejects Enlightenment ideas, while also trying to avoid relativism. And Durkheim's reconceptualization of individualism is an attempt to vigorously uphold the political and ethical substance of individualistic values (tempered, to be sure, by aspirations for maintaining community) while totally rejecting any grounding of individualism that does not account for cultural and historical factors. Individual liberty, Durkheim tells us, does not stem from human nature or from destroying collective social and cultural structures, but from a particular line of development of these structures in the modern West.

Ideas that black-box cultural processes discourage progressives from analyzing how the views they hold come into existence. The frequent although usually only implicit assumption is that progressive politics is less driven by cultural factors, and needs less cultural work, than conservative politics. One manifestation of this assumption is that while there is a whole industry of scholars churning out books and articles on the religious right, there is relatively little research on the cultural factors working in favor of progressive politics. This is because the researchers are on the average fairly progressive themselves. They believe that the "wrong" views on political issues are explained by the influence of irrational factors, while implicitly assuming that the "correct" ones happen when people are not seduced into error. Since "correct" ideas are natural, they do not need explaining. But the truth is that all effective movements with more than very narrow goals—whether progressive or conservative—have a strong cultural dimension, including moral language, links to other cultural traditions, narratives, images, and rituals. The problem is that progressives sometimes hold views that make them unaware of the culturality of their own work. Correctly wishing to assert the principle of individual liberty, they sometimes mistakenly tell a story in which liberty is achieved by freeing the individual from all but self-chosen social ties.

Further, social critics and activists sometimes think of the politics of economic issues as more natural than that of cultural issues. It is obvious that views inimical to gay rights need to be challenged or changed by cultural effort. But it is not as obvious that support for economic justice requires cultural work. This is one reason that people fall into conflating the cultural versus economic dimension of issues to be addressed with the dimension of expansive or richly cultural versus constrained modes of discourse.

It is easy to think of material "interests" as a natural phenomenon. To be sure, economic issues are very practical.[11] But interests do not come into existence without cultural work. People need to develop a concept of their interests and learn to conceptualize their own experience in relation to that concept. To see this, one need only recall how much cultural effort community organizing devotes to imbuing participants with a robust sense of their "self-interest" and convincing them that pursuing it is a legitimate part of public life. More generally, many Americans profess to believe that self-interest is the natural wellspring of human behavior. Yet in fact enormous energy goes into inculcating this supposedly natural phenomenon: schools, sports, television, and print media constantly encourage Americans to conceive of life using the model of competitive individualism. Thus self-interest becomes articulate and politically relevant through cultural processes. The same is true of the sense of injustice, when applied to economic inequality—such a sense does not emerge automatically from oppression. That it is right and sensible to become involved in social movements challenging injustice requires yet another cultural leap.

In sum, progressives need to be aware of cultural factors and get involved in substantive discussions about justice and liberty, the kind of America one should hope for, and the values that should guide progressive politics. To avoid black-boxing cultural factors does not require either liking or disliking the traditions one encounters. What it *does* require is that progressives be conscious of how they are drawing upon or struggling with these traditions, and that they talk among themselves about this part of their work. This is especially important, although harder to do, with regard to economic issues.

Issues about Expansive and Constrained Discourse

Many social-critical issues about the role of culture in politics concern the strengths and weaknesses of constrained and expansive discourse. Let us examine a few of these issues.

Progressive politics varies in the "temperature" of its discourse, the degree to which it links varied issues, and the connections it makes to civil-societal traditions. On all these dimensions expansive discourse has its critics. In the fifteen years after World War II, a group of prominent historians and social scientists, reacting to fascism, the Holocaust, and postwar McCarthyism, developed several related lines of thinking manifesting fear of popular mobilizations. Richard Hoftstadter, Daniel Bell, William Kornhauser, and Seymour Martin Lipset were central figures in this intellectual trajectory. For these intellectuals, passionate politics, ideology, and anything (including religion) that might be construed as irrational were enemies of healthy politics. They advocated instead the political center, interest-based politics, and pragmatic problem solving by elites. As pointed out by Michael Rogin, a critic of this strand of social theory, writings on McCarthyism often conflated it with populism. "Populism" thus became a term with stronger connotations of irrationalism and threats to freedom than of pursuit of social justice. Yet these thinkers were not right-wingers. On the whole, they favored a moderate liberalism or even social democracy. But they were more concerned with styles of political engagement than with substantive issues. Out of that concern they feared popular mobilizations of the left and right almost equally—and in fact stressed the similarities between such mobilizations.[12]

Today similar views may be encouraged by unhappy memories of red-hot discourse in the 1960s, which was sometimes a barrier to effective cultural work, and by the intolerant proposals of some religious right leaders. Perhaps the most articulate proponent of constrained discourse at the turn of the millennium is pragmatist philosopher Richard Rorty. Rorty argues strenuously for what he calls "banal politics." In striking contrast to the authors of *Habits of the Heart*, Rorty gets worried when public engagement, idealism, and altruism run high. He is especially skeptical of the most frequent way in which Americans bring civil-societal cultural traditions to bear on politics, which is to use religious ideas to help address public issues. Religious influences on politics, in Rorty's view, are likely to promote intolerance, division, incivility, absolutism, and irrationality. Rorty's worries are shared by some activists, such as the Amnesty members who said that there would be grave internal conflict if discursive constraints were loosened.[13]

Rorty favors keeping not only religion but any kind of perspective involving ultimate or metaphysical commitments out of politics. To preserve democracy, he believes, it is advisable to exclude all questions of philosophy and religion from public discussion. Interpreting the perspective of fellow philosopher John Rawls, but also expressing his own views, he says that "a liberal democracy will not only exempt opinions on [questions about the meaning of life, or God, or human nature] from legal coercion, but also aim at disengaging discussions of such questions from discussions of social policy." He advocates "a society that encourages the 'end of ideology.'" In Rorty's view, we should conceptualize public life using the model of the "bazaar." That is, in the public sphere we should simply work out the best deal we can, in a purely instrumental way, confining to private life our efforts at forging moral community and expressing our true values.

While Rorty has a special fear of religion, he objects to secular but transcendent discourse almost as much. Kant is almost as unacceptable as Ignatius. From a sociological standpoint this shows consistency, in that the cultural processes used by religions—transcendence, invocation of sacredness, ritual, and so on—are as much responsible for their political impact as the particular content of their worldviews, and can be used by nonreligious worldviews as well.[14]

Yet it is far from clear that transcendent points of view, as they function in America, are inimical to democracy. Consider first the secular scene. A significant number of Americans consider themselves socialists, and yet totalitarian Leninist Americans who truly believe in abolishing civil liberties could be counted on the fingers of a hand or two. To take a transcendent but secular view with a wider following, think of the somewhat Durkheimian individualism that can be found in Amnesty International, the American Civil Liberties Union (ACLU), and other organizations. This sort of individualism is absolutist and has much in common with religious frameworks, and would therefore be suspect on Rorty's premises. Yet its absolutism is probably, as Durkheim argued, a better protection for freedom than any more compromising, more utilitarian, less transcendent grounding for democratic values. What other tradition can we rely upon for advocating liberty at moments when utilitarian grounds are weak, such as wartime or periods of social disorder?[15]

Turning to religion, Rorty's analysis of its implications seems like a caricature. His examples, such as Ignatius, are taken from the authoritarian end of the spectrum of religious thinkers and are quite removed in time and culture from the contemporary American religious scene. As a pragmatist he might be expected to analyze the actual functioning of ideas when applied to specific situations. Instead, he conceptualizes religion in an abstract and *a priori* way, as if it were a single entity following the worst hypothetical consequences of what he regards as its central principles. Through this lens he sees religion as an enemy of democracy.

In a parallel vein, one could argue that connecting religion to politics, even in the name of progressive goals, is dangerous because it opens the door to the fanaticism of the religious right. The many descriptions of culture-wars atrocities that one encounters in progressive and scholarly periodicals usually portray this danger in somewhat the same way Gitlin pictures identity politics.

However, the worries of Rorty and many culture-wars analysts are contradicted by the best evidence about the ways in which religions work, most of the time, in late-twentieth-century America. To be sure, there are authoritarian and antidemocratic strands within American religion. Some religious right groups are quite intolerant. But evidence from systematic research suggests that the real base of support for the religious right agenda is small—perhaps 6 percent of the American public—and that even among evangelicals and fundamentalists few ordinary believers are interested in enlisting in culture wars. The reason for this limited support is that the potential for intolerance in some American theologies is countered, in actual American activism and among actual American adherents of these theologies, by other strands that are stronger, such as commitment to individual conscience and democratic procedures. Religious traditions, even the ones drawn upon by the religious right, contain powerful strands that counter intolerance. In particular, theologically conservative Protestantism generally stresses voluntary and personal decisions in matters of conscience. The ideal of freedom of conscience is also deeply embedded in democratic political traditions that influence religious traditionalists along with other Americans. As a result of these religious and political influences, few Christians have much sympathy with inquisitors. The more intolerant proposals of the religious right have not been able to gather mass support, and its shrill mode of politics has alienated even those who have some sympathy with its goals. Alan Wolfe, in his portrait of middle-class moral thinking—and people who consider themselves middle-class make up the vast majority of Americans—shows a strong aspiration for unity and dislike for extremes, and a large degree of common ground in terms of shared basic values that can inform political discussion.[16]

The evidence in this book points in the same direction. Faith-based community organizing shows none of the baleful qualities that Rorty expects from incursion of religion into public discourse, and Amnesty does not have the absolutist character one might expect from Rorty's account of what happens when transcendent perspectives enter politics. Nor have I seen these qualities in other progressive groups with relatively expansive discourse that I have observed. On the contrary, activist groups typically value democracy more than their particular goals.

In short, there are two factors that make the risks from transcendent politics, issue links, and links to civil-societal culture less than Rorty and other social critics imagine. One is that the cultural traditions that worry them are in fact ambiguous, containing potentialities for tolerance as well as absolutism. The other is the success of liberal politics over the past century. For example, in contrast to the situation only a few decades earlier, at the beginning of the twenty-first century antisemitic statements meet with condemnation in all but the most marginal circles. That government should not promote Protestantism over Catholicism, or work against any religions other than the few demonized as cults, or discriminate against atheists is accepted even by most of the religious right. The basic secularity of government, and of the business world, has become assumed and accepted. In the realm of secular ideology, the repression of dissent carried on in the decade after World War II, through blacklists, loyalty oaths, jailings, and firings, seems unlikely to recur. Although the need for the ACLU's vigilance is not gone, overall the state of civil liberties is considerably healthier at the turn of the millennium than it was fifty years earlier.

While the risks of expansive discourse are quite limited, the potential gains are substantial. Chapter 7 argued that many of the problems blamed on weakness in civil society might better be attributed to weakness in the links—cultural and organizational—between civil society and politics. Progressive cultural work, in my view, should try to strengthen these links. In effect, that means being an advocate of radical democracy and the broadest possible politicization of ordinary Americans, since most Americans live far more in civil society than in the realm of explicit politics. Links between politics and civil society mean that more Americans will be interested in becoming active and have a context in which it is possible for them to do so. The energy and concern they invest in politics will be greater, and they will be more likely to develop the capacity to be articulate participants in public discourse. Links between civil society and politics also increase the likelihood of nonindividualistic values flourishing in public life, since these are more present in civil society than in Washington politics.

Nonetheless, to engage in a culturally rich politics is to take the risk that the cultural commitments of ordinary Americans could work against one's cause. Progressives should accept this risk partly out of a realistic hope that these commitments will work in their favor more often than not, partly because strategies for social change that bypass ordinary Americans are unlikely to succeed, and partly because democracy is as fundamental to progressive values as economic justice and civil liberties. A politics worth having is going to be accountable to Americans in all their variety and with all their values and passions. If progressives do not put culture in a black box, they will know that the current form of American cultural commitments is not a force of nature but the outcome of cultural work. On occasion, progressives will challenge civil-societal cultural traditions and endeavor to change them, or at least the ways in which they are understood and used. But this can happen in a useful way only within a basically affirmative stance toward American culture.

Adopting a Realistic and Critically Affirmative Stance toward American Culture and Engaging in Dialogue across Lines of Cultural Difference

To be realistic means assessing the actual cultural traditions found in the United States and the range of political implications they actually support, as opposed to limiting one's analysis to stereotypes or unexamined assumptions. Richard Rorty's way of thinking about the role of religion, described earlier, caricatures American cultural reality. On the other hand, the hopeful assumptions of the Christian reform teleology can only be sustained by putting on blinders. There may be a "tilt" toward social justice and concern for the dignity of the human person in Christian traditions, but the variety of social interpretations of which Christianity has proved capable suggests that it is not realistic to rely on Christians adopting any particular interpretation.

To be critically affirmative means avoiding the kind of populism that questions almost nothing in American cultural traditions, sometimes not even the ways those traditions are currently understood. Robert Westbrook correctly criticizes those he describes as "radical traditionalists," such as Jean Bethke Elshtain, for their inability "to clearly distinguish the features of traditional mediating institutions which they find indispensable to human welfare from those that are not."[17]

But progressives often have a harder time adopting an affirmative relationship to American cultural traditions. Indeed, these traditions are not always progressives' friends. It is reasonable that cultural radicals would be alienated from the worship of the traditional family that is common in the United States. The alliance of the Christian Coalition with Republicans representing the interests of wealth is off-putting, to say the least. But sometimes progressives denigrate the actually existing cultural forms that command the allegiance of ordinary Americans on the basis of prejudice and stereotype. Many secular progressives, like Rorty, hide from themselves the potential for an affirmative relationship with religious traditions. They also seem insufficiently aware of the continuing power of the tradition of radical democracy—a tradition that is still deeply resonant for many Americans. Or else, such progressives are uncomfortable with this tradition. It has the potential, which many intellectuals find worrisome, of inspiring in ordinary people a passionate and moralistic involvement that does not lend itself to an end of ideology or to letting policy experts work out the "best" policy directions quietly and without political "interference."

Whatever the obstacles, only by making connections with the life-affirming aspects of American culture can progressive politics succeed. No matter how much progressives may find wrong in contemporary American values and attitudes, they are almost sure to be drawing extensively on indigenous American culture. The areas of convergence often become most apparent in action. In fact, activists are likely to have a more positive view of mass culture than social critics. An activist knows from concrete, daily experience that many Americans are public spirited and have a deep concern to preserve and strengthen the bonds of solidarity and community that potentially unite Americans. Thus being active is one of the best ways to sustain an affirmative relationship with American culture.

We have mentioned the postmodernist emphasis on cultural particularity. This perspective is absolutely correct in saying that an attempt to be universal can result in losing all the power and value of cultural forms. Yet it is still necessary to justify one's claims to cultural others if one is to get beyond a politics that simply bargains with others on the basis of the numbers and power of one's group. Fortunately, that is possible. American culture is not as "decentered" as some intellectuals believe, and cultural others are typically different only in some respects. Furthermore, one can, like Milwaukee Innercity Congregations Allied for Hope (MICAH) in its housing march, articulate claims in terms of the specific cultural traditions that command one's primary allegiance, but also translate claims into the terms of other traditions. By doing this, one accepts the reality and value of American multiculturality and engages in dialogue across lines of cultural difference. For secular people, this means treating religious traditions with care and respect. For people of religious faith, it means dealing with other religions, and even more importantly with secularity, as perspectives with their own integrity and without which America would be poorer.

Moving in the direction of more expansive discourse is not easy and entails risks. One obstacle is that it requires a certain degree of organizational altruism. What is in the best interests of a particular organization is not always the best contribution to achieving the broader goals of the organization's participants and supporters. Immediate victories help build one's organization, but attaining them sometimes involves narrowing or compromising one's goals to the degree that it is no longer clear whether the victories advance the social vision participants hold. Expansive modes of discourse are essential for the development of progressive politics as a whole and for changing the terms of public debate, but they are not always the best for winning particular short-term struggles, expanding an organization's contributor base, and minimizing risks of conflict within the organization.

Sometimes expansive discourse is impossible or inappropriate. During the war in Indochina, broad coalitions developed that involved people as different as the head of the Socialist Workers Party and the CEO of the Bank of America. These coalitions would not have been promising sites for expansive discourse, but they were one ingredient in popular mobilization against the war. Even when such practical considerations are absent, expansive discourse can go to extremes that are harmful. A politics that constantly ran at a very high ethical temperature could become intolerant or turn into a politics of witness that made no difference to the world. Addressing all the issues, all the time—as opposed to finding occasions to talk about broader social visions and situating specific projects within a broader agenda of social change—would destroy the focus or else fracture most activist organizations. A politics that tried to draw all of its principles directly from civil-societal traditions, without respect for the specificity of politics, could end up with absurdities such as trying to use religious scriptures as codes of law.

Perhaps the most immediate drawback of expansive discourse is that it can slow down action. The constant press of daily activities makes the efficiency rationale for constraint alluring. The urgency of these activities, however, should not be overestimated. The United States does not appear to be on the threshold of either fascism or a radical progressive transformation. The immediate issues progressives face are not so ultimate that one should leave aside tasks required for a long-term approach to social change. Such tasks include the political education and development of activists, helping them develop cultural capacities for involvement in public life. These tasks also include building stable, coherent, independent institutions; strengthening the political impact of civil society; and carrying out an ideological struggle for the allegiance of American citizens. Such tasks require a significant degree of expansive discourse.

The potential risks of expansive discourse have been extensively described by social critics and by the activists we have seen articulating accounts for constraint. For instance, a more culturally engaged politics can increase the risks of division within an organization or among different groups of progressives.

Despite all these considerations, as we look back at the trends of the last quarter of the twentieth century, it is hard to see how progressives could have fared much worse than they have in the politics of economic issues. Caution and constrained discourse have not paid off. This is an argument for trying more risky approaches in these early years of the twenty-first century. Progressives are unlikely to do better in the future without effective mobilization in social movements and third parties. But cultural work is equally essential: there is little hope of recent political trends reversing unless progressives engage with great seriousness and care the moral issues that arise in discussions about equality, economic democracy, the role of government, and other basic questions about the kind of economic order America ought to have. This kind of attention to the ethical dimension of economic life is not impossible or something of interest only to philosophers and clergy. It is what workers did when they made the English working class; what radical trade unions have done over and over again in the United States; what populist and poor people's movements have done; and what the civil rights movement did. It is what progressives need to do again, in new ways to respond to new times. Only if those of us who hope for vastly greater economic justice than America currently provides are as culturally attuned as conservatives, take the necessity of forming human values as seriously in the realm of economic issues as of cultural ones, and engage the cultural traditions that Americans care about will we be able to assist in the birth of a better nation.

Appendix A

RESULTS FROM TWO NATIONAL SURVEYS OF CONGREGATION-BASED COMMUNITY ORGANIZING

In 1994 I conducted a survey of congregation-based community organizing projects in the United States. In that survey I sent a questionnaire to all ninety projects active at that time. About two-thirds responded; for the remainder, I obtained more limited information from the Catholic Campaign for Human Development (CCHD) and the networks.[1] In late 1999 and early 2000, I was the consultant for a survey sponsored by Interfaith Funders, which provides considerable financial support to faith-based organizing. This survey produced returns from 75 percent of the 133 local projects active in early 2000. The new survey asked many of the same questions as the earlier one, allowing one to compare the state of faith-based organizing in 1994 and 2000. In the following account, the national figures are projections from the respondents to the entire field of organizations.

The field has clearly grown: there are 48 percent more local organizations than there were six years earlier. Actually, the growth is greater than this figure indicates, since the average size of the projects has increased from twenty to twenty-six congregations. (Some of the networks have followed a systematic policy of merging nearby affiliates in order to create organizations with more capacity to address public policy issues. Absent this policy, the number of organizations would have grown more but their size would not have grown as much.) As a result, the total number of congregations involved in the local organizations has grown from approximately 1,800 in 1994 to an estimated 3,515 in early 2000, a 95 percent increase. However, in other respects the field has not changed greatly: the ethnic and religious makeup of the organizations, for instance, is roughly the same as before. I will therefore refer to the 1994 survey results only where they provide information not collected in 2000 or where a significant shift has taken place over the period between the two surveys.

These congregations are official members of the local organizations. This is not just a paper membership or endorsement, since organizing projects charge their member congregations significant dues and also expect major contributions of time and energy. In 1994 the number of adherents in the member congregations, on average, totaled about seventeen thousand per organizing project. Nationwide, these figures indicate that in 1994 about 1.53 million Americans belonged to congregations involved in this kind of organizing. The number of individual adherents was not asked in the new survey, but if the average size of member congregations has remained the same, they now comprise 2.99 million Americans. Naturally the majority of these people are not involved personally, but in member congregations there is typically a steady stream of information and exhortation with regard to the organizing work. The idea that faith should be connected to the public realm and the congregation to its neighborhood is articulated and argued for repeatedly. For crucial occasions such as large public meetings, pressure is put on most members, often by personal solicitation, to turn out. And many members are interviewed in the kind of one-on-one's Joan Hauser conducted (see chapter 2). Therefore the organizing process touches in a significant way many of these people.

What about more substantial kinds of involvement in organizing? "Core teams" like the ones in Milwaukee Innercity Congregations Allied for Hope, or some equivalent structure, were normative in almost all the local organizations and were reported to be operative, in 1994, in 45 percent of congregations nationwide. Such teams comprise anywhere from six to twenty (or even more) persons; if we take ten as a conservative estimate of the average, about 8,100 people nationwide were members of core teams in 1994. Unfortunately we do not have comparable data from the new survey.

The cadre of people who are actually doing volunteer work on a regular basis (belong to a work committee, for instance) reported in the survey averages 179 per organization, or 23,768 nationwide. In 1994, the organizations ran an average of four local training events (typically a half or full day) per year, with a combined attendance of 292; thus an estimated 26,280 people per year nationally were getting exposure to this kind of training. These events are usually provided by the organization's consultant. The training typically includes considerable blocks of time devoted to learning skills and techniques—how to do a one-on-one interview, how to "cut" an issue, how to analyze the power structure of one's local community, and so on. But they put even more emphasis on learning new ideas, terms, languages, and forms of discourse. All of the networks also provide longer, more intensive residential training retreats ranging from five to ten days. These are powerful experiences, sometimes inducing a kind of conversion. The new survey did not ask about one-day trainings, but it did ask about these longer events. An average of 169 persons per organization, or 22,644 nationally, have had this kind of training. Overall, these figures show an impressive level of involvement and also of investment by community organizations in the development of individual participants.[2]

The budgets of church-based community organizations are high by comparison with most social movement organizations. They average about $171,454, for an estimated national total of nearly $23 million. This is tiny on a corporate scale and modest in comparison with nationwide, professionalized, direct-mail organizations such as the Sierra Club. But as a budget for the work of grassroots social change, in comparison with the resources going to such work in other movements, it is a very substantial sum. Salaries for organizers are high by the standards of social change work: typically $40,000 or more, and higher in high-cost cities, for a lead organizer. Such salaries reflect the understanding that organizing is a profession that demands high skills and levels of performance. And in fact, organizers are typically experienced; a lead organizer has usually had several years of previous experience in assisting roles, has been trained and vetted by a network, and is a mature and seasoned person in her or his thirties or forties, with considerable skills and savvy. By offering salaries that a person can really live on for the long term, community organizations can attract numerous candidates from around the country for organizing positions. Since the organizer is not subsidizing the organization (as one would if working at sacrificial wages), the elected leadership has an easier time setting the agenda. Most social change organizations are staff-driven, and of course this is so to some extent in organizing, but less than in other sectors.

In addition to staff, the organizations make major investments in training programs for their participants and pay substantial fees—an average of $19,427 per organization, or about 14 percent of their budgets—to the networks or consulting organizations that assist them in their work. These funds not only pay for training and consulting services from the networks, but also provide the networks with the resources to embark on new directions in organizing and to provide consultation at a low fee to new projects in development.

The sources of the funds used in organizing are diverse. Averaging across all the organizations that responded, currently about 16 percent of the income of the local projects comes from CCHD and another 12 percent from other religious funders. Foundations (community, corporate, and social change) contribute 36 percent. Eighteen percent comes from dues paid by congregations, 14 percent from other local fundraising, and 4 percent from miscellaneous sources. This pattern of fund sources is a significant shift from 1994, when a little over one-third of the funds came from CCHD and a little under one-third from congregational dues.[3] Community organizations typically do not seek or accept public funds, but nowadays they often receive grants from corporate charitable giving programs or foundations. Tapping new sources of funding is one way in which local projects have been able to expand their budgets over the past six years.

What kind of congregations are involved in faith-based organizing?

Viewed as a whole, at the national level, organizing is extremely diverse ethnically and racially: 35 percent of the congregations are predominantly African American, 21 percent Hispanic, 2 percent Asian or Native American, 36 percent European American, and 6 percent interracial. The survey collected data on the predominant ethnicity of congregations, rather than the ethnicity of individual participants. (Since relatively few religious congregations in America are ethnically or racially diverse internally, it is usually reasonable to speak of a black, white, or Hispanic congregation.) These figures may underestimate the presence of Hispanics among *individual* participants, and overestimate the other groups, since predominantly Hispanic congregations involved with organizing are mostly Catholic and therefore tend to be bigger.

The local groups reflect local conditions and vary considerably in degree and kind of diversity. Twenty-seven percent of the projects are highly diverse internally. In these, no single racial/ethnic group (among the four just mentioned) is predominant in a majority of the congregations. But other organizations are almost entirely European American, Hispanic, or African American, partly because of the characteristics of their territories and partly because of the strategies and networks of relationships used in organizing. For whatever reason, 15 percent of the projects might be called "monocultural." In these projects, there is a majority ethnic/racial group and no other group makes up even 10 percent of the congregations.[4] The remaining 58 percent of the local organizations, including MICAH, are in the middle, with one group forming the majority but significant representation of at least one other group. Compared with six years ago, the diversity of local projects has increased somewhat.

The national surveys also requested information on the denominations to which congregations belong.[5] Overall, 33 percent of the congregations are Catholic. Another 34 percent of the congregations belong to "mainline" (that is, theologically liberal or moderate) denominations: Presbyterians, Lutherans, Episcopalians, United Church of Christ, United Methodist Church, and the like. Of the remaining congregations, the bulk are Baptist or affiliated with black denominations, such as the Church of God in Christ or African Methodist Episcopal Church. (Remember that some of the Catholic and mainline Protestant congregations, and many of the Baptist ones, are also predominantly black.)

Christian congregations are the overwhelming majority; only about 2 percent are Jewish, another 2 percent are Unitarian, and a handful belong to other religious groups, such as Muslims and Baha'i. There are a few Mormon congregations, and about 3 percent belong to traditionalist and predominantly white Protestant denominations such as the Evangelical Covenant Church; but the movement is basically composed of Catholics, mainline Protestants, and the black churches. Comparing this with the makeup of the American religious scene at large, the absence of non-Christian groups is not surprising. What *is* striking is that white traditionalist Protestants (evangelicals, fundamentalists, and the like), who comprise over one quarter of the American population, were almost entirely absent from congregation-based community organizing. This discrepancy is felt as a lack by community organizers, and attempts are being made to bring more congregations from this sector of American religion into community organizing.[6] Compared with six years ago, there is a little more religious diversity in organizing, but the change is small and the absence of traditionalist white Protestants is still striking.

The 1999–2000 survey obtained considerable information on the organizers. A little over one-half of the organizations have one or two organizers; amost one-third have three or four; and one-eighth have five or more organizers. Forty-four percent of the organizers are women, 28 percent are black, and 17 percent are Latino/a. Their median age is 41. Religiously, 42 percent are Catholics, 23 percent mainline Protestants, and 14 percent Baptists. Jews are much more evident in the organizer corps than among the congregations, holding down 8 percent of the posts. Aside from that the organizers are fairly similar, religiously and ethnically, to the congregations with which they work.

Overall, the results from the survey indicate a movement with much more diversity and a much broader base than is usually associated with political activism. Whereas many social movements of the left are largely European American and others are based in ethical or racial minorities, faith-based organizing manages to be strongly multiracial. It is also a large and growing movement. While it is far from attaining the kind of scale required to compete for political power nationally—it reaches about 1 percent of Americans and a similar proportion of religious congregations—it operates on a vastly larger scale than other progressive movements with a religious base, or than comparable social justice movements.[7]

Appendix B

A CATHOLIC FRAMEWORK FOR ECONOMIC LIFE

This document was published in 1996 (some editions are dated 1997) by the U.S. Catholic Conference on the occasion of the tenth anniversary of "Economic Justice for All," a pastoral letter by the U.S. Catholic Bishops. Downloaded from <http://www.nccbuscc.org/sdwp/framework/education.htm>.

As followers of Jesus Christ and participants in a powerful economy, Catholics in the United States are called to work for greater economic justice in the face of persistent poverty, growing income gaps, and increasing discussion of economic issues in the United States and around the world. We urge Catholics to use the following ethical framework for economic life as principles for reflection, criteria for judgment and directions for action. These principles are drawn from Catholic teaching on economic life.

TEN POINTS FOR ECONOMIC LIFE

1. The economy exists for the person, not the person for the economy.
2. All economic life should be shaped by moral principles. Economic choices and institutions must be judged by how they protect or undermine the life and dignity of the human person, support the family, and serve the common good.
3. A fundamental moral measure of any economy is how the poor and vulnerable are faring.
4. All people have a right to life and to secure the basic necessities of life (e.g., food, clothing, shelter, education, health care, safe environment, economic security).
5. All people have the right to economic initiative, to productive work, to just wages and benefits, to decent working conditions as well as to organize and join unions or other associations.

6. All people, to the extent they are able, have a corresponding duty to work, a responsibility to provide for the needs of their families, and an obligation to contribute to the broader society.

7. In economic life, free markets have both clear advantages and limits; government has essential responsibilities and limitations; voluntary groups have irreplaceable roles, but cannot substitute for the proper working of the market and the just policies of the state.

8. Society has a moral obligation, including governmental action where necessary, to assure opportunity, meet basic human needs, and pursue justice in economic life.

9. Workers, owners, managers, stockholders and consumers are moral agents in economic life. By our choices, initiative, creativity and investment, we enhance or diminish economic opportunity, community life, and social justice.

10. The global economy has moral dimensions and human consequences. Decisions on investment, trade, aid, and development should protect human life and promote human rights, especially for those most in need wherever they might live on this globe.

Appendix C

DECLARATION OF THE RIGHTS OF MAN AND OF THE CITIZEN

The declaration was approved by the National Assembly of France, 26 August 1789. This translation is provided by the Ministry of Justice, Government of France. Downloaded from <http://www.justice.gouv.fr/anglais/addhc.htm>.

The French people, as represented at the National Assembly, consider that the ignorance, disregard or contempt of human rights are the sole causes of the nation's misfortunes and of the corruption of governments and have resolved to state the natural, inalienable and sacred human rights in a solemn declaration, so that this declaration be a constant reminder to the members of the body politic of their rights and their duties; so that as the actions of the legislative and those of the executive power may be compared at any time with the aim of all political institutions, these actions shall be more respectful of that aim; so that the claims of the citizens, based henceforth on simple and indisputable principles, always be turned towards upholding the Constitution and the common good.

Consequently, the National Assembly acknowledges and declares in the presence of and under the auspices of the Supreme Being, the following rights of man and citizen.

ARTICLE 1

All people shall have equal rights upon birth and ever after. General utility is the only permissible basis for social distinctions.

ARTICLE 2

The aim of all political associations shall be to preserve man's natural and imprescriptible rights. These are the right to freedom, property, safety and the right to resist oppression.

ARTICLE 3

The principle of all sovereignty resides in the Nation. No body or individual may exercise any power other than that expressly emanating from the Nation.

ARTICLE 4

Freedom is the power to do anything which does not harm another: therefore, the only limits to the exercise of each person's natural rights are those which ensure that the other members of the community enjoy those same rights. Legislation only may set these limits.

ARTICLE 5

Only actions harmful to the community may be made illegal. No one may be prevented from doing that which the law does not forbid, nor be forced to do that which the law does not command.

ARTICLE 6

Legislation expresses the overall will. All citizens, either in person or through their representatives, are entitled to contribute to its formation. Legislation must be the same for all, whether it serves to protect or to punish. As all citizens are equal in the eye of the law, positions of high rank, public office and employment are open to all on an equal basis according to ability and without any distinction other than that based on their merit or skill.

ARTICLE 7

A person may be accused, arrested or detained only in the cases specified by law and in accordance with the procedures which the law provides. Those who solicit, forward, carry out or have arbitrary orders carried out shall be punished; however, any citizen summoned or apprehended pursuant to law must obey forthwith; by resisting, he admits his guilt.

ARTICLE 8

Only penalties which are strictly and clearly necessary may be established by law, and no one may be punished other than pursuant to a law established and enacted prior to the offence, and applied lawfully.

ARTICLE 9

As all persons are presumed innocent until declared guilty, force used in making indispensable arrests which exceeds that needed, shall be severely punished by law.

ARTICLE 10

No one may be troubled due to his opinions, whether or not they are on religious issues provided that the expression of these opinions does not disturb the peace.

ARTICLE 11

Free communication of ideas and opinions is one of the most precious human rights; all citizens may therefore speak, write and print freely, though they may be required to answer for abusing this right in cases specified by law.

ARTICLE 12

The protection of the rights of man and the citizen requires a police force; consequently this force is established in the interest of all, not in that of those to whom it has been entrusted.

ARTICLE 13

The maintenance of the police force and administration expenses require public contributions. These contributions are to be borne by the citizens equally according to their resources.

ARTICLE 14

All citizens have the right, either in person or through their representatives, to ascertain the need for the public contributions, to freely authorize these contributions, to monitor their use, and to determine the amount, basis, collection and duration of contributions.

ARTICLE 15

The community has the right to ask any public officer to account for his service.

ARTICLE 16

Any society in which rights are not guaranteed, nor the scope of power determined, has no Constitution.

ARTICLE 17

The right of ownership is an inviolable and sacred right; one may not be deprived of one's property, unless where public need, duly ascertained by law, clearly requires it, and subject to the condition that fair and prior compensation be made.

Appendix D

THE BILL OF RIGHTS AND SUPPORTING DOCUMENTS

The Bill of Rights comprises the first ten amendments to the U.S. Constitution. They were ratified 15 December 1791. Downloaded from <http://www.nara.gov/exhall/charters/billrights/billrights.html>.

I. Congress shall make no law respecting an establishment of religion, or prohibiting the free exercise thereof; or abridging the freedom of speech, or of the press; or the right of the people peaceably to assemble, and to petition the Government for a redress of grievances.

II. A well regulated Militia, being necessary to the security of a free State, the right of the people to keep and bear Arms, shall not be infringed.

III. No Soldier shall, in time of peace be quartered in any house, without the consent of the Owner, nor in time of war, but in a manner to be prescribed by law.

IV. The right of the people to be secure in their persons, houses, papers, and effects, against unreasonable searches and seizures, shall not be violated, and no Warrants shall issue, but upon probable cause, supported by Oath or affirmation, and particularly describing the place to be searched, and the persons or things to be seized.

V. No person shall be held to answer for a capital, or otherwise infamous crime, unless on a presentment or indictment of a Grand Jury, except in cases arising in the land or naval forces, or in the Militia, when in actual service in time of War or public danger; nor shall any person be subject for the same offence to be twice put in jeopardy of life or limb; nor shall be compelled in any criminal case to be a witness against himself, nor be deprived of life, liberty, or property, without due process of law; nor shall private property be taken for public use, without just compensation.

VI. In all criminal prosecutions, the accused shall enjoy the right to a speedy and public trial, by an impartial jury of the State and district wherein the crime shall have been committed, which district shall have been previously ascertained by law, and to be informed of the nature and cause of the accusation; to be confronted with the witnesses against him; to have compulsory process for obtaining witnesses in his favor, and to have the Assistance of Counsel for his defence.

VII. In suits at common law, where the value in controversy shall exceed twenty dollars, the right of trial by jury shall be preserved, and no fact tried by a jury, shall be otherwise reexamined in any Court of the United States, than according to the rules of the common law.

VIII. Excessive bail shall not be required, nor excessive fines imposed, nor cruel and unusual punishments inflicted.

IX. The enumeration in the Constitution, of certain rights, shall not be construed to deny or disparage others retained by the people.

X. The powers not delegated to the United States by the Constitution, nor prohibited by it to the States, are reserved to the States respectively, or to the people.

PREAMBLE TO THE BILL OF RIGHTS

Adopted 4 March 1789. Downloaded from <http://www.nara.gov/exhall/charters/billrights/preamble.html>.

The Conventions of a number of the States, having at the time of their adopting the Constitution, expressed a desire, in order to prevent misconstruction or abuse of its powers, that further declaratory and restrictive clauses should be added: And as extending the ground of public confidence in the Government, will best ensure the beneficent ends of its institution.

Resolved by the Senate and House of Representatives of the United States of America, in Congress assembled, two thirds of both Houses concurring, that the following Articles be proposed to the Legislatures of the several States as amendments to the Constitution of the United States, all, or any of which articles, when ratified by three fourths of the said Legislatures, to be valid to all intents and purposes, as part of the said Constitution; viz.

Articles in addition to, and Amendment of the Constitution of the United States of America, proposed by Congress and ratified by the Legislatures of the several States, pursuant to the fifth Article of the original Constitution.

PREAMBLE TO THE CONSTITUTION

Downloaded from <http://www.nara.gov/exhall/charters/constitution/constitution.html>.

We the People of the United States, in Order to form a more perfect Union, establish Justice, insure domestic Tranquility, provide for the common defense, promote the general Welfare, and secure the Blessings of Liberty to ourselves and our Posterity, do ordain and establish this Constitution for the United States of America.

SECOND PARAGRAPH OF THE DECLARATION OF INDEPENDENCE

Downloaded from <http://www.nara.gov/exhall/charters/declaration/declaration.html>.

We hold these truths to be self-evident, that all men are created equal, that they are endowed by their Creator with certain unalienable Rights, that among these are Life, Liberty and the pursuit of Happiness.—That to secure these rights, Governments are instituted among Men, deriving their just powers from the consent of the governed,—That whenever any Form of Government becomes destructive of these ends, it is the Right of the People to alter or to abolish it, and to institute new Government, laying its foundation on such principles and organizing its powers in such form, as to them shall seem most likely to effect their Safety and Happiness. Prudence, indeed, will dictate that Governments long established should not be changed for light and transient causes; and accordingly all experience hath shewn, that mankind are more disposed to suffer, while evils are sufferable, than to right themselves by abolishing the forms to which they are accustomed. But when a long train of abuses and usurpations, pursuing invariably the same Object evinces a design to reduce them under absolute Despotism, it is their right, it is their duty, to throw off such Government, and to provide new Guards for their future security.—Such has been the patient sufferance of these Colonies; and such is now the necessity which constrains them to alter their former Systems of Government. The history of the present King of Great Britain is a history of repeated injuries and usurpations, all having in direct object the establishment of an absolute Tyranny over these States. To prove this, let Facts be submitted to a candid world.

Appendix E

UNIVERSAL DECLARATION OF HUMAN RIGHTS

This declaration was adopted by the General Assembly of the United Nations, 10 December 1948. Downloaded from <http://www.un.org/Overview/rights.html>.

Whereas recognition of the inherent dignity and of the equal and inalienable rights of all members of the human family is the foundation of freedom, justice and peace in the world,

Whereas disregard and contempt for human rights have resulted in barbarous acts which have outraged the conscience of mankind, and the advent of a world in which human beings shall enjoy freedom of speech and belief and freedom from fear and want has been proclaimed as the highest aspiration of the common people,

Whereas it is essential, if man is not to be compelled to have recourse, as a last resort, to rebellion against tyranny and oppression, that human rights should be protected by the rule of law,

Whereas it is essential to promote the development of friendly relations between nations,

Whereas the peoples of the United Nations have in the Charter reaffirmed their faith in fundamental human rights, in the dignity and worth of the human person and in the equal rights of men and women and have determined to promote social progress and better standards of life in larger freedom,

Whereas Member States have pledged themselves to achieve, in co-operation with the United Nations, the promotion of universal respect for and observance of human rights and fundamental freedoms,

Whereas a common understanding of these rights and freedoms is of the greatest importance for the full realization of this pledge,

Now, therefore, THE GENERAL ASSEMBLY

Proclaims this Universal Declaration of Human Rights as a common standard of achievement for all peoples and all nations, to the end that every individual and every organ of society, keeping this Declaration constantly in mind, shall strive by teaching and education to promote respect for these rights and freedoms and by progressive measures, national and international, to secure their universal and effective recognition and observance, both among the peoples of Member States themselves and among the peoples of territories under their jurisdiction.

ARTICLE 1

All human beings are born free and equal in dignity and rights. They are endowed with reason and conscience and should act towards one another in a spirit of brotherhood.

ARTICLE 2

Everyone is entitled to all the rights and freedoms set forth in this Declaration, without distinction of any kind, such as race, colour, sex, language, religion, political or other opinion, national or social origin, property, birth or other status. Furthermore, no distinction shall be made on the basis of the political, jurisdictional or international status of the country or territory to which a person belongs, whether it be independent, trust, non-self-governing or under any other limitation of sovereignty.

ARTICLE 3

Everyone has the right to life, liberty and the security of person.

ARTICLE 4

No one shall be held in slavery or servitude; slavery and the slave trade shall be prohibited in all their forms.

ARTICLE 5

No one shall be subjected to torture or to cruel, inhuman or degrading treatment or punishment.

ARTICLE 6

Everyone has the right to recognition everywhere as a person before the law.

ARTICLE 7

All are equal before the law and are entitled without any discrimination to equal protection against any discrimination in violation of this Declaration and against any incitement to such discrimination.

ARTICLE 8

Everyone has the right to an effective remedy by the competent national tribunals for acts violating the fundamental rights granted him by the constitution or by law.

ARTICLE 9

No one shall be subjected to arbitrary arrest, detention or exile.

ARTICLE 10

Everyone is entitled in full equality to a fair and public hearing by an independent and impartial tribunal, in the determination of his rights and obligations and of any criminal charge against him.

ARTICLE 11

(1) Everyone charged with a penal offence has the right to be presumed innocent until proven guilty according to law in a public trial at which he has had all the guarantees necessary for his defence.

(2) No one shall be held guilty of any penal offence on account of any act or omission which did not constitute a penal offence, under national or international law, at the time when it was committed. Nor shall a heavier penalty be imposed than the one that was applicable at the time the penal offence was committed.

ARTICLE 12

No one shall be subjected to arbitrary interference with his privacy, family, home or correspondence, nor to attacks upon his honour and reputation. Everyone has the right to the protection of the law against such interference or attacks.

ARTICLE 13

(1) Everyone has the right to freedom of movement and residence within the borders of each State.

(2) Everyone has the right to leave any country, including his own, and to return to his country.

ARTICLE 14

(1) Everyone has the right to seek and to enjoy in other countries asylum from persecution.

(2) This right may not be invoked in the case of prosecutions genuinely arising from non-political crimes or from acts contrary to the purposes and principles of the United Nations.

ARTICLE 15

(1) Everyone has the right to a nationality.

(2) No one shall be arbitrarily deprived of his nationality nor denied the right to change his nationality.

ARTICLE 16

(1) Men and women of full age, without any limitation due to race, nationality or religion, have the right to marry and to found a family. They are entitled to equal rights as to marriage, during marriage and at its dissolution.

(2) Marriage shall be entered into only with the free and full consent of the intending spouses.

(3) The family is the natural and fundamental group unit of society and is entitled to protection by society and the State.

ARTICLE 17

(1) Everyone has the right to own property alone as well as in association with others.

(2) No one shall be arbitrarily deprived of his property.

ARTICLE 18

Everyone has the right to freedom of thought, conscience and religion; this right includes freedom to change his religion or belief, and freedom, either alone or in community with others and in public or private, to manifest his religion or belief in teaching, practice, worship and observance.

ARTICLE 19

Everyone has the right to freedom of opinion and expression; this right includes freedom to hold opinions without interference and to seek, receive and impart information and ideas through any media and regardless of frontiers.

ARTICLE 20

(1) Everyone has the right to freedom of peaceful assembly and association.

(2) No one may be compelled to belong to an association.

ARTICLE 21

(1) Everyone has the right to take part in the government of his country, directly or through freely chosen representatives.

(2) Everyone has the right of equal access to public service in his country.

(3) The will of the people shall be the basis of the authority of government; this will shall be expressed in periodic and genuine elections which shall be by universal and equal suffrage and shall be held by secret vote or by equivalent free voting procedures.

ARTICLE 22

Everyone, as a member of society, has the right to social security and is entitled to realization, through national effort and international co-operation and in accordance with the organization and resources of each State, of the economic, social and cultural rights indispensable for his dignity and the free development of his personality.

ARTICLE 23

(1) Everyone has the right to work, to free choice of employment, to just and favourable conditions of work and to protection against unemployment.

(2) Everyone, without any discrimination, has the right to equal pay for equal work.

(3) Everyone who works has the right to just and favourable remuneration ensuring for himself and his family an existence worthy of human dignity, and supplemented, if necessary, by other means of social protection.

(4) Everyone has the right to form and to join trade unions for the protection of his interests.

ARTICLE 24

Everyone has the right to rest and leisure, including reasonable limitation of working hours and periodic holidays with pay.

ARTICLE 25

(1) Everyone has the right to a standard of living adequate for the health and well-being of himself and of his family, including food, clothing, housing and medical care and necessary social services, and the right to security in the event of unemployment, sickness, disability, widowhood, old age or other lack of livelihood in circumstances beyond his control.

(2) Motherhood and childhood are entitled to special care and assistance. All children, whether born in or out of wedlock, shall enjoy the same social protection.

ARTICLE 26

(1) Everyone has the right to education. Education shall be free, at least in the elementary and fundamental stages. Elementary education shall be compulsory. Technical and professional education shall be made generally available and higher education shall be equally accessible to all on the basis of merit.

(2) Education shall be directed to the full development of the human personality and to the strengthening of respect for human rights and fundamental freedoms. It shall promote understanding, tolerance and friendship among all nations, racial or religious groups, and shall further the activities of the United Nations for the maintenance of peace.

(3) Parents have a prior right to choose the kind of education that shall be given to their children.

ARTICLE 27

(1) Everyone has the right freely to participate in the cultural life of the community, to enjoy the arts and to share in scientific advancement and its benefits.

(2) Everyone has the right to the protection of the moral and material interests resulting from any scientific, literary or artistic production of which he is the author.

ARTICLE 28

Everyone is entitled to a social and international order in which the rights and freedoms set forth in this Declaration can be fully realized.

ARTICLE 29

(1) Everyone has duties to the community in which alone the free and full development of his personality is possible.

(2) In the exercise of his rights and freedoms, everyone shall be subject only to such limitations as are determined by law solely for the purpose of securing due recognition and respect for the rights and freedoms of others and of meeting the just requirements of morality, public order and the general welfare in a democratic society.

(3) These rights and freedoms may in no case be exercised contrary to the purposes and principles of the United Nations.

ARTICLE 30

Nothing in this Declaration may be interpreted as implying for any State, group or person any right to engage in any activity or to perform any act aimed at the destruction of any of the rights and freedoms set forth herein.

Appendix F

EXCERPTS FROM THE STATUTE OF AMNESTY INTERNATIONAL

These excerpts are as amended by the Twenty-third International Council Meeting, Cape Town, South Africa, 12–19 December 1997. They include the entire sections on "object and mandate" and "methods," and a small part of the section on "organization." Minor corrections have been made to the text as posted on the Amnesty International web site. Downloaded from <http://www.web.amnesty.org/web/aboutai.nsf/5451236ceac8ca36802567750034ca9a/94f6012357992016802567 7f004b90a5?OpenDocument>. AI index number POL 20/01/95.

OBJECT AND MANDATE

1. The object of Amnesty International is to contribute to the observance throughout the world of human rights as set out in the Universal Declaration of Human Rights.

In pursuance of this object, and recognizing the obligation on each person to extend to others rights and freedoms equal to his or her own, Amnesty International adopts as its mandate:

To promote awareness of and adherence to the Universal Declaration of Human Rights and other internationally recognized human rights instruments, the values enshrined in them, and the indivisibility and interdependence of all human rights and freedoms;

To oppose grave violations of the rights of every person freely to hold and to express his or her convictions and to be free from discrimination and of the right of every person to physical and mental integrity, and, in particular, to oppose by all appropriate means irrespective of political considerations:

a) the imprisonment, detention or other physical restrictions imposed on any person by reason of his or her political, religious or other conscientiously held beliefs or by reason of his or her ethnic origin, sex, colour, language, national or social origin, economic status, birth or other status, provided that he or she has not used or advocated violence (hereinafter referred to as 'prisoners of conscience'); Amnesty International shall work towards the release of and shall provide assistance to prisoners of conscience;

b) the detention of any political prisoner without fair trial within a reasonable time or any trial procedures relating to such prisoners that do not conform to internationally recognized norms;

c) the death penalty, and the torture or other cruel, inhuman or degrading treatment or punishment of prisoners or other detained or restricted persons, whether or not the persons affected have used or advocated violence;

d) the extrajudicial execution of persons whether or not imprisoned, detained or restricted, and "disappearances," whether or not the persons affected have used or advocated violence.

METHODS

2. In order to achieve the aforesaid object and mandate, Amnesty International shall:

a) at all times make clear its impartiality as regards countries adhering to the different world political ideologies and groupings;

b) promote as appears appropriate the adoption of constitutions, conventions, treaties and other measures which guarantee the rights contained in the provisions referred to in Article 1 hereof;

c) support and publicize the activities of and cooperate with international organizations and agencies which work for the implementation of the aforesaid provisions;

d) take all necessary steps to establish an effective organization of sections, affiliated groups and individual members;

e) secure the adoption by groups of members or supporters of individual prisoners of conscience or entrust to such groups other tasks in support of the object and mandate set out in Article 1;

f) provide financial and other relief to prisoners of conscience and their dependants and to persons who have lately been prisoners of conscience or who might reasonably be expected to be prisoners of conscience or to become prisoners of conscience if convicted or if they were to return to their own countries, to the dependants of such persons and to victims of torture in need of medical care as a direct result thereof;

g) provide legal aid, where necessary and possible, to prisoners of conscience and to persons who might reasonably be expected to be prisoners of conscience or to become prisoners of conscience if convicted or if they were to return to their own countries, and, where desirable, send observers to attend the trials of such persons;

h) publicize the cases of prisoners of conscience or persons who have otherwise been subjected to disabilities in violation of the aforesaid provisions;

i) investigate and publicize the disappearance of persons where there is reason to believe that they may be victims of violations of the rights set out in Article 1 hereof;

j) oppose the sending of persons from one country to another where they can reasonably be expected to become prisoners of conscience or to face torture or the death penalty;

k) send investigators, where appropriate, to investigate allegations that the rights of individuals under the aforesaid provisions have been violated or threatened;

l) make representations to international organizations and to governments whenever it appears that an individual is a prisoner of conscience or has otherwise been subjected to disabilities in violation of the aforesaid provisions;

m) promote and support the granting of general amnesties of which the beneficiaries will include prisoners of conscience;

n) adopt any other appropriate methods for the securing of its object and mandate. . . .

ORGANIZATION

8. Responsibility for Amnesty International work on violations of human rights in any country or territory, including the collection and evaluation of information, and the sending of delegations, lies with the international governing bodies of the organization, and not with the section, groups or members in the country or territory concerned.

9. . . . Sections shall take no action on matters that do not fall within the stated object and mandate of Amnesty International.

10. Groups . . . shall accept for adoption such prisoners as may from time to time be allotted to [them] by the International Secretariat, and shall adopt no others as long as [they] remain affiliated to Amnesty International. No group shall be allotted a prisoner of conscience detained in its own country. Groups shall take no action on matters that do not fall within the stated object and mandate of Amnesty International.

Notes

CHAPTER ONE

1. Throughout this book I use the terms *progressive* and *conservative*. I recognize that there are grave problems about such terms. "Progressive" can be confused with progressivism as a specific political movement, and has connotations of faith in progress. Also, some social critics, such as Anthony Giddens, argue that the conservative/progressive dichotomy is outmoded. Nonetheless, I think "progressive" is a less unfortunate term than the alternatives. "Liberal" has such a variety of frequently invoked meanings, ranging from a philosophical preference for the individual—the meaning on which critics such as Alasdair MacIntyre and Stanley Hauerwas focus—to the journalistic meaning of favoring economic equality and civil liberties, that the term is deeply confusing. "Left" also has severe problems. In using the term *progressive,* let me be clear that I imply nothing about progress or any other teleology. Nor do I mean to imply that the political views Americans hold exist in neat packages all easily arranged on a single progressive–conservative dimension. On the contrary, it is clear that the patterning of political views takes diverse forms. Nonetheless, the kind of progressive politics embodied in support for human rights and that manifested by struggles for economic justice have things in common, and are empirically associated to some degree.

2. Opinion poll data conclusively show that there is no connection between religious traditionalism and conservatism on economic issues, or indeed on most issues outside the areas of sexuality, reproduction, gender roles, and schooling. See Stephen Hart, *What Does the Lord Require? How American Christians Think about Economic Justice* (New York: Oxford University Press, 1992; expanded edition: New Brunswick, N.J.: Rutgers University Press, 1996) for survey data on this point and references to other authors reaching the same conclusion.

3. In past writings I have spoken of "thick" and "thin" discourse. There is no essential difference in that to which the old and new terms are meant to refer. But the new terminology, I hope, has a smaller overload of evaluative connotations and will therefore be less confusing and off-putting. Another

reason for changing terminology is to avoid confusion with the terminology found in Michael Walzer's *Thick and Thin: Moral Argument at Home and Abroad* (Notre Dame: University of Notre Dame Press, 1994), which has appeared since I started using these terms. Walzer's distinction is related to mine but is not by any means the same. Confusion has also come from people's familiarity with Clifford Geertz's concept of "thick description." (Geertz, of course, was speaking of thick qualities in the social scientific narrative about culture, whereas Walzer and I are concerned with the cultural forms themselves.)

4. One could distinguish between "primary" discourse, dealing with the world, and "secondary" discourse that tries to govern primary discourse. This distinction is analogous to the way legal theorist H. L. A. Hart defines primary and secondary rules in *The Concept of Law* (Oxford: Clarendon Press, 1961).

5. This is not to be confused with the philosophical perspective of the same name, associated with French thinkers such as Henri Bergson and Emmanuel Mounier. In the United States, the most obvious political manifestation of personalism in this more traditional sense is the Catholic Worker movement.

6. Paul Lichterman, *The Search for Political Community: American Activists Reinventing Commitment* (Cambridge: Cambridge University Press, 1996), 34.

7. Here Peter and the apostles are speaking to a Jewish priestly council. This and all other scriptural quotations and citations are taken from the New Revised Standard Bible.

8. The basic argument for the social and political significance of transcendent religious frameworks was first made, within social-scientific analysis, by the sociologist Max Weber. In *The Protestant Ethic and the Spirit of Capitalism* (New York: Scribner, 1958 [German original, 1904]), Weber showed how world-rejecting stances could transform the world (paradoxically, more than stances backing the pursuit of self-interest). He made the argument even more pointedly, and in a way that applies more directly to politics, in the conclusion to *The Religion of China* (New York: Free Press, 1951 [not published in Weber's lifetime]). Michael Walzer's *The Revolution of the Saints* (Cambridge: Harvard University Press, 1965) carries forward this intellectual perspective, applying it explicitly and in detail to the religious genesis of modern revolutions. Robert Bellah's seminal article "Religious Evolution" (*American Sociological Review,* 29 [June 1964]: 358–74) puts the argument in an ambitiously comparative context. My own *What Does the Lord Require? How American Christians Think about Economic Justice* (expanded edition), an empirical analysis of grassroots viewpoints based mostly on in-depth interviews, shows how the capacity of Christians of many theological stripes to assert transcendent values and images of reality against what they see around them persists today, often with progressive political implications. The line of argument of all of these scholars applies fully to the Greens and ex-communists described here. In other words, they meet the analytical requirements of this model even though concretely their worldviews are very far from the ones Weber, Walzer, and Bellah discuss.

9. On this subject, see Tom Smith, "Liberal and Conservative Trends in the United States since World War II," *Public Opinion Quarterly* 54 (1990): 479–507; James Davis, "Changeable Weather in a Cooling Climate Atop the Liberal Plateau: Conversion and Replacement in Forty-two General Social Survey

Items, 1972–89," *Public Opinion Quarterly* 56 (1992): 261–306; and the preface to the 1996 edition of Hart, *What Does the Lord Require? How American Christians Think about Economic Justice.* A more journalistic treatment is found in Thomas Ferguson's *Golden Rule: The Investment Theory of Politics* (Chicago: University of Chicago Press, 1995). The reason for my focus on issue positions in this argument is that voting and party preference do not really measure where people stand on issues. Also, some of the shift in party allegiance is in the South and may be a move from being conservative Democrats to being Republicans without any shift in political philosophy.

10. A not very empirical but nonetheless insightful argument about the enduring strength of American moral discourses is found in Jeffrey Stout's *Ethics after Babel: The Languages of Morals and Their Discontents* (Boston: Beacon Press, 1988); see especially chapter 9. The debate about whether American civil society is declining has been spirited in recent years, particularly in response to Robert Putnam's widely influential essay "Bowling Alone: America's Declining Social Capital," *Journal of Democracy* 6 (1995): 65–78. One important critique of Putnam is Theda Skocpol's "Unraveling from Above," *American Prospect* 7, no. 25 (March–April 1996): 20–25. For a study of how American voluntary associational involvement stacks up against other countries (way above average, including religion; a little above average not including religion), see James Curtis, Edward Grabb, and Douglas Baer, "Voluntary Association Membership in Fifteen Countries: A Comparative Analysis," *American Sociological Review* 57, no. 2 (April 1992): 139–52.

11. Dan Clawson, Alan Neustadtl, and Mark Weller, *Dollars and Votes: How Business Campaign Contributions Subvert Democracy* (Philadelphia: Temple University Press, 1998). See also Thomas Ferguson, *Golden Rule: The Investment Theory of Politics* (Chicago: University of Chicago Press, 1995).

CHAPTER TWO

1. As terminologies, "congregation-based" seems to put the focus on organizational factors while "faith-based" sounds as if it referred to beliefs and personal commitments. But in practice the two terms are used almost interchangeably, and people who use one term do not, as far as I can tell, do their organizing any differently from people who use the other. The former is the term most often used by the Gamaliel Foundation, while the latter is the dominant usage in the Pacific Institute for Community Organizing (PICO). The Industrial Areas Foundation (IAF) speaks of "broad-based" organizing, but the local projects they assist are composed entirely or almost entirely of congregations and faith is almost as central to the organizing process as in PICO or Gamaliel projects. A fourth term, "institution-based organizing," is sometimes used by people outside the networks into which local community organizations are gathered, in an effort to subsume all the other usages and be neutral among them. Thus preferences among these terminologies sometimes reflect differences among the networks. Each network regards its work as distinctive. I am persuaded, however, and most other observers agree, that the arguments between networks reflect their organizational rivalry more than differences in how they organize. Those differences, while real, are relatively subtle, and

would not generate the heat of the inter-network debates were it not for the competition with each other in which they are frequently engaged.

2. In saying this, I am not comparing faith-based organizing to movements that have "mail-order" memberships where participants make contributions to a national office that works on their behalf but are not personally engaged in political activity beyond an occasional phone call or letter. Such groups may have many supporters but few active participants. Nor am I comparing it to the environmental movement. Only part of that movement is centrally concerned with economic justice, and environmental activism is so varied that it is only in the loosest sense a single movement. Congregation-based community organizing, on the contrary, is a quite coherent (if not organizationally unified) movement.

Some of the terms I am using here, such as "congregation-based," "community organizing," and "movement" can be understood in various ways. Preferences among these usages are sometimes passionate, and the choice among them obviously affects one's views as to whether one should call congregation-based organizing a "movement." However, one can say without minimizing the differences among them that these 133 organizations are more similar to each other, in both spirit and organization, than to other ways in which Americans seek social justice, democracy, and community—and *a fortiori* to organizations with other goals. What is shared is more, in fact, than among peace organizations or environmental ones, and this provides warrant for thinking of these organizations as constituting a single, coherent social movement. The term *movement* is controversial, however, since community organizers often contrast their work, quite polemically, to "social movements." Some would be more comfortable speaking of an approach, strategy, or philosophy. Here we will use the term *movement* in a generic sense—removing the specific and pejorative meanings added in polemics—to speak about taking organized action, outside of government and other established channels, to seek social change. A particular movement could then be considered to be a family of organizations operating at the same time with similar purposes and means, some degree of shared consciousness, and shared channels of communication. In this sense, community organizing easily qualifies as a movement.

3. This is Ms. Spivey-Perry's real name. Except where noted, names of organizers and clergy are real while names of volunteer lay participants are pseudonyms. In the interviews, I did not make promises of anonymity, and in fact there are only rare occasions where a respondent said anything sensitive—anything they would be likely to be worried about having reported under their own names. Nonetheless, it seemed better to preserve the privacy of the volunteer lay participants. For the organizers and clergy, it is almost impossible to do so because they serve as spokespersons and are widely known.

4. The main interview was conducted August 11, 1992, at Ms. Spivey-Perry's house in Milwaukee, at a time when she was preparing to leave for a new position in Washington, D.C. I had many less formal discussions with her earlier, and I have had a few since.

5. Quotes from Galluzzo in this chapter come from extended interviews with him on May 1, 1992, and July 20, 1992. I have also had dozens of more informal conversations with him. The history of MICAH's development is also

based on interviews with CCHD staff and Jack Murtagh of the Milwaukee Interfaith Conference, and on documents in the MICAH files.

6. See, for instance, John Meyer, "Institutionalized Organizations: Formal Structure as Myth and Ceremony," in *The New Institutionalism in Organizational Analysis,* ed. Walter Powell and Paul DiMaggio (Chicago: University of Chicago Press, 1991), 41–62.

7. Gary Delgado has argued that one should think of communities of interest and identity rather than of only locality. In reply, Mike Miller says that this is what community organizing has always done, and that a focus on locality has resulted from the common interests found in local communities. I think that place is actually more integral to community organizing, and that Delgado's challenge is actually a more serious one, than Miller realizes. To some extent, to be sure, sharing a place means sharing a set of common circumstances, and the organizing is really about these circumstances. Local communities typically have a lot more in common than a set of zip codes. Since government is organized in terms of spatial units, a particular geographic area will have specific neighborhood schools, patterns of policing, and so on that create particular interests. Furthermore, real estate, industrial, and commercial development are patterned spatially, resulting in neighborhoods with differing characteristics in terms of racial composition, kind and quality of housing stock, and so forth.

Nonetheless, organizing based on locality is different from other kinds of organizing. It both requires and allows different methodologies. For instance, it allows a great deal of face-to-face interaction and requires dealing with more ideological and religious diversity than other kinds of organizing. It also engages people in a different part of their lives and thus around different kinds of issues. The first and most obvious (far from the only) role of the participants in locality-based organizing is as a "resident," rather than a citizen or worker. One important example of the implications of this role-focus is that in locality-based organizing, more than other kinds, housing conditions almost always surface as a major issue. See Gary Delgado, *Beyond the Politics of Place: New Directions in Community Organizing in the 1990s* (Oakland, Calif.: Applied Research Center, 1994); Mike Miller, "'Beyond the Politics of Place': A Critical Review," written in 1995, published on the Internet, downloaded from <http://h-net2.msu.edu/~urban/comm-organization/miller/miller.html> on 16 March 1997.

8. Emile Durkheim, *The Elementary Forms of the Religious Life* (New York: Free Press, 1915 [1912]).

9. Because of the importance of this characteristic, some people speak of "institution-based" organizing. By contrast, much community organizing recruits *individuals* as members, sometimes in combination with local structures such as block clubs. See also note 1, p. 255.

10. Almost all the MICAH pastors were interviewed in 1993, and all the interviews included a structured section about the impact on their congregations of involvement in MICAH.

11. Conversation with Dennis Jacobsen, 11 November 1991.

12. This is an example of seeking consensus on a democratic process rather than any substantive image of a good society. The tension between

these two approaches is an important issue and will come up at many points in this book.

13. Figures from the web site of the Employment Policy Institute, which strongly opposes fair wage initiatives (information downloaded from <http://epionline.org/enacted.htm> on 8 December 1999). Other information on these initiatives comes from an interview with Arnold Graff and Jonathan Lange, BUILD organizers, conducted 7 December 1999. These organizers referred me to the Employment Policy Institute as a reliable source of information.

14. The numbers given here will undoubtedly seem too low to some organizing leaders and researchers. In 1994, I was frequently given estimates that 150 or more organizations existed, but I was only able to locate ninety, and in 1999–2000 there was a similar gap between insider estimates and the data I was able to obtain. Also, each network tends to claim a higher number of affiliates than I have found. For both the 1994 and 1999–2000 surveys, however, CCHD and the networks provided lists that were used as the initial basis for the research, and it is unlikely that many organizations were missed. Some that were on the initial lists were later determined not to be congregation-based organizing projects or not really to exist. (The criterion for "really existing" was that an organization have at least one paid organizer and a known, valid phone number or address.) The reason for such discrepancies is that some organizations listed by networks are embryonic and others are inactive or defunct.

15. Interview with Spence Limbocker, 6 November 1991; interview with Mike Miller, 18 April 1997.

CHAPTER THREE

1. U.S. Catholic Conference, *A Catholic Framework for Economic Life* (Washington, D.C.: National Conference of Catholic Bishops, 1996), reprinted in this book as appendix B. The original pastoral letter upon which this statement draws is U.S. Catholic Conference, *Economic Justice for All: Pastoral Letter on Catholic Social Teaching and the U.S. Economy* (Washington, D.C.: National Conference of Catholic Bishops, 1986). Some sources show the years as 1987 and 1997.

2. Bernard Doering, ed., *The Philosopher and the Provocateur: The Correspondence of Jacques Maritain and Saul Alinsky* (Notre Dame: University of Notre Dame Press, 1994).

3. James Cone, "Black Religious Thought," in *Encyclopedia of the American Religious Experience: Studies of Traditions and Movements,* ed. Charles Lippy and Peter Williams (New York: Scribners, 1987), 1173–87, at 1181.

4. Interview with David Mann, 17 April 1997.

5. Personal communication from Richard Wood, 25 June 1998.

6. Sydney Ahlstrom, *A Religious History of the American People* (New Haven: Yale University Press, 1972), 786.

7. Conversation with Dan Weir, 18 April 1999; interview with David Mann, 17 April 1997.

8. Interview with Jim Dammier, 10 June 1993. Pope Paul VI and the Second Vatican Council, *Gaudium et Spes: Pastoral Constitution on the Church in the Modern World,* promulgated 7 December 1965.

9. Conversation with Dan Weir, 18 April 1999.

10. Saul Alinsky, *Reveille for Radicals* (Chicago: University of Chicago Press, 1969 [1946]), 199.

11. Ibid., 40–42. The term *People's Organizations* is reminiscent of the name of the party representing the populist movement, the People's Party.

12. Saul Alinsky, *Rules for Radicals* (New York: Vintage, 1971). The Back of the Yards organization held its first public meeting on the 150th anniversary of Bastille Day—a fitting coincidence given the rooting of Alinsky's work in radical democracy.

13. For an engaging if somewhat uncritical account of Cortes and his work, see Mary Beth Rogers, *Cold Anger* (Denton: University of North Texas Press, 1990). See also Ed Chambers, *Organizing for Families and Congregations* (Franklin Square, N.Y.: Industrial Areas Foundation, 1978).

14. A few organizers today are still direct students of Alinsky; many are students of Alinsky's students or associates; and some are yet another generation removed.

15. The quotes and most paraphrases for Phil Reifenberg are from an interview conducted on June 8, 1993. The remainder are from other conversations.

16. Field notes from my observation of Gamaliel seven-day residential training, 10–16 November 1991, held at the Techny Conference Center near Chicago. In describing training, I also use notes from my observations of one-day trainings in Milwaukee in 1992 and 1993, Richard Wood's notes of a PICO residential training, 24–29 July 1993, and Phil Reifenberg's account (in our interview, 8 June 1993) of the IAF and Gamaliel trainings he attended.

17. Max Weber, *From Max Weber: Essays in Sociology*, ed. Hans Gerth and C. Wright Mills (New York: Oxford University Press, 1946 [in German, posthumous]), 180.

18. One does not have to adopt a cynical or even a positivist view of law and politics to reach the point of having to confront the possibility of one person's power binding another. Legal theorist H. L. A. Hart, for instance, adopts as a model for law not the traditional one—the order of a sovereign to subjects, backed up by threats of punishment—but one that includes, even stresses, law as a process for acting efficaciously; one might think of the example of making a will, where one follows the law in order to achieve personal purposes. But of course by doing so one overrides the government's "default" distribution of property (a default that expresses some kind of social norm) and also the desires of one's potential heirs, and part of why one pays attention to the law of wills is to make sure that people who are unhappy with one's choices cannot successfully challenge them. Thus, in situations where legal tools provide a capacity to act rather than domination there remains an element of constraining the actions of others. H. L. A. Hart, *The Concept of Law* (Oxford: Clarendon Press, 1961).

19. Notes from Barbara Beck on MICAH public meeting at Greater Galilee Baptist Church, 28 June 1993. Beck attended the meeting as my research assistant.

20. Interview with Nathan Johnson (pseudonym), June 1993.

21. Paul Lichterman, *The Search for Political Community: American Activists Reinventing Commitment* (Cambridge: Cambridge University Press, 1998).

22. Address by Pat Speer at conference on community organizing, 12 May 1994, Hartford Seminary; interview with Ed Chambers, 8 December 1993; interview with David Mann, 17 April 1997.

23. This philosophical tradition of personalism has nothing to do with what Lichterman calls "personalism."

24. Jesus' healing miracles presumably would not fall under the same critique, since there the miracles are performed to heal an afflicted person, not gratuitously or primarily to demonstrate Jesus' special relationship with God.

25. Robert Bellah et al., *Habits of the Heart: Individualism and Commitment in American Life* (Berkeley: University of California Press, 1985). Utilitarian individualism is a perspective that regards the pursuit of individual, material interests as the necessary and appropriate organizing principle for human life. Self-interest is also different from the other form of individualism that Bellah and his coauthors criticize, expressive individualism.

26. Interview with David Boyd, 15 July 1993.

27. Interview with Samuel Jones, 6 July 1993.

28. Notes from one-day training, 15 May 1993.

29. Meeting of the MICAH crime and drugs task force, 22 June 1993. Alternative customary phrases include ". . . in His name" or ". . . in the Lord's name."

30. Alinsky, *Reveille for Radicals,* 67–69 and passim.

31. This term is used in many of Bourdieu's works; see, e.g., *Distinction: A Social Critique of the Judgment of Taste* (Cambridge: Harvard University Press, 1984 [1979]), 53–54.

32. Alinsky, *Reveille for Radicals,* 69.

33. Ibid., 93.

34. Sermon by James Leary, 23 February 1992.

35. Alinsky, *Reveille for Radicals,* 44.

36. "The Gamaliel Foundation, 1994," unpublished document provided by the Gamaliel Foundation, at 6–7; Gamaliel Foundation funding proposal to the Ameritech Corporation, unpublished document provided by Gamaliel Foundation, 1993, at 2–3.

37. Interview with José Carrasco, 22 April 1997. The interview was recorded on tape but conducted in a Jack-in-the-Box restaurant—an acoustically challenging environment. For this reason the following quotations bristle with bracketed explanatory words.

38. Ernie Cortes's work is documented journalistically in Rogers, *Cold Anger.*

CHAPTER FOUR

1. In speaking of cultural practices, I am really using a shorthand for identifying what sociological theorists would call one "analytical dimension" of actions that are not divisible concretely. For example, the PACT public meeting described later in this chapter was in part a practical means to organizational ends—a way of pressuring the mayor and extracting more resources for the less affluent parts of San Jose. But many aspects of what happened at the event are better understood in terms of their expressive and symbolic value, that is,

how they enacted PACT's values and view of the world and enriched the ritual and discursive life of the organization. It was a single event "concretely" but had various dimensions "analytically," which is to say, in terms of what kind of explanations might best account for what happened. Strictly speaking, therefore, we might speak, not of cultural practices, but of the symbolic/expressive dimension of practices. Such a dimension is never entirely absent. However, in faith-based organizing this dimension is rich and carefully attended to, which was less the case, say, in the antiwar coalition in Cincinnati. (We might also note that discourse itself is also a practice: it consists of oral or written statements to audiences in particular social contexts. The communicative intent is normally so dominant in the practice of discourse, however, that I have focused on the ideas or content flowing through this practice.)

2. Interview with Pearl Cabanilla (pseudonym), 23 April 1997.

3. Talk by Kathy Fish at Gamaliel residential training, 10–16 November 1991.

4. Talk by Betty Smith at Gamaliel residential training, 10–16 November 1991.

5. Presentation by Joe Marino at Gamaliel residential training, 10–16 November 1991.

6. Saul Alinsky, *Reveille for Radicals* (Chicago: University of Chicago Press, 1969 [1946]), 23, 43.

7. The information on the housing task force and its march comes from personal observation. In my possession are the source documents, such as the flyer distributed at the march; a letter dated July 10, 1992, from Leo Ries, director of Housing and Neighborhood Development, describing the city administration's position; and the text of the ordinance.

8. City of Milwaukee, Common Council file number 900641, Substitute 4, submitted by Ald. Johnson, Henningsen, Pratt, McNulty, and Richards, "A substitute ordinance relating to use of certain tax deed properties for public housing," revising sections 304-49-2, 304-49-2-d, and 304-49-3.5 of the city code. It also "encourage[s]" the use of "city residents and/or current public housing tenants" as employees and contractors on the rehabilitation work.

9. Interview with David Boyd, 15 July 1993.

10. Jean-François Lyotard, *The Postmodern Condition: A Report on Knowledge* (Minneapolis: University of Minnesota Press, 1984 [original French edition 1979]).

11. PICO training, 24–29 May 1993. Notes provided by Richard Wood.

12. Interview with an anonymous Milwaukee city official, 28 August 1995.

13. The account of this public meeting comes from a videotape provided by PACT. I was in the city the week before, observing preparation for the meeting.

14. PICO training, 24–29 May 1993. Notes provided by Richard Wood.

CONCLUSION TO PART TWO

1. This pattern in which public self-presentations are if anything *less* high-minded than what is spoken in private is not unique. In an elegant portrayal of the discourse of local recreational, volunteer, and activist groups, Nina

Eliasoph gives examples of a pattern in which discourse gets more constrained as it becomes more public. Nina Eliasoph, *Avoiding Politics: How Americans Produce Apathy in Everyday Life* (Cambridge: Cambridge University Press, 1998).

2. For Alinsky's views on this subject, see the chapter entitled "Of Means and Ends," in *Rules for Radicals* (New York: Vintage, 1971). See Mary Beth Rogers, *Cold Anger* (Denton: University of North Texas Press, 1990), an account of the work of Ernie Cortes and the Texas IAF.

3. Sociologist Jeffrey Alexander and others have argued that there is a vocabulary of democratic concepts that has almost universal appeal. The only problem with this argument is that these ideas are capable of being interpreted in an enormous variety of ways and are not the only basis on which Americans conceptualize politics. Jeffrey Alexander and Steven Smith, "The Discourse of American Civil Society: A New Proposal for Cultural Studies," *Theory and Society* 22 (1993): 151–207.

4. PICO training, 24–29 July 1993. Notes provided by Richard Wood. This perspective has much in common with what political theorists call "pluralism."

5. Saul Alinsky, *Reveille for Radicals* (Chicago: University of Chicago Press, 1969 [1946]), 169ff. (here he takes up unionism and antiracism; there are other examples scattered throughout the book). Alinsky also argued (167ff.) for connecting local issues to nationwide ones. In practice, however, community organizations tend to be focused on their specific localities. The process of cutting issues tends to encourage a local focus, since the organization can exert significant influence locally but would be swamped by larger forces if it tried to address even statewide issues. The solution is for local organizations to work together, and the networks have all started promoting that strategy where they have several affiliates within the same state. But in practice, most work is quite local and sometimes a bit isolated. In the MICAH housing task force, for example, there was not one person who subscribed to *ShelterForce*, the principal national periodical for people working on low-income housing issues.

The local focus has a number of sources beyond the desire for winnable issues. Such a focus was implicit in the approach to empowering people articulated in chapter 3 by José Carrasco. Another factor is the strong commitment to working in and with one's local neighborhood felt by many congregations involved in faith-based organizing.

6. This was, of course, during the Popular Front period of American communism, and before the Cold War.

7. Gary Delgado, *Beyond the Politics of Place: New Directions in Community Organizing in the 1990s* (Oakland, Calif.: Applied Research Center, 1994); Mike Miller, "'Beyond the Politics of Place': A Critical Review," a 1995 essay published on the Internet; downloaded from <http://h-net2.msu.edu/~urban/comm-organization/miller/miller.html> on March 3, 1997. In such debates, one key term is "ideology," which is sometimes used as a pejorative label. One wants, organizing intellectuals frequently say, to avoid ideologues. In order not to enter into such debates over terminology, it may be better simply to refer to highly structured and comprehensive political perspectives.

8. Alinsky, *Reveille for Radicals*, 54; quotes from Gamaliel training, 10–16 November 1991.

9. Actually, Catholic social teachings put more emphasis on substantive goals than on increased democracy.

10. Interview with David Mann, 17 April 1997. Jim Shaul joined us for part of the interview.

11. Robert Bellah, "Civil Religion in America," *Dædalus* 96 (winter 1967): 1–21.

12. In addition, what will come out of a black box is either constant or can be predicted based on what goes in. A psychology that simply analyzes stimuli and responses and how they correlate, without giving an account of what happens between them, is treating the organism in question as a black box.

13. The term *teleology* is used to imply that this way of thinking includes the assumption that we can understand human events in terms of an end or *telos*—a goal or direction—toward which historical phenomena tend. Christianity, in this teleology, has an inherent directionality toward social reform. The Christian reform teleology is one of the two central bases in the modern West for belief in progress. The other is the Enlightenment teleology, found on occasion in human rights work, which posits historical movement toward overcoming superstition, prejudice, and other nonrational understandings that divide humans from each other.

14. Interview with José Carrasco, 22 April 1997.

15. Biblical interpretation is a fine art, and one can find a progressive meaning in even the texts that superficially look most unpromising. So I am not claiming that Paul's writings objectively and necessarily have antifeminist implications. But they have been widely used to support reserving certain roles to men and lend themselves fairly easily to that purpose. In saying this, I also do not mean to argue that all use of Scripture is opportunistic, that religious traditions have no real influence, or that there is no basis for deciding what social implications one is going to draw from one's own tradition. Any person of faith can and in my view should decide what he or she finds to be the most authentic way of applying faith to the social world. And debates about what that way might be can and should be carried on; this is not just a matter of taste. Yet *empirically* there are enormous variations in the social interpretations of faith. Furthermore, speaking more personally and theologically, I do not find it plausible to claim that all such variations result from bad faith or ignorance, without which everybody would presumably adopt my interpretation. Reasonable, good-faith, historically precedented interpretations of faith cover a wide range. One should, I believe, argue with people who adopt interpretations one rejects, but not claim that these interpretations are inauthentic or that adopting them makes a person any less a member in good standing of one's faith community.

16. PICO training, 24–29 July 1993. Notes provided by Richard Wood. Interview with Pearl Cabanilla, 23 April 1997.

17. Interview with David Mann, 17 April 1997.

18. "The Gamaliel Foundation, 1994," unpublished document provided by the Gamaliel Foundation, at 1, 6.

19. I am speaking here of the contemporary United States. In contexts where traditional community structures—religion, family, tribe, or the like—have more capacity to coerce people than is normally the case in the United

States today, progressive principles might lead to a preference for *weakening* civil society.

20. This is also manifest in the kind of relativism described with regard to the tone of discourse.

21. Talk by Pat Speer at conference on community organizing, Hartford Seminary, 12 May 1994.

CHAPTER FIVE

1. Voltaire, "Treatise on Toleration," in *Les Philosophes,* ed. Norman L. Torrey (New York: Capricorn, 1960 [1763]), 267–71, at 267.

2. Articles 4 and 7 contain similar balancing provisions.

3. In practice, of course, American constitutional jurisprudence recognizes limits to the rights of citizens, but the difference in the formal text still matters.

4. That is, if one examines the uses of "man" and "citizen" in the Declaration, one cannot find any distinction that works for all the instances in the text. The terms seem to have been chosen haphazardly rather than with any clear idea of their having different meanings. This is important in part because Karl Marx would later try to read such a distinction into the text. The primary source where Marx analyzes the French Declaration (along with American human rights documents) is in his 1843 essay, "On the Jewish Question," found in many collections; see, e.g., Robert Tucker, ed., *The Marx-Engels Reader,* 2d ed. (New York: Norton, 1978), 26–52.

5. T. H. Marshall, "Citizenship and Social Class," in *Class, Citizenship, and Social Development* (Garden City, N.Y.: Anchor Books, 1965 [1950]), 71–134. The essay was first published in 1950 as a revision of the Marshall Lectures delivered at Cambridge University in 1949. An irony is that the term *citizenship* is so fiercely used by a person who was, by the legal terminology of his country at his time, a "subject" of the queen rather than a citizen. Marshall's conceptualization of stages of development of human rights is of course not unique; there are various others that parallel his. Another sign of how Marshall represented not something unique but a kind of *Zeitgeist* is that he shows no sign of being aware of the UDHR, adopted only months before he gave the Marshall Lectures. He does not refer to the United Nations, and the term *human rights* is not found in his index.

6. Alternate evolutionary trajectories about citizenship that have less progressive implications are found in the work of other social scientists. Talcott Parsons, for instance, speaks of a historical trajectory toward "upward inclusion" that is a cousin of Marshall's evolutionary assumptions only with a moderate liberal rather than social democratic political tinge. See Talcott Parsons, "Comparative Studies and Evolutionary Change," in *Social Systems and the Evolution of Action Theory* (New York: Free Press, 1977), 193–97. Gabriel Almond and Sidney Verba articulate ideas of civility and citizenship as preconditions for democracy, taking human rights to be manifestations of a fully modern political culture that had accepted a pluralistic framework for political competition. Gabriel Almond and Sidney Verba, *The Civic Culture: Political Attitudes and Democracy in Five Nations* (Princeton: Princeton University Press, 1963).

7. News release issued by the International Secretariat of Amnesty International, 16 June 1999 (AI index: ORG 10/03/99).

8. Amnesty International–USA, *The Policy Manual* (New York: Amnesty International, 1992).

9. There are two notable exceptions in the United States: locals of labor unions and congregations in denominations with a relatively "connectional" polity do accept serious constraints.

10. These figures come from organizational documents given to me by Hans Wahl and other AI national staff.

11. The group number constitutes a pseudonym, since the group wished to remain anonymous; but all AI groups in the United States are named in this fashion—e.g., Group 999. I was an active member of this group from April 1995 through December 1996. The group requested the opportunity to see and comment on a draft of the part of the manuscript concerning Amnesty International. I fulfilled that request and received in return a number of very useful comments, particularly from the member here called Daniel Levine.

12. Interview with Michael Cresci (pseudonym), 6 July 1995.

13. Amnesty International–USA, no title, not dated (circa 1992–96), not published. This consists of a four-page information packet, sent to me by national staff. It appears to be an introductory packet mailed to people who call in to inquire about the organization. From internal evidence, it appears to date from the middle months of 1995.

14. The eight subsections clearly relating only to individual victims are e) through l). Subsection m), the ambiguous item, is about seeking general amnesties that will include POCs. This is broader than working for individual prisoners, but could be seen as simply a "wholesale" version of casework rather than dealing with broader issues. The subsection clearly dealing with a broader concerns is b), about promoting the adoption of human rights treaties. Note that none of the provisions speaks of changing the factors that according to some analyses tend to increase or be associated with political imprisonment, such as arms sales to dictators, lack of free elections, or severe social inequality. There are, incidentally, four other subsections. These are generic or infrastructural: a) on impartiality, c) on cooperating with other human rights organizations, d) on building AI as an organization, and n) on doing anything else required to fulfill the mandate. The text referred to here is the *Statute of Amnesty International* as amended at the International Council meeting in December 1997, which can be found on the AI web site <www.amnesty.org>.

15. *Statute of Amnesty International,* Art. 2, sec. a.

16. Amnesty International–USA, *Amnesty International Handbook* (New York: Amnesty International, 1991), 17.

17. Amnesty International, "Amnesty International: Independence and Impartiality" (London: Amnesty International, 1984).

18. Interview with Hans Wahl, 17 July 1995.

19. For how local groups can work on treaties, see, e.g., an untitled pamphlet interpreting the rule against working in one's own country published by Amnesty International (London: Amnesty International, 1992). Nationally, Amnesty has also worked on military assistance at least to the extent of doing

research and publication, putting out a report on the harm done to human rights by U.S. military aid (Amnesty International–USA, *Human Rights and U.S. Security Assistance* [New York: Amnesty International, 1996]). It is unclear whether local groups ever work on this question.

20. Amnesty International–USA, no title, not dated (circa 1992–96), not published (four-page information packet cited in note 13).

21. Interview with Hans Wahl, 17 July 1995.

22. *Amnesty International Handbook,* 15.

23. Final Report of the Mandate Review Committee, April 1991. This is defined explicitly as an "internal" document, restricted to members. I was able to obtain it because I am a member of Amnesty, but am not free to quote directly from it.

24. Michael Ignatieff, "Human Rights: The Midlife Crisis," *New York Review of Books,* 20 May 1999, 58–62.

25. Interview with Hans Wahl, 17 July 1995.

26. This analysis is based on reading every version of the mandate, from the earliest (in 1961) to, at the time of this writing, the most recent (1997). The specific quotes are from the versions of 1968 and 1997. The earliest versions were provided by the International Secretariat. The more recent ones are found in the yearly editions of the *Amnesty International Annual Report* (e.g., Amnesty International, *Annual Report 1968–69* [London: Amnesty International, 1969]), and the current version is found on the AI web site.

The change with regard to gays was adopted through a resolution without changing the text of the mandate. Note that imprisonment for advocating gay rights had of course always qualified people as POCs; the change was in adopting people imprisoned for gay sexual conduct.

CHAPTER SIX

1. Interview with Catherine Duncan and two other Group 425 activists, 24 June 1996. All names of local Amnesty activists are pseudonyms. Group 425 is also, since the group requested that its identity be disguised.

2. Talk by Catherine Duncan at candlelight vigil, 13 December 1995; text provided to the author by Duncan.

3. Talk by Pat Speer at conference on community organizing, Hartford Seminary, 12 May 1994.

4. Robert Bellah et al., *Habits of the Heart: Individualism and Commitment in American Life* (Berkeley: University of California Press, 1985), 221.

5. This practice disappeared near the end of my observation of Group 425. Why this happened is not clear. The explanation group members gave was that the person who had provided the letters (downloading them from an AI web site and then printing multiple copies) had ceased to do so. But the practical problem would have been easy to solve if there had been a real will to continue.

6. Amnesty International–USA, introductory packet for people inquiring about the organization, no title, not dated (but probably 1995), not published; Amnesty International–USA, "Guide to Writing Appeals for Prisoners of Conscience," not dated, not published, 2; personal communication from Daniel

Levine, 13 April 1997 (punctuation as in Levine's letter); interview with Catherine Duncan and two other Group 425 activists, 24 June 1996.

7. This draws on a deep-seated cultural structure in the United States, which Alexander and Smith call the democratic code. Jeffrey Alexander and Steven Smith, "The Discourse of American Civil Society: A New Proposal for Cultural Studies," *Theory and Society* 22 (1993): 151–207.

8. Postcard from Group 425 to its members, October 1996; in author's possession.

9. Interview with Catherine Duncan and two other Group 425 activists, 24 June 1996; interview with Hans Wahl, 17 July 1995; talk by Daniel Levine at a commemoration of the Chinese student democracy movement of 1989, 9 June 1996; interview with three Group 425 members, 24 June 1996; conversations with Margaret Marsh, April 1995.

Wahl wants local groups to be more strategic about what will advance human rights, moving beyond letter writing and thinking about what leverage they can find working in their local areas to get governments abroad to change their practices. Governments, he says, have become more sophisticated, and merely sending them a lot of letters does not have as much effect as it used to.

10. The reasons for abandoning this ritual practice are not clear. Some members told me that the object was too large and prickly (with the barbed wire) to carry to meetings easily. Others referred to an occasion when the candle was knocked over and wax spilled on the table as the reason for the demise of this practice. But Catherine Duncan felt these reasons were inadequate and wanted to revive it. Interview with Catherine Duncan and two other Group 425 activists, 24 June 1996.

11. In addition to the nuts and bolts work done at meetings, much work was done behind the scenes, some—such as maintaining the mailing list and producing the address labels for the newsletter each month—by people who did not come to a single meeting during the eighteen months I attended.

12. Letter from Group 425 to William Schulz, director of Amnesty International–USA, 20 September 1995. The letter does say "mandates," not "mandate."

13. Interview with Sarah Browning and Daniel Levine, 19 June 1996.

14. Ibid.

15. Telephone conversation with Bob Antonucci, 20 June 1997.

16. Interview with a member of an AI group in Brooklyn, New York, 5 August 1997.

17. In addition to their narrative and subjective mode of grounding human rights, Group 425 members also refused to give any definition of human rights, even when asked explicitly in interviews. Three people I interviewed together established in collaborative fashion a position not requiring an explicit definition: "It's like art. People say, I don't know art, [but] I know what I like. I don't know what human rights are, but when I hear about human rights" being violated "you sense it." "Instead of saying what the rights are, you can quickly [tell] when people are being denied them." Interview with three members of Group 425, 24 June 1996. Essentially the same position is attributed to Eleanor Roosevelt, who chaired the commission that drafted the UDHR.

18. Interview with Catherine Duncan and two other Group 425 members, 24 June 1996; personal communication from Daniel Levine, 13 April 1997.

19. Interview with Sarah Browning and Daniel Levine, 19 June 1996.

20. Interview with a member of an AI group in Brooklyn, New York, 5 August 1997. Another account that was somewhat similar to the one concerning unanimity came about in the context of preparing for the national, annual Amnesty General Meeting. The agenda for that meeting included matters of principle and mandate controversies, but the group did not carry out any discussion of these issues. Members were united and emphatic in explaining why: such discussions were unspeakably boring because the resolutions to be debated at the meetings were framed in such a technical and bureaucratic way.

21. Interview with a member of an AI group in Brooklyn, New York, 5 August 1997; interview with Sarah Browning and Daniel Levine, 19 June 1996.

22. Personal communication from Daniel Levine, 13 April 1997. Another account for constraint, articulated by a member of the Brooklyn group, similarly sought a least common denominator. It defended the single-minded focus on casework on the grounds that this was the way to evoke human interest, to get people interested in human rights.

23. Interview with Catherine Duncan and two other Group 425 members, 24 June 1996.

24. Ibid.

25. Interview with Sarah Browning and Daniel Levine, 19 June 1996.

26. Another account for constraint that occasionally was given concerned hospitality. It would have been wrong to debate political issues in the educational meetings because the speakers were invited guests who should not have to fend off attacks on their views.

27. Personal communication from Daniel Levine, 13 April 1997.

28. Personal communication from Nina Eliasoph, 13 June 1997.

CONCLUSION TO PART THREE

1. Program for the Workers' Organizing Committee Second Delegate Convention, 3 February 1997, at 8 (not published). The history, philosophy, and projects of the organization are described elsewhere in this program, in other documents provided by the WOC and in the author's possession, and in personal communications from a WOC organizer to the author.

CHAPTER SEVEN

1. With regard to the political impact of individualism, see Robert Bellah, *The Broken Covenant: American Civil Religion in Time of Trial* (New York: Seabury Books, 1975); Robert Bellah et al., *Habits of the Heart: Individualism and Commitment in American Life* (Berkeley: University of California Press, 1985); Robert Putnam, "Bowling Alone: America's Declining Social Capital," *Journal of Democracy* 6 (1995): 65–78.

2. Bellah et al., *Habits of the Heart.* Exact definitions of the two kinds of individualism are given at 336 and 333–34. Expressive individualism, in these definitions, is taken to be an outcome of the romantic reaction against utilitar-

ianism; I would want also to emphasize the influence of the strong antinomian strands in American religious traditions. The concept of expressive individualism is a potentially controversial one insofar as there are disagreements about how to understand the kind of cultural and social movements and trends that might be tagged expressive individualist. This label, along with the argument made in the book that expressive individualism is only slightly less harmful to American life than utilitarian individualism, implicitly discounts the claims of the counterculture, and perhaps of feminism and other movements drawing on the cultural trends of the 1960s and early 1970s, that they radically departed from the values of their cultural environment. Like any conceptualization, the one in *Habits* draws attention to some things and downplays others. In particular, it highlights the antistructural aspect of the cultural currents of the 1960s and downplays the substance of their critique of older gender roles, sexual moralities, family patterns, orientations toward work, and so forth. In addition to the two forms of individualism, *Habits* sees America as possessing, but not much using, biblical and "republican" traditions. This last, in their view, is a secular tradition that "presupposes that the citizens of a republic are motivated by civic virtue as well as self-interest" (335). This allows individuals to be active participants in public life on behalf of justice and the common good.

3. Jeffrey Stout, *Ethics after Babel* (Boston: Beacon Press, 1988).

4. Ibid., 271.

5. In arguing for the need for discourse that has generality, I am not taking a "foundationalist" position, asking everyone to have a systematic general philosophy from which all ethics and politics can be derived. I am talking only about having some kind of tools for addressing the issues that actually come up in contemporary politics. Such recurring issues as the competing claims of diverse groups (which comes up even in local politics) and the question of whether to enforce moral standards through law go beyond what sphere-specific languages can address. To address such issues does *not* require a general philosophy. But these issues are not hypothetical; they come up all the time. Therefore to participate in public discourse one has to have *some* tools to address them. Note also that some observers, such as Robert Putnam, want to argue that even civil-societal activities that are totally apolitical can contribute to the strength of civil society and therefore (in their view) democracy. This is a complex issue, but in any case here I am speaking only of what civil-societal involvements mean for people's political-cultural capacities—their ability to participate in public discourse. See Putnam's "Bowling Alone," discussed later in this chapter.

6. Organizing also links politics and civil society organizationally, which is important in relationship to the debate between Putnam and Skocpol discussed below.

7. Talk by Pat Speer at conference on community organizing, Hartford Seminary, 12 May 1994.

8. Alexis de Tocqueville, *Democracy in America* (New York: Vintage Books, 1945 [1835]); Putnam, "Bowling Alone."

9. Putnam believes that almost any kind of involvement contributes to democracy, but this argument is controversial. One example of the complex

debate about Putnam's argument is the article by Theda Skocpol discussed below. Another is an attempt at a more comprehensive and systematic assessment than Putnam conducted, "Is Social Capital Declining in the United States? A Multiple Indicator Assessment," by Pamela Paxton, in *American Journal of Sociology* 105, no. 1 (July 1999): 88–127. Paxton concludes that there is decline on some measures but not others. A systematic comparative survey of voluntary-associational involvement is James Curtis et al., "Voluntary Association Membership in Fifteen Countries: A Comparative Analysis," *American Sociological Review* 57, no. 2 (April 1992): 139–152, which concludes that American involvement is on the high side but not extraordinary if religious involvements are not included, but way above all other countries when they are.

10. Theda Skocpol, "Advocates without Members: The Recent Transformation of American Civic Life," in *Civic Engagement in American Democracy,* ed. Theda Skocpol and Morris P. Fiorina (Washington and New York: Brookings Institution Press and Russell Sage Foundation, 1999).

11. The existence and independence of civil society as we now understand it are of course not natural and universal phenomena, but a development in Western history. Karl Marx's 1843 essay "On the Jewish Question" is a classic statement of how modern Western societies, using concepts of rights and freedom, have established the idea that the economic market and equally religion should be areas for each person to pursue egoistic interests, material or spiritual, while collective life is confined to the state. Marx sees the difference between "man" and the "citizen" in the French Declaration as corresponding to this bifurcated existence in civil society and the public realm. Actually, as I mentioned in note 4 to chapter 5, the usage of the terms in the Declaration does not follow Marx's logic: they are often used interchangeably, and at other times in ways that are inconsistent with Marx's interpretation. But the use of the two terms as a metaphor for the ways in which private and public are understood in many of the ideologies of modern Western societies is illuminating. Marx's essay is found in various collections; see, e.g., Robert Tucker, ed., *The Marx-Engels Reader,* 2d ed. (New York: Norton, 1978), 26–52.

12. Nelson Lichtenstein, "Workers' Rights Are Civil Rights: How to Put the Labor Movement Back at the Center of American Political Culture," *WorkingUSA* (March/April 1998): 57–66; quote from 60.

13. Ibid., 62.

14. Ibid., 65, 64.

15. *Habits of the Heart* acknowledges the existence of political languages, such as "republicanism," that combine individualism with public concern. But these are understood as largely absent from the contemporary scene, and the authors of *Habits* would probably be skeptical of the role of personalism in American public discourse, seeing it as doing harm as well as good. See Paul Lichterman, "Beyond the Seesaw Model: Public Commitment in a Culture of Self-Fulfillment," *Sociological Theory* 13 (1995): 275–300; Paul Lichterman, *The Search for Political Community: American Activists Reinventing Commitment* (Cambridge: Cambridge University Press, 1996).

16. Louis Hartz, in *The Liberal Tradition in America: An Interpretation of American Political Thought since the Revolution* (New York: Harcourt Brace, 1955), argued that Americans were basically all liberals. In the 1990s Jeffrey

Alexander and Steven Smith, drawing on Hartz's thinking but recasting it in terms of "late Durkheimian" sociology, proposed that American public discourse operates within a hegemonic "democratic code" that provides a unified and coherent cultural basis. All particular ideologies are special cases operating within this code. The code can be used by political actors of varied stripes, but it still provides shape to public discourse, a shape that transcends utilitarianism and individualism. However, the determinacy and causal efficacy of this code are quite dubious, and it is clear that American public discourse is also deeply influenced by other cultural traditions, such as utilitarianism and religions. See Jeffrey Alexander and Steven Smith, "The Discourse of American Civil Society: A New Proposal for Cultural Studies," *Theory and Society* 22 (1993): 151–207.

17. Lichterman, "Beyond the Seesaw Model," 276 (emphasis in original). The cultural forms to which Lichterman's term refers should not be confused with personalism as a movement in social philosophy, found in thinkers such as Henri Bergson and Emmanuel Mounier. Lichterman equates personalism with expressive individualism (as described in *Habits of the Heart*) in note 2 of his article.

18. Whether "personalism," as Lichterman understands it, is an ideology is an ambiguous point. He argues (in personal communications, in the author's possession) that instead it is a mode of life and action within the activist groups he studies. On the other hand, he describes propositions that personalism upholds, and the "ism" at the end of the term is suggestive. I think that actually it is both a perspective and a mode of action. The distinction between the two, in any case, is unclear given that Lichterman conceptualizes culture as incorporating both dimensions.

19. Lichterman acknowledges this in a footnote. See "Beyond the Seesaw Model," 288 n. 9.

20. Emile Durkheim, "Individualism and the Intellectuals," in *Emile Durkheim on Morality and Society,* ed. Robert Bellah (Chicago: University of Chicago Press, 1973 [1898]), 43–57. The specific occasion for this essay was the Dreyfus Affair, a controversy surrounding the conviction of a Jewish army officer on spying charges that later proved false. The case became an arena in which questions not fully resolved previously in French politics—about tradition, authority, order, liberty, religion, and reason—were once again hashed over.

21. In fact, Durkheim calls individualism a religion. However, I think it is more helpful to restrict the range of the term *religion* to its more commonsense meaning and to deal conceptually, separate from such terminology, with the processes and characteristics of cultural traditions that are most obvious in religions but also found in other perspectives. That is, sacredness, transcendence, and ritual are cultural processes found both in religions and secular cultural traditions.

22. Durkheim's acceptance of these arguments is often described as a concern with the bases for social order. This may be true, but it sees Durkheim through functionalist lenses. While of course there are functionalist strands in Durkheim's thinking, there are also others. Here something more substantive is at stake: under what cultural conditions can we experience the characteristic advantages of the social organization of the modern West—which Durkheim

saw in terms of freedom, the use of reason, and richness of cultural possibilities rather than material prosperity—and yet overcome the dangers of modern life—social injustice, unbridled competition, and social conflict, or loss of meaning and direction in life and social isolation, which are the characteristic sufferings we moderns inflict on each other and ourselves? The central question is not so much how to maintain order for its own sake, but what kind of order, with what quality of life (socially and ethically), we are going to have.

23. Emile Durkheim, *The Division of Labor in Society* (New York: Free Press, 1933 [1893]).

24. Within the human rights movement, there are naturally many others who propose this kind of integration. One of the best advocates of this kind is Canadian sociologist Rhoda Howard; see her *Human Rights and the Search for Community* (Boulder, Colo.: Westview Press, 1995).

25. Durkheim, "Individualism and the Intellectuals," 231 n. 6. Durkheim focuses on the nonrational as well as the collective elements of our individualistic heritage. But by doing this he does not mean to take sides with conservative critics of rational examination. On the contrary, in "Individualism and the Intellectuals" he is an unqualified advocate of the right to use rational examination, and his whole body of work in fact exercises that right, piercing conventional illusions at many points. But the cultural *basis* for that right, Durkheim says, is found in passion and sacredness, and in our collective cultural life, not in the cerebrations of the isolated individual.

26. At least implicitly, all evangelism is also prohibited. It would not do, for instance, for a Baptist involved in MICAH to try to convert a Catholic or Lutheran participant.

CHAPTER EIGHT

1. I am not attempting to portray the central ideas of postmodernism, but only the ideas of this movement with most relevance to the issues under consideration here.

2. The term *culture wars* first reached a wide audience through James Davison Hunter's influential book *Culture Wars: The Struggle to Define America* (New York: Basic Books, 1991). Primarily criticizing the right, exponents of the notion of culture wars see U.S. politics as tending more and more into a battle between cultural modernists and traditionalists—a battle about sexuality, gender roles, the family, and of course religion. Christian Smith, "The Myth of Culture Wars," in *Cultural Wars in American Politics: Critical Reviews of a Popular Myth,* ed. Rhys Williams (Hawthorne, N.Y.: Aldine de Gruyter, 1997), 175–95, has documented the enormous quantity of commentaries on this topic. There have been, he found, hundreds of articles and at least six books on the subject since the publication of Hunter's book. Despite this fecundity, the empirical evidence for a number of propositions related to the culture wars framework is thin. For instance, it has not been shown by any rigorous analysis of evidence that voting is increasingly primarily based on cultural issues, or that polarization on cultural issues has increased at the grass roots (as opposed to the rhetoric heard at elite ideological gatherings such as Republi-

can national conventions), or that Americans are increasingly adopting a unified worldview centered on cultural issues, as opposed to holding the complex and varied combinations of relatively disconnected views on different issues that characterize American public opinion, according to survey evidence. Smith shows that even among evangelical Christians only a small proportion of people have any desire to join in culture wars. In "Worldviews or Social Groups as the Source of Moral Value Attitudes: Implications for the Culture Wars Thesis" (*Sociological Forum* 12, no. 3 [1997]: 371–404), John Evans demonstrates that there is only weak and ambiguous empirical support in public opinion data for the kind of attitude structures that the theory of culture wars implies. My own research, reported in *What Does the Lord Require? How American Christians Think about Economic Justice* (New Brunswick, N.J.: Rutgers University Press, 1996, xv–xvii), has also shown how small the constituency for the religious right agenda is—only about one quarter even of evangelicals and fundamentalists, which results in the figure given in the text of 6 percent of Americans. Despite such evidence, the argument continues to be made that the cultural politics of the religious right and its allies is highly divisive and threatens civility in public discourse, brings a dangerous set of irrational forces into politics, and distracts public attention from the "real" issues such as the economy.

3. Talk by Ellen Willis at opening plenary of Socialist Scholars Conference, 13 April 1996. This is an event held annually in New York City.

4. In a way, this is a critical description of exactly the cultural situation celebrated by many postmodernists.

5. Todd Gitlin, *The Twilight of Common Dreams: Why America Is Wracked by Culture Wars* (New York: Holt/Metropolitan, 1995), 23, 31, 34, 35–36.

6. In addition, cultural processes can be ignored through the "policy wonk" mode often used in progressive policy proposals. That is, the proposals consist of a set of cleverly designed solutions to problems whose nature is defined by careful research. Such proposals seem technocratic, in that there is no way for nonexperts to make intelligent comment. Perhaps a kind of elitism sometimes motivates them, but probably this is more an outcome than a motive. (The technocratic cast of policy proposals may also serve as a way of disguising what the actual goals of the proponents are. President Clinton's failed health care proposals were amazingly complex but did actually aim at a significant equalization of access to health care. The value of equality, however, was not very evident nor much spoken about. Perhaps the president and his advisers felt that there would not be much public support for this value and that they were better off trying to get it instituted by stealth. If so, they miscalculated; their enemies could figure out what was at stake.) The more critical problem is that such proposals evade having to define the political and ethical goals policy is supposed to serve. Such an evasion assumes either that those goals are shared and self-evident, so that only questions of technique need to be debated, or else that the goals are purely individual and that policy is supposed to be formed on a basis of relativism, simply responding to the individual value preferences that exist in American society. In either case, the value element of policy is treated as a black box.

7. The document was authored by Eric Prokosch, theme research coordi-

nator for Amnesty International, and was issued in December 1998. It carries AI index number ACT 50/13/98. As of August 8, 1999, it was located at <http://www.amnesty.org/ailib/aipub/1998/ACT/A5001398.htm>. It was in July 1999 that I searched the Amnesty web site and found this as the only substantial philosophical statement. Note that the UDHR says nothing about the death penalty, but Prokosch argues that the principles enunciated in it should exclude capital punishment.

8. Quoted in Saul Alinsky, *Reveille for Radicals* (Chicago: University of Chicago Press, 1969 [1946]), 155.

9. Jean-François Lyotard, *The Postmodern Condition: A Report on Knowledge* (Minneapolis: University of Minnesota Press, 1984 [original French edition, 1979]). The term *meta-narrative* is a misleading although technically accurate translation, since meta-narratives actually contain explanatory theory as much as story telling.

10. MacIntyre has made such arguments repeatedly. See, for example, *Whose Justice? Whose Rationality?* (Notre Dame: University of Notre Dame Press, 1988).

11. Actually, cultural issues can also be quite practical: think of the impact that theological debates have on the career prospects of gay and lesbian clergy—who are thick on the ground in many religious bodies.

12. Seminal writings in this tradition include Richard Hofstadter, *The Age of Reform* (New York: Knopf, 1955); Daniel Bell, *The End of Ideology* (Glencoe, Ill.: Free Press, 1959); William Kornhauser, *The Politics of Mass Society* (Glencoe, Ill.: Free Press, 1959); and Seymour Martin Lipset, "Working-Class Authoritarianism" and "Fascism—Left, Right, and Center," chaps. 4 and 5 in *Political Man* (Garden City, N.Y.: Doubleday, 1960). Michael Rogin's critique is found in the introduction to *The Intellectuals and McCarthy: The Radical Specter* (Cambridge: MIT Press, 1967), 1–7.

13. Richard Rorty, "For a More Banal Politics," *Harper's*, May 1992, 16–21.

14. Note that the expression "end of ideology" was first popularized by Daniel Bell in the 1950s, in writings that played an important part in the development of negative views of popular mobilization among postwar intellectuals. Richard Rorty, "The Priority of Democracy to Philosophy," in *Objectivity, Relativism, and Truth* (Cambridge: Cambridge University Press, 1991), 183, 184. The image of the bazaar is in "On Ethnocentrism: A Reply to Clifford Geertz," ibid., 209–10. With regard to using "religious" processes in secular cultural pursuits, an example is Durkheim's conception of individualism. Durkheim views individualism as a religion, and has no discomfort with that entailing rituals, taboos, sacred objects, and so forth.

15. The main way in which one might detect intolerance within this kind of individualism is that it favors individual rights over the autonomy of cultural groups. We saw that Amnesty activists are not relativists when it comes to female circumcision, and one could imagine them supporting (probably as individuals rather than through Amnesty) laws that prohibited groups that have traditionally practiced this ritual from performing it in the United States, at least on minors or by coercion. This dilemma of individual versus group rights is unavoidable in human rights thinking, as Rhoda Howard convincingly argues in *Human Rights and the Search for Community* (Boulder, Colo.: Westview Press, 1995).

16. Alan Wolfe, *One Nation, after All: What Middle-Class Americans Really Think about God, Country, Family, Racism, Welfare, Immigration, Homosexuality, World, the Right, the Left, and Each Other* (New York: Viking Penguin, 1998).

For a comprehensive and challenging review of evidence on the impact of American religion, with conclusions very much at odds with Rorty's, see R. Stephen Warner's "Work in Progress: A New Paradigm for the Study of American Religion," *American Journal of Sociology* 98 (1993): 1044–93. The empirical evidence on "culture wars," discussed in note 1, also contradicts Rorty's image. One important influence making quite traditionalist religion reasonably tolerant is the strong tradition of voluntarism—the belief that all valid religious and ethical decisions have to be made through the voluntary exercise of individual conscience—within Christianity. Even in sectarian religion, voluntarism is often strong. For instance, a Jehovah's Witness I interviewed (reported in Stephen Hart, *What Does the Lord Require? How American Christians Think about Economic Justice* [New Brunswick, N.J.: Rutgers University Press, 1996]) spoke of his distress about his son's not having yet adopted his faith. He believes that his son is objectively wrong and is literally headed for hell. But he also believes that only his son's own decision, made without coercion or even strong pressure, can save him. Such a position hardly implies trying to impose religiously based ethical absolutes on others.

The figure of 6 percent support for the religious right agenda comes from the analysis reported in the preface to the 1996 edition of Hart, *What Does the Lord Require?* See note 1 for more details and for a discussion of culture wars research and its problems.

17. Robert Westbrook, "Good-bye to All That: Eileen Kraditor and Radical History," *Radical History Review* no. 28–30 (1984): 69–89, at 86.

APPENDIX A

1. In the 1994 survey, I included all active groups known to CCHD or to any of the four national networks. It is unlikely that there were any other groups actively doing congregation-based community organizing at that time. Groups were included only if they seemed to really exist and be active. If I could not locate an organizer or an office, I ruled the project out. At the time I was doing the survey, I heard claims that 150 faith-based organizing projects existed around the country, but I never saw a *list* of projects to back such claims. My guess is that these were hopeful estimates based on numbers given out by networks that included, for each network, embryonic and moribund as well as active projects.

The response rate was relatively high for a mail survey and was obtained only after extensive telephone follow-up. There can be bias due to nonresponse, of course. Probably the smaller and weaker organizations were less likely to respond, and it is clear that affiliates of the Industrial Areas Foundation (IAF) were underrepresented. The IAF organizations tend to be larger than the others, however, and so one can reasonably hope that these two biases partly cancel each other out. A somewhat similar survey conducted by John McCarthy yielded very similar results. (The results have not yet been published, but McCarthy shared with me an unpublished report, John D. McCarthy and

Jim Castelli, "Working for Justice: The Campaign for Human Development and Poor Empowerment Groups," prepared for the Aspen Institute Nonprofit Sector Research Fund, issued by the Life Cycle Institute, Catholic University of America, November 1994.)

The 1999–2000 survey also used lists from CCHD and the networks. This survey was done by telephone, with questions and worksheets mailed out in advance and materials faxed in afterwards. This mode of surveying may have helped the response rate, but the interviewers were many and only minimally trained, resulting in a long and difficult fieldwork process to obtain the 75 percent return rate finally achieved. The estimated national figures reported here are projections from the responding organizations to the whole field of organizing. I used weights in calculating these projections to compensate for differences in response rate from one network to another.

2. The survey instructions said to report the number of *different* people who took training, so this does not include repeat trainees.

3. Some of this is from the CCHD national office and some from diocesan CCHD operations.

4. Sometimes, of course, they have cultural diversity of other kinds: of groups within a given racial categorization (e.g., Vietnamese and Pakistanis, both categorized as Asian) or of other kinds (e.g., a large gay/lesbian membership).

5. The data provided were not always complete or as specific as one might wish.

6. Mike Miller of the Organize Training Center in San Francisco is heading a major effort to promote community organizing among evangelicals.

7. The best estimate from reliable data of the total number of religious congregations in the United States is 355,000—almost exactly 100 times the number of congregations involved with community organizing. Virginia Hodgkinson and Murray Weitzman, *From Belief to Commitment* (Washington, D.C.: Independent Sector, 1993), 116.

Index